GARDENING
IN THE
SOUTH

GARDENING

IN THE

SOUTH

THE
COMPLETE
Homeowner's
GUIDE

PLANT PICKS • GROWING ADVICE • STYLE TIPS

MARK WEATHINGTON

Timber Press
Portland, Oregon

Frontispiece: Blue sages and geraniums make a cool splash in the early summer garden.

Photography credits appear on page 307.
Map on page 18 © Benchmark Maps.

The Haseltine Building
133 S.W. Second Avenue, Suite 450
Portland, Oregon 97204-3527
timberpress.com

Printed in China
Cover design by Laura Palese
Text design by Jane Jeszeck/www.jigsawseattle.com

Third printing 2018

Library of Congress Cataloging-in-Publication Data

Names: Weathington, Mark, author.
Title: Gardening in the South: the complete homeowner's guide / Mark
    Weathington.
Description: Portland, Oregon: Timber Press, 2017. | Includes bibli-
    ographical references and index.
Identifiers: LCCN 2016036944 | ISBN 9781604695915 (pbk.)
Subjects: LCSH: Plants, Ornamental—Southern States. |
    Gardening—Southern States.
Classification: LCC SB405 .W43 2017 | DDC 635.90975—dc23 LC
record available at https://lccn.loc.gov/2016036944

A catalog record for this book is also available from the British Library.

For my wife and best friend, Mary, without whose support I wouldn't be where I am today.

Contents

PREFACE

A GARDENING BOOK is a very personal glimpse into the mind of the author, so you may be interested to know a bit more about me and my philosophy regarding gardening. I am a lifelong resident of the Southeast, having grown up in south-central Virginia. Unlike those lucky folks who talk about gardening as a child at the side of their grandmother, I did not find my passion for horticulture until I went to college in the mountains. After trying on and discarding several majors (architecture, business, English) I took a plant propagation class on a lark and discovered immediately that I would spend the rest of my life in this field.

My passion for the intersection of plants and people led to undergraduate degrees in both horticulture and sociology and a master's degree in horticulture. I encountered the steepest learning curve, however, from my experience working in a retail garden center during my college years. That job threw me into all facets of gardening, from outdoor landscaping, to interiorscaping, to sales. There is perhaps no better way to learn than to help the tremendous assortment of people who come through a garden center's doors. After college I headed to Atlanta for my first taste of public horticulture at the Atlanta Botanical Garden, where my enthusiasm for new plants and great horticultural displays only grew. After several years I moved to coastal Virginia and the Norfolk Botanical Garden where I learned to deal with sandy soils and salt spray as well as the occasional hurricane. A decade spent at the seaside seemed like enough, and I yearned to be back in the rolling hills of the Piedmont where I grew up.

The opportunity to work with the fantastic staff of the JC Raulston Arboretum (JCRA) at North Carolina State University was too tempting to pass up. Few public gardens have had as great an impact on the field of horticulture in as short a timeframe as the JCRA. The Arboretum not only has a reputation for introducing new plants to cultivation, but perhaps more important, for introducing the right people to the right plants and getting them into production and available to the general public. The ethos of sharing is integral to the JCRA and makes it a unique place to be. Whether it is plant material or

A garden gateway beckons you to explore.

information, the desire to make as much as possible available to as wide an audience as possible carries through everything we do.

After two and a half decades in horticulture I've learned several lessons—there is nothing more important than being well-rooted, a garden without people to see it isn't worth the effort, and a plant shared equals a friend made. I still get excited by a new plant, a well-designed garden, or a stunning combination, but the sharing of these moments with other people is what makes gardening so enjoyable. My gardening philosophy is, first and foremost, your garden should make you happy. Gardening "rules" have their place and can help guide design, but throw them out the window if they interfere with your unique sense of style. I am personally a plant lover—while I know in my heart that my garden would be best served by planting out masses of perennials, I can't make myself plant in anything but drifts of one. Ultimately the most memorable gardens are the ones which truly reflect their owners. I hope reading this book will inspire you to go out and garden and more importantly to share your garden with a friend.

Hostas, ferns, azaleas, and other shade lovers create a lush, vibrant woodland garden.

INTRODUCTION

Welcome! Few regions of the country offer the immense rewards that gardening in the South can provide. The long growing season allows us to garden almost all year long, and a well-planned garden in all but the coldest areas can have blooms 12 months of the year. And while we mostly don't have to deal with snow, we do get to experience all four seasons. Quite a few trees and shrubs that struggle to grow or flower in the Pacific Northwest or in Great Britain thrive with our high heat and mild winters. Few temperate regions can be as successful with such a wide a range of plants as we can be in the South.

Borrowed views should be accentuated wherever possible to extend your landscape.

ALONG WITH THE REWARDS, the challenges can, at times, seem daunting. Sauna-like summer heat and humidity can make gardening a chore at best. And while precipitation comes mostly regularly throughout the year, two weeks with no rain and 90°F temperatures can shrivel even established plants. Along with the thriving plants, pests are often very happy in the region and can spread quickly from garden to garden. Soils throughout tend to be sandy, heavy red clay, or barely concealed bedrock. Where soils are deeper and richer, they are often old crop fields which can be quite nutrient poor after a couple centuries of farming.

The southeastern United States is an interesting region with a long and storied history of great gardeners and deep ties to the land, from backyard dirt farms to the estates of the Charleston area where plants like camellias and osmanthus were first introduced to the New World. The region is composed of all or part of a dozen states, including North Carolina south through north Florida and west through Tennessee to Arkansas and east Texas. Such a large area presents a great variety of climatic and geologic differences to discuss. Whether you are new to the area—five of the fastest growing states by population are found here—or have been a lifelong resident, I'm sure you will find something to help make you a better gardener in these pages, perhaps a new plant, an improved gardening technique, or a design inspiration.

In the following pages we'll take a closer look at gardening in the South, providing all the tools you'll need to be successful, whether you call the mountains or coast home. After exploring the weather, soils, and other vagaries of the eco-regions of the South, we'll look at some design inspirations to whet your appetite for getting out and getting dirty. Once you have a vision for your garden, I'll provide the tools for you to create a successful landscape. Starting with the basic building blocks—plants—you'll get a sense of what can be grown across the region. We'll finish up with how-tos for turning your inspiration into a thriving garden and keeping it in top shape.

LEFT Bold tropical color provides the wow factor in any combination (*Canna* 'Phasion'). RIGHT Foliage color, form, and texture create an interesting tableau, even with minimal flowers.

A SENSE OF PLACE

THE SOUTH AS DEFINED for our purposes includes Alabama, Arkansas, Georgia, Kentucky, Louisiana, Mississippi, North Carolina, South Carolina, Tennessee, Virginia, West Virginia, eastern Texas, and northern Florida. As could be expected from such a large area, many climatic and geologic differences are here to explore.

GEOGRAPHY OF THE SOUTH

The southeastern United States can be broadly divided into three major regions based on their climate and geological features: the Southeastern Coastal Plain, including the Mississippi River Valley; the Piedmont; and the Eastern Highlands, including the Appalachian Mountains and the Ozarks. A fourth unofficial region is urban areas—the metropolitan hubs across the South, which are often characterized by non-native plants, droughty conditions, pollution, and higher temperatures than the surrounding countryside.

Southeastern Coastal Plain

Much of the population of the Southeast has traditionally been along the coasts of the Atlantic Ocean and Gulf of Mexico, and many of the largest cities are still found in this region. The coastal plain is the typically flat region along the coastline, stretching inland for about 100 miles from the Atlantic coast and narrowing to a thin band across the Florida panhandle and the coasts of Alabama and Mississippi. The region expands to nearly 250 miles deep in Louisiana and along the gulf coast of Texas. The Mississippi River Valley up through Arkansas, while exhibiting some differences from the rest of the coastal plain, can be included in this eco-region due to its low, flat topography.

Gardens in the coastal plain can grow a wide variety of plants from subtropicals to Mediterranean herbs but are best characterized by the signature native live oak (*Quercus virginiana*) draped with Spanish moss (*Tillandsia usneoides*). Gardening is a way of life throughout this region dating to the earliest settlers, and every home from the largest antebellum plantations to small country shacks seems to cultivate something in the landscape.

Few plants evoke the southern coastal plain like a live oak draped in Spanish moss.

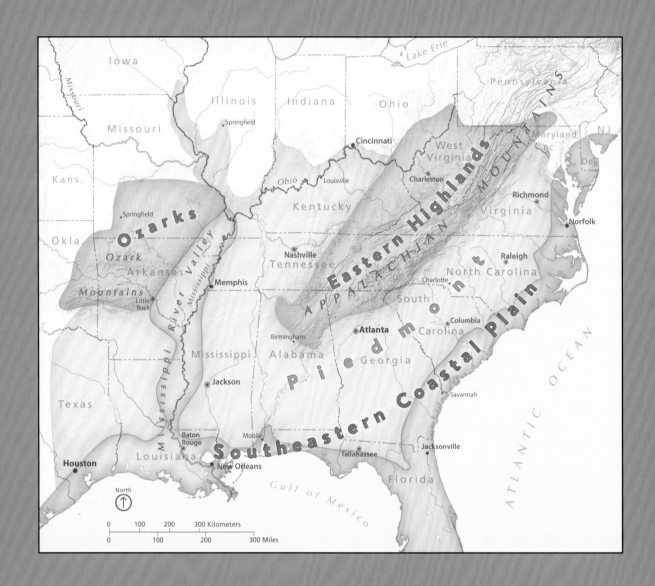

The southeastern United States includes three geographic and climatic regions (Southeastern Coastal Plain, Piedmont, Eastern Highlands and Ozarks) that are not bound by hard lines but represent distinct growing conditions. This map is only for general designations to help gardeners in their planning.

Dense forests and rocky outcrops characterize much of the Appalachian Mountains.

Piedmont

By far the largest eco-region of the Southeast is the Piedmont, which gets its name from an Italian town at the base of the Alps. The term *piedmont* literally translates to *foothill* and is the low plateau between the coastal lowlands and the mountains. It covers a broad band nearly 300 miles deep. Its rolling topography stretches along the Atlantic states and back up the western side of the Appalachian Mountains, jumping across the Mississippi River Valley into southwestern Arkansas where it meets with Texas and Louisiana.

The Piedmont begins at the fall line where the level, navigable rivers of the coastal plain develop falls and historically, ships carrying goods had to be unloaded. The Piedmont's rolling hills, like all the South, have a history of agriculture but also have traditionally been home to much of the business of the region. The gardens across this region are perhaps the most eclectic.

Eastern Highlands and Ozarks

The mountains along the North Carolina–Tennessee border extending through northern Georgia and into central Alabama form the bulk of the highlands of the region. The geographically separate but ecologically similar Ozarks in northwestern Arkansas, while having some distinctions, have many of the same gardening challenges, including rocky soils and some of the coldest temperatures in the Southeast.

The highlands are characterized by a close connection to the natural habitats of the region. Gardens across the area often blend with the native forests. Many gardeners focus on the local flora, and even where gardens are full of exotics, planting styles often mimic the woodlands of the region.

Urban regions

The unofficial fourth region encompasses the metropolitan areas across the Southeast. Cities like

Charlotte, Atlanta, Nashville, Little Rock, and Baton Rouge have more in common with each other than they do with their respective native eco-regions. The urban, built environment is a significant portion of our gardening space and should not be ignored. Green infrastructure will soon be a major way many people interact with the natural world.

Urban plantscapes vary but they share the characteristics of non-native, often low organic and compacted soils; restricted root zones; typically droughty conditions; pollution; and temperatures which can be much greater than the surrounding countryside. An increase in green infrastructure—green walls, green roofs, rain gardens, and pocket gardens—will make our cities much more livable in the long run.

SEASONS IN THE SOUTHEAST

The Southeast is a relatively mild climate allowing us to grow a wide variety of plants. With average annual minimum temperatures ranging from -15°F to 25°F, we fall into hardiness zones 5 to 9 according to the United States Department of Agriculture's Plant Hardiness Zone Map. The updated map reflects the regional differences in climate. Search the Internet for USDA Hardiness Zones or visit planthardiness.ars.usda.gov to find your exact zone by entering your zip code.

Rainfall is generally high and while summers often feel bone dry, precipitation is relatively even throughout the year. Most of the region receives 3–4 in. of rain per month, although a small portion of the mountains in North Carolina has some of the

A green wall at the very urban Mexico City International Airport.

WINTER WONDERS

Winter-flowering plants extend the southern gardening season well beyond the typical spring to fall of other regions. As an added bonus, many winter-flowering plants are exceptionally fragrant, perhaps in an attempt to attract the few pollinators active during the cooler months.

SCIENTIFIC NAME	COMMON NAME	DECEMBER	JANUARY	FEBRUARY	MARCH
Camellia	camellia	●	●	●	●
Chionodoxa	glory-of-the-snow			●	●
Clematis cirrhosa	winter clematis		●	●	
Crocus	crocus		●	●	●
Cyclamen	cyclamen	●	●		
Daphne odora	winter daphne		●	●	●
Edgeworthia	paperbush			●	●
Eriobotrya	loquat	●	●		
Galanthus	snowdrops		●	●	
Hamamelis	witchhazel		●	●	●
Helleborus	hellebore	●	●	●	●
Iris reticulata	reticulate iris			●	●
Iris unguicularis	Algerian iris	●	●		●
Mahonia ×media	grape-holly	●	●		
Muscari	grape hyacinth			●	●
Parrotia	ironwood			●	●
Prunus mume	Japanese apricot		●	●	
Sarcococca	sweetbox	●	●	●	
Scilla	squill			●	●
Stachyurus	spiketail			●	●

highest rainfall averages in the continental United States, with yearly totals of more than 90 in. Other spots are in rain shadows where they miss most of the regular precipitation.

Winter

There's a good reason the South is home to so many displaced Northerners and Midwesterners—the winters are mild and fairly short. In the Deep South, winter is more of a suggestion than a season, and the Gulf Coast often remains mostly frost free. Even the mountains, excepting the highest peaks, rarely stay below freezing through 24 consecutive hours. These mild temperatures allow for cultivating a wide range of plants. Gardening in the Southeast is truly a four-season endeavor, and winter brings low humidity and keeps the pesky mosquitoes at bay. Luckily we have many plants to enjoy during the winter even beyond the numerous broadleaf evergreens.

Garden hardscapes provide interest throughout the year.

Away from the moderating effects of the Atlantic Ocean or Gulf of Mexico, temperatures can be volatile, all too commonly with swings from 20 to 40 degrees between the high and low temperatures within 24 hours. These wide temperature fluctuations are harder on many plants than the consistent cold of some other regions. Early fall or late spring freezes while plants are actively growing is also a common problem especially across the Piedmont. The lack of reliable snow cover means that some perennials which perform well under the moderating effects of a blanket of snow actually suffer more in the South where they are more exposed than in northern gardens.

Spring

Despite our mild winters, spring is as welcome in the South as it is in colder climates. Warm temperatures start as early as the beginning of March in many years, and after a few of these short winters, novice gardeners are lulled into planting too early. Those of us who have purchased tomatoes three times in a single spring have learned to wait until the regular frost-free date to plant out our tender new starts. This doesn't stop the nurseries from selling plants to the overly naive or optimistic gardeners who can't wait to get planting.

Spring is a mixed prospect across the Southeast. The Deep South often gets only a glance at spring before jumping right into summer with temperatures in the 80s by the end of April. Even in other areas spring can start early and last for a few months, but it rarely if ever extends beyond early May. By the end of May, the entire region is firmly in the grip of summer.

Spring is a great time for planting in the Southeast, with mild to warm temperatures and regular rains being the norm. April across much of the region has some of the lowest monthly rainfall totals of the year, but the winter moisture and the sporadic rain keep plants going.

Summer

Summer is the defining season of the South, with sweltering temperatures in the 80s and 90s which barely cool down in the evening. There's a reason we like our tea cold and sweet—the ice helps us cool down, the caffeine overcomes the enervating effects of the oppressive humidity, the liquid keeps us hydrated, and much like juice and cookies when donating blood, the sugar helps replenish the blood lost to the swarms of mosquitoes.

Warm soils and regular rain help us create some of the lushest and greenest gardens in the temperate zone. By mid- to late summer the rain often feels as though it has abandoned us and a look at the average monthly totals can be deceiving. The 4 in. or so of monthly rain in July, August, and September looks great on paper, but it often comes in one or two rain events that flatten perennials and run off the baked soil instead of soaking into the ground. It isn't a bad idea when soils are bone dry and rain is in the forecast to run sprinklers for a bit to encourage the rainfall to soak in deeply rather than run off the surface.

A late summer to early fall reality for much of the coastal region is the threat of hurricanes with high winds and flooding. The salt spray carried inland by storms can be devastating, and gardens close to the shore will benefit from a windbreak to block the worst of it.

If watering is an option for your garden, plants can be installed all summer long, but they will need some special care to survive the often brutal heat. As a gardening professional, my spring and fall seasons are often so busy that I don't manage to get anything in the ground before July, and while not ideal, it can be done.

Fall

By the end of a blazing hot summer with humidity like a sauna, fall is quite welcome. But like a teenager with a license and some freedom, there's no telling when it will show up. In some years we begin feeling a bit of fall by early September, especially in the form of cooler evenings. Summer seems to last into almost November in other years. The highlands, and to a lesser extent the Piedmont, do usually experience a true autumn. The coastal plain can occasionally miss autumn entirely. Like spring, it can be a fleeting season but we can take solace that our winter isn't much colder than a northern fall.

If you are outside the highlands, which can have spectacular autumn color, the fall foliage season can be disappointing, especially to a displaced Vermonter. Gardeners in the Piedmont can select plants to provide reliable color, but the effect still isn't quite the same. Coastal plain gardeners can revel instead in the huge diversity of broadleaf evergreens that keep their landscapes lush and vibrant 12 months of the year.

Fall is for planting in the South. While I do garden around the year, there is no better time to put plants in the ground than autumn. Cooling air temperatures mean plants are under much less water stress as they establish. The warm soil encourages the roots, giving plants a head start on spring, when they'll be ready to leap into growth.

DESIGN INSPIRATIONS

A LANDSCAPE IS UNIQUE among creative endeavors as it changes through the seasons and transforms over the course of years. Inevitably a garden's design will need to be tweaked, adjusted, and edited as time goes by—plants grow, perhaps they die, and your needs and desires may change. When initially planning a garden, or when planning how to remake one, you will always find the job easier by keeping in mind the characteristics unique to your space, the needs and desires you have for your garden, and your personal aspirations and limits. Once you have these considerations defined, take the time to plan the details of your garden space and the plants you want to fill it, before taking shovel to soil or wallet to garden center.

CONSIDERATIONS

Before jumping into the excitement of plant selection, you will benefit from considering those aspects that underlie a successful garden. Familiarize yourself with the environmental details of your space, decide how you want to use the space, and honestly determine how much time you can invest.

A dry streambed can be used to move water during downpours and serve as an attractive garden feature at other times.

Know your space

When planning a garden, you must first understand what you have to work with, what constrains the design, and what problems need to be solved. Sun is perhaps the most important factor in the Southeast. A patio placed in blazing afternoon sun will likely get less use than one that is protected from summer heat. Study the sun patterns across your yard. Take into account that sun exposure will change based on the season.

Pay attention to water movement—water flow patterns, low spots, and dry patches are much easier to deal with earlier in a garden's development rather than later. Wait for a rainstorm and walk through the garden to see potential problems firsthand. Often these issues can be solved by simple landscape features like a rain garden or a dry streambed to direct water flow. In most cases, keeping water above ground is more efficient than trying to move it underground through drains and piping. Permanently damp areas can be converted to bog gardens, allowing for a wider variety of plants, or French drains can be installed to move the water away.

Wind can be a factor to consider in some areas, especially on the coast where salt spray can be a severe problem. The prevailing winds in highland regions can also affect plant growth and garden use in exposed areas. Hedges may be needed as a wind buffer. On the other hand, you may want to take advantage of cooling breezes to create pleasant and mosquito-free sitting spaces.

Know your needs

Consider honestly how you will be using your garden on a regular basis. If the yard will be a soccer field for children, then a broad expanse of turf may be important. As children age out, is a lawn necessary? Too many homeowners fertilize, spray, mow, and otherwise spend a great deal of time on a yard that is used only to fertilize, spray, and mow. Lawns have a high need for input and are usually underutilized.

If you plan to do a lot of outdoor entertaining, patios, firepits, and gathering spaces may be important. Avid cooks often want a kitchen garden or potager near the house for easy harvesting of vegetables and herbs from a beautiful garden space.

Make a list of needs and wants in order of importance and overlay those needs on a plan of your property. Often this will quickly help create a simple design—a hedge here to block the loud and nosy neighbor, a patio and firepit outside the family room, a natural shade garden with wildlife-friendly plants toward the back of the property for bird watching, and a rain garden to the side where the gutters drain.

Make a new list every five to seven years as your needs change. Have you become a more passionate birder? Perhaps expanding the wildlife garden is in order. Haven't entertained like you thought you would? Maybe remove the firepit to make space for a formal herb garden to satisfy a newfound joy of cooking. Rethinking the garden on a regular basis will keep you enthusiastic about your landscape and make sure it meets your changing needs.

Know your limitations

The biggest mistake many new gardeners make is to bite off more than they can chew. The desire to create a whole landscape or a large new garden can be overpowering but starting small is almost always wise. Nothing will discourage a gardener like feeling overwhelmed by their landscape. If you've never had a shade garden before, for example, start with a small plot of tried and true shade-loving plants. If that just whets your appetite, expand it the next year after you have a realistic sense of the input needed.

You will find more satisfaction in succeeding on a small scale and expanding as time, money, and desire allow. Starting too big stretches you thin and leads to a feeling that the garden is in charge. Give time for your gardening skills to develop, for plants to grow and fill in, and to get each piece of the garden under control. Once a space has had a year or two to establish, maintenance becomes much easier and your attention can shift to the next garden area. Be patient. A design often takes years to really come together as the plants grow and develop. In the meantime, parts of the garden may be bare or at best seem thin and sparse. If this isn't acceptable to you, fill with annuals or quick-growing groundcovers, with the plan to remove them over time as the garden fills in.

Remember that gardening is all experimentation and that even the best gardener fails regularly. Anyone with significant experience will proudly tell you about the plants they've killed, the gardens that went awry, and the great ideas that weren't. The joys of success are all the sweeter after a few mishaps along the way. The real reason some people seem to have a green thumb is that they have a lot of compost made from all the plants they've killed.

Even when a garden thrives and the plants grow, the design may just not come out the way you envisioned. Often a few tweaks will fix the problem, but sometimes going back to a blank slate is the best solution. I regularly dig plants and move them to another spot if they don't seem to be growing well or if they just don't look quite right. Don't be afraid to get in and switch things up. A garden is never finished. Its ever-changing, growing, and developing nature make trying to keep a garden static an exercise in futility.

WORKING WITH SPACE

To plan the layout and specific plantings for your garden, think of the space three-dimensionally. Plants can create rooms in the landscape. The different rooms can fulfill different purposes and evoke different feelings, from a grand cathedral-like sense of awe to a cozy sitting-room intimacy. Creating a room in the garden necessitates creating walls, doorways, a ceiling, and a floor, but much like a room in a house, it is the furnishings which give the space a purpose and sense of style. An intricate Persian rug, a dining room table, or a focal piece of art may add that final touch of pizzazz. In the same way, you can create and embellish a garden room by thoughtfully combining the same sorts of elements.

Floor

Every garden room will have a floor since the ground serves as the foundation of the space. Often the floor is turf, a carpet of mixed perennials, or a layer of low-growing shrubs. Other flooring options include decking, stone, pavers, or a mixture of plants and

TOP RIGHT A grit path cleanly edged with stone opens to a floor with a geometric pattern, for a formal look complemented by a container with a clipped arborvitae.
RIGHT The floor of the garden can make a strong statement when carefully composed. Here, three elements—stone, dwarf mondo grass, and a ground-covering sedum—create a peaceful labyrinth suitable for quiet reflection.

Moss, ferns, and irregular stone edging give a much different feel than a mulched path would provide.

hardscape. What happens under your feet is the basis for how a room feels. A hardwood mulch base will rarely lend itself to a formal landscape but instead works better in a shade garden, while an intricate stonework pathway will give a different impression.

Pathways are an important part of the floor, and an easy way to transition from one garden space to another is to change the path material. The transition may be abrupt with a sharp delineation between rooms, or the path may break apart to ease the movement through the different spaces.

Light and shadow play across a path inspired by Japanese nobedan.

Walls

Actual walls, fences, and trellises obviously create walls in the garden which may separate garden rooms or provide a barrier between your garden and a neighbor. Large shrubs, hedges, tree trunks, and tall perennials can create walls and separation between garden spaces as well. Unlike indoor walls, walls in a garden may be see-through, providing tantalizing peeks into other garden rooms. Doorways between rooms, like the pathways which lead through them, are transition zones between garden spaces.

A hedge can provide more than just a barrier between spaces if it is clipped to create a textured wall.

A garden wall does not need to be solid. Here, a line of small trees creates separation between garden spaces.

A round portal invites you to step through and discover what's on the other side while also effectively framing the view.

Trees can be trained into an archway to create a low roof, like the famed laburnum walk at Bodnant Castle in Wales.

Ceiling

Perhaps the most neglected feature of the garden room is the ceiling. Often the ceiling will simply be the sky above, which helps even a small garden space feel large and airy. Medium and small trees may give a more intimate and cozy sense, especially when planted under a higher overstory. Tall, mature trees without lower limbs can give the garden a sense of grandeur similar to a cathedral. Creating this imposing sense would be difficult to do from scratch, but where suitable trees are already part of the landscape you may accentuate height by limiting or removing understory trees.

Furnishings

Once your garden rooms are created, the real fun begins. The furnishings are what make your garden unique and give it a sense of individuality. Garden art, specimen plants, benches, and memorable combinations bring flair, and talented gardeners will use these features to make each space feel different from the others.

Depending on the chosen pieces, garden art can add whimsy, formality, or a sense of age. Traditional statuary often evokes themes of grand European estates and, when combined with elements like clipped hedges and geometric beds, will turn any garden into a formal space. Whimsical elements create

A cement statue filled with succulents provides a color echo in the garden.

A simple container with a single plant can add drama to a garden when edged and planted in a formal manner.

BOTTOM Repeating elements in small containers can be more effective than a single large pot.

a fun environment and lend themselves to gardeners with eclectic taste and a sense of irreverence.

Perhaps the most common garden furnishing other than the plants themselves are containers. Pots provide focal points, allow for a different look from year to year, and change across the seasons. Containers are often planted with tropicals or annuals, but they can also be ideal for a specimen Japanese maple or tough evergreen perennial.

The furniture you choose for a garden room hints at the uses you imagine for the space. A single seat may be an invitation for quiet reflection, while a table and chairs provides a spot for a garden get-together. Garden furniture can add to the sense of place as well. A rough-hewn bench fits into a woodland garden, and a brightly painted swing acts as a focal point in a whimsical space.

TOP A grouping of potted plants can make use of neglected patio corners or unused garden space. Massing also makes them easier to water. LEFT A pot containing a mix of drought-tolerant plants is an easy-care garden element for busy gardeners and frequent travelers. RIGHT A single mixed container can become a focal point, so carefully consider its site.

TOP A woodland table and benches of natural materials blend into the landscape and invite you to spend time in the cool shade. LEFT A white metal bench becomes a focal point in this meadow garden. RIGHT Old tiles are repurposed to create a mosaic seat on a rustic bench.

GREEN INFRASTRUCTURE

Green infrastructure is a broad concept that includes various ways of incorporating plants into our built environment, especially highly urban areas, often with the intent of managing water. Perhaps the most common form is the green roof. Planted rooftops provide insect and bird habitats that would otherwise be lost to both permanent residents and migrating populations. Green roofs can also reduce particulate pollution; clean, reduce, and delay water entering storm systems; and moderate indoor temperatures. Green walls provide many of the same benefits and in conjunction with green roofs have the potential to significantly reduce the heat island effect of our cities. In addition to the environmental benefits green roofs and walls provide, they can significantly improve our quality of life.

Dense and diverse plantings like this roof at Moore Farms Botanical Garden in South Carolina can create a sense of place. (Yes, this is a roof!)

Modern-looking green roofs with a minimalist planting plan can reinforce contemporary architectural design.

Rain gardens can be beautiful as well as functional landscape features.

Rain gardens are another form of green infrastructure which help reduce the pollutants entering our streams and rivers. Urban rain gardens can capture the water running through gutters before it reaches the storm drains. This helps reduce the initial rush of water which can overwhelm the system. Rain gardens also capture that first flush of the most highly polluted and contaminated water. Plants have a remarkable ability to clean water significantly, and the water that exits these gardens and enters the storm drain system has fewer pollutants, like oils, when it discharges into rivers. Discharged water will also be significantly cooler which can help prevent algae outbreaks and fish kills.

Other green infrastructure concepts include permeable paving to allow water to soak into the soil rather than running off, bioswales to move and direct the flow of water, and cisterns or other rainwater storage systems. Cities have also started looking to the advantages of increasing neighborhood tree canopies.

SOME OUTSTANDING SOUTHEASTERN GARDENS

Discussions of general design principles are all well and good, but seeing them put into practice in actual gardens drives home the realization that good design matters—particularly when it accompanies a sensitivity to the unique qualities of a particular site. The following gardens exemplify the many ways that design can transform a garden from something merely pleasant into an extraordinary blend of plants, hardscape, and that elusive quality, "sense of place."

A jewelbox garden

Montrose, the garden of Nancy and Craufurd Goodwin in Hillsborough, North Carolina, is a showcase for interesting plants used in creative ways. Offering a variety of habitats on a spacious site, it accommodates woodland gems like cardiocrinums, formal features such as the undulating, 19th-century boxwood hedges, and scores of sun-loving plants that thrive in the North Carolina heat and humidity. Especially notable are Nancy's color-themed gardens, which concentrate bursts of vivid color in relatively confined areas. The orange and purple garden is a riot of hot hues fearlessly deployed, while the blue and yellow garden deftly juxtaposes these two gentler colors. In both cases, tender perennials and annuals contribute mightily to the length of the display and the ultimate success of the plantings. Also noteworthy are the garden's displays of winter-blooming plants, especially cyclamen and snowdrops. Guided tours are available from September to May by appointment; go to visitnc.com/listing/montrose-gardens for more information.

Among Nancy Goodwin's most stunning achievements at Montrose are her color-themed gardens, which blend heat-tolerant annuals, perennials, bulbs, and shrubs into a dazzling tapestry. Here, the orange-and-purple garden is framed by the gothic arch of the shade house; coreopsis, gomphrenas, setcreaseas, ornamental grasses, and cannas romp in the foreground.

Woodland wonder

In a southeastern garden, the cooling effect of mature deciduous trees is an asset to be cherished—not to mention the fact that deciduous hardwood forest is the default setting, so to speak, for much of the South. Although woodland gardening means forgoing exclusively sun-loving plants, stunning effects can be achieved with a palette of shade-loving native plants and their noninvasive Asian counterparts. This is nowhere more evident than in C. Colston Burrell's Virginia garden. Burrell, a lecturer, garden designer, writer, and photographer, is the principal of Native Landscape Design and Restoration, and his work shows a finely tuned sensitivity to the role of native plants in the landscape—although he readily admits to using and collecting what he calls "the best plants of the global garden." His 10-acre garden, Bird Hill, encompasses meadows as well as woodland, although shade plantings dominate near the house. Here, Burrell has employed circular spaces inspired by the Danish-American landscape architect Jens Jensen, and filled them with a rich tapestry of ferns, bulbs, wildflowers, shrubs, and flowering trees. Seeing what Burrell has accomplished, it's clear that woodland conditions are compatible with the highest goals of garden design.

The blue-and-yellow garden at Montrose, with its masses of salvias and asters, forms a cool and sparkling counterpart to the orange-and-purple garden. RIGHT TOP The bright blossoms of primulas, native bleeding hearts, trilliums, and Virginia bluebells take center stage before ferns and other foliage plants take over. RIGHT BOTTOM Wild blue phlox, tiarella, and yellow corydalis usher the visitor to a shaded sitting spot.

An air of formality

With so many cities rich in historic architecture, the Southeast has a strong tradition of formal garden design. This is particularly apparent in Charleston, South Carolina, where the gardening legacy of the 17th and 18th centuries got a big boost from Loutrel Briggs (1893–1977), a New York–born landscape architect who worked in Charleston for 40 years. Briggs felt it was important to create gardens that were in harmony with their spatial and architectural surroundings, and the result was the formality so in evidence today in the historic district.

Patti and Peter McGee inherited the framework of a Briggs landscape when they began their former garden in Charleston's Ansonborough neighborhood. Rather than hewing to a strictly formal planting scheme, Patti chose to introduce a note of lushness and exuberant color by planting flowering shrubs and vines and using an abundance of potted specimens like clivias and begonias. The result was spectacular: burgeoning plants within a crisp, classically proportioned hardscape—proof, if any were needed, that the formal style can easily accommodate the passions of a plant-loving gardener.

The central terrace of the McGees' garden, shaded by an enormous live oak, is almost tropical in its lushness and bright color. RIGHT In another part of the garden, axial paths and clipped boxwoods reflect Loutrel Briggs's lingering influence.

In May, this cool-colored corner of Pamela Harper's garden brims with *Veronica incana*, *Verbascum chaixii* 'Album', dianthus, and *Papaver somniferum*, all woven among the feathery plumes of *Stipa tenuissima*.

An exceptional Tidewater garden

Writer and garden photographer Pam Harper readily admits she doesn't have to cope with the salt-laden winds and harsh sun that afflict many coastal gardens, but her Tidewater Virginia garden certainly experiences its share of challenges. The infertile, acidic, sandy soil she encountered when she first began gardening on the site, some 45 years ago, has been modified by the addition of countless truckloads of compost and mulch, so that today it is humus-rich and accommodating to a wide range of plants. Summer drought is also a frequent problem, as is flooding. Harper's main strategy has been to garden in the more sheltered parts of the property, while allowing native plants to form a buffer zone behind the house, close to the brackish water where the Chesapeake Bay meets the James and York Rivers (although Hurricane Isabel wreaked a fair amount of havoc here in 2013). By concentrating on creating suitable conditions in a clearly defined part of her property, Harper has succeeded in creating a richly diverse garden that anyone would envy—a testament to her understanding of a sometimes problematic site and her intelligent use of resources, not to mention her artistic eye and profound knowledge and love of plants.

Despite a challenging climate and soil, Pamela Harper created this exuberant border, bright with pink phlox, scarlet dahlias, rosy sedums, white Japanese anemones, and flaming orange kniphofias.

A SOUTHEAST PLANT PALETTE

PLANTS ARE THE PRIMARY BUILDING BLOCKS of the garden, and even the best-designed garden will suffer if plants are selected improperly. The South can grow numerous evergreens, which provide the skeleton of the garden, giving weight and substance twelve months of the year. Large shade trees provide a ceiling for your garden, and in neighborhoods can establish continuity between one garden and the next, creating a sense of community instead of a collection of individual properties. Flowering trees and shrubs give flashes of color throughout the season, and herbaceous perennials bring texture variation and tie everything else together. All season long, color from flowering annuals provides cheery interest whether planted out en masse or dotted sparingly between permanent plantings.

A well-planted garden will have elements of most or all of these plants. Their thoughtful combination will transform a garden throughout the seasons. Perhaps your garden space is filled with white-flowering bulbs and shrubs in early spring mixed with evergreens for an elegant display, but becomes a riot of bright reds and golds by midsummer. Or perhaps it is a soothing tapestry of shades of green for a peaceful sanctuary. Plants can also delineate different garden rooms or spaces with different looks and uses. In purely utilitarian terms, plantings can solve landscape problems, like shielding your house from nosy neighbors with a dense hedge or dealing with a low spot that floods by installing a rain garden.

This plant palette contains many of the plants I have found most useful and enjoyable in my years of gardening. I have grouped the plants in this palette into eight basic forms, found on the following page.

Calycanthus ×*raulstonii* 'Hartlage Wine', a hybrid sweetshrub developed at the JC Raulston Arboretum, offers glossy leaves and large burgundy flowers.

While it is useful to break plants into these manageable groups, the plants do not always want to follow along. Consider, for instance, *Colocasia* (elephant ear). This genus could be grouped with the tropicals since it is certainly not hardy throughout the entire Southeast and some species will not tolerate a freeze. It could also be grouped with the perennials since many will survive in large swaths of the region and return year after year. But here you will find *Colocasia* with the bulbs, because its underground storage organ is one of its defining features.

EIGHT BASIC PLANT FORMS

Annuals and tropicals	Plants which either grow, flower, and die in one growing season or are generally not winter hardy through most of the Southeast.
Bulbs	Plants which form some underground storage structure such as a bulb, corm, or tuber.
Grasses	True ornamental grasses and grass-like plants with narrow strappy leaves which don't have the traditional showy flowers of other herbaceous perennials.
Groundcovers	Spreading herbaceous perennials or low-growing woody plants which are traditionally used to provide cover for large areas in the landscape.
Perennials	Plants which do not form woody tissue but return year after year in the garden.
Shrubs	Plants which form true wood, are often multi-stemmed, and generally reach less than 15 ft. tall.
Trees	Plants which form true wood, are typically (but not always) single trunked, and grow to more than 15 ft. tall.
Vines	Plants which may be woody or herbaceous and will form long stems that clamber and climb.

Each plant entry names a single genus, but in some cases the plants within that genus vary widely either between species or among selections. Consequently, size ranges may cover a wide span and winter hardiness may range from truly tropical to almost the coldest areas of the region. Additional characteristics that predominate in each genus I have highlighted through the use of the following symbols.

PLANT LISTINGS KEY

Full sun	☀	Six or more hours of direct summer sunlight per day including at least some intense afternoon sun.
Part sun	☼	Four to six hours of direct summer sunlight per day usually including some hot afternoon sun.
Part shade	◐	Two to four hours of direct summer morning sunlight or very bright dappled sunlight as through a tall canopy of widely spaced trees.
Shade	●	Less than two hours of direct summer sunlight or lightly dappled light from a relatively dense overstory.
Drought tolerant	☼	These plants will tolerate significant periods of drought once established. No plant is drought tolerant until its root system has had time to spread and grow. In general, perennials need one to two years, two years for shrubs and trees, plus one additional year for each inch of tree trunk caliper (diameter) in order to be well-rooted in the soil.
Salt tolerant	S	These plants will tolerate salt spray when grown in coastal conditions and will be more tolerant of limited flooding with salt water.
Deer resistant	🦌	Deer tend to avoid these plants but when deer populations are high, no plant is completely safe.
Evergreen	🌲	Plants which keep their leaves throughout the entire year.
Semi-evergreen	🌲	Plants which will retain most of their leaves in a typical winter.
Fragrant	✿	Plants which have fragrant flowers.
Attractive to pollinators	🐝	Plants which attract significant numbers of pollinators, especially honeybees, butterflies, and hummingbirds.
Native	📍	Plants native to the Southeast.

Annuals and Tropicals

Annuals, tropicals, and tender perennials are the spice which allows the garden to change from year to year. Perhaps one year a palette of white and pastel gives a subdued and elegant effect while the next year's is a melange of hot orange and gold. Whether planted out in traditional bedding displays, arranged in containers, or simply mixed into perennial beds, these tender plants can provide some of the greatest impact on the garden display. A well-placed banana plant can elevate the typical to the extraordinary.

Several plants in this section are reliable perennials in the warmer areas of the Southeast, especially along the mild coastal regions. Others would require the frost-free zones of southern Florida for any chance of survival, while a handful are true annuals whose entire life cycle is completed in a single season. For those plants which can be kept from year to year, I have included some information to assist you, but part of the fun with these plants is their offer of new experiences. Don't feel bad about composting your tropicals and trying something different every year. After all, even an expensive specimen tropical that will give enjoyment for an entire season costs less than a meal at a midrange restaurant.

All these quick-growing and often long-flowering plants require supplemental fertilization and irrigation to reach their maximum potential, unless otherwise noted. Flowering in particular takes a lot of energy and benefits from a regular liquid feed of fertilizer. Many of the plants will also continue flowering much longer if you deadhead or remove the spent flowers after they fade but before the plants develop seed.

Annuals and tropicals such as *Ipomoea lobata* or candy corn vine provide vivid color and interest to the summer garden and can be switched out from year to year.

Allamanda

Allamanda, yellow mandevilla

BLOOM PERIOD: May to October

SIZE: 2–12 ft. tall, depending on species

HARDINESS: Zones 9–11

Allamandas are a group of trees, shrubs, and vines ranging from Mexico south through much of South America. Most commonly seen in cultivation are the shrubby *Allamanda cathartica* and vining *A. hendersonii*, both with bright gold, 2-in. tubular flowers, and the vining *A. blanchetii* with rosy pink flowers. They are hardy in the warmest areas of the Southeast but should otherwise be grown in annual displays. The vines can provide quick, long-season color growing up mailboxes or along fences. A full 10-in. container purchased in spring can easily grow to 6 ft. or more in a season. The shrubby species will top out at about 4 ft.

The subtropical *Allamanda cathartica* can be grown as a shrub or trained into a small patio tree.

Alternanthera

Joseph's coat

BLOOM PERIOD: May to September

SIZE: 8–30 in. tall

HARDINESS: Zones 10–11

Joseph's coat is grown for its often brightly colored foliage and occasionally fine texture. The small-growing *Alternanthera ficoidea* often has extremely narrow leaves in shades of burgundy, pink, green, or chartreuse, or variegated with several colors. It makes a tight plant used extensively for intricate bedding schemes and edging annual beds. Larger forms become focal points for beds or containers. *Alternanthera dentata* has dark burgundy foliage ideal for cascading from containers. Joseph's coat is easy to propagate, and cuttings taken before frost can be rooted in a light potting mix indoors if kept moist.

The broad leaves and dark color of *Alternanthera dentata* 'Purple Knight' make an excellent midsize plant for annual combinations.

Angelonia

Angelonia, angel flower

BLOOM PERIOD: May to September

SIZE: 10–30 in. tall

HARDINESS: Zones 9–11

Angelonia angustifolia is a popular summer annual with upright spikes of blue, pink, white, or bicolor flowers. Older cultivars would often cycle through flowering periods, with several weeks of heavy bloom followed by little or no flowering. More recent selections flower heavily and uniformly throughout the growing season. Taller forms make good focal plants in small containers or beds. The smaller selections can be planted 12 in. apart for bedding or edging. Deadheading the taller forms will keep them looking their best but isn't necessary for smaller cultivars.

The compact forms of angelonia are long-blooming, easy plants for bedding out or using in containers.

CREATING CONTAINERS

An effective way to use annuals and tropical plants is in containers that can either be moved indoors during the winter or replanted every year to create new displays. A well-planted pot adds drama and can draw your attention, which is why they are so often placed near garden entrances or used to lead you through the garden. Larger containers used singly or en masse can hide uglier or more functional areas of the garden or separate the garden into rooms.

The typical container often has a central, very dramatic specimen surrounded by lower groupings of plants, and is completed by cascading or trailing plants hanging over the edges of the pot. However, containers can be just as effective with a single specimen plant, whether it is a special Japanese maple or a massive elephant ear.

Containers can be used to create special environments for plants which wouldn't otherwise survive in the garden. Excellent drainage can be provided for desert or Mediterranean climate plants that would quickly turn up their toes in the wet Southeast. If your garden doesn't have a pond, a pot with no drainage can be used to grow miniature waterlilies and cattails. For those in drier areas who garden with drought-tolerant plants, a single container with lush plants is a smart way to get the most bang for the buck with limited water use.

Place your containers needing the most water closest to a water source, perhaps near your front entrance. Containers with lower water needs can be put further out in the garden where they will require less maintenance. Grouping containers is both visually effective and can make them easier to maintain.

Begonia

Begonia

BLOOM PERIOD: **May to September**
SIZE: **8–24 in. tall**
HARDINESS: **Zones 9–11**

Begonias are a large group, making them difficult to generalize, but most have succulent stems and do not tolerate drought. The common wax begonias used traditionally for bedding have rounded green to burgundy foliage with white, pink, or red flowers. Other begonias suitable for annual plantings in the Southeast include the colorful-foliaged rex-type selections. These often have burgundy, silver, and other shades on textured leaves; flowering for these is typically not showy. *Begonia grandis* is much hardier than other species, spreading well even in warm zone 6 gardens. Grow begonias in shade in a loose, consistently moist soil.

TOP Tropical begonias like *Begonia* 'Passing Storm' often have striking foliage that can make an average annual display exceptional. BOTTOM The common wax begonias will flower all summer long and make easy, low-care annual displays.

Beta

Ornamental beet, Swiss chard

BLOOM PERIOD: Non-flowering

SIZE: 8–18 in. tall

HARDINESS: Zones 4–11

The traditional edible beet and Swiss chard, both forms of *Beta vulgaris*, can be grown as ornamentals as well as for food by choosing one of the dark-leaved cultivars like 'Bull's Blood' or a colorful stalked form such as 'Bright Lights'. Sow seeds in late winter or early fall and leaves will appear about five weeks later. They are best in a moist, loose soil with some protection from hot, afternoon sun. Betas will suffer under high heat in Deep South gardens but are excellent as winter annuals.

The brilliant leaf stalks of *Beta vulgaris* 'Bright Lights' Swiss chard are beautiful in the garden or on a dinner plate.

Brassica

Ornamental cabbage, ornamental kale

BLOOM PERIOD: April to May

SIZE: 12–18 in. tall

HARDINESS: Zones 4–11

Brassica is an important genus of edible plants which includes cabbage, kale, turnips, broccoli, and Brussels sprouts. The showy forms of *B. oleracea* known as ornamental cabbages and kales are excellent for planting with pansies and other winter annuals. You can purchase plants in early fall or start seed indoors in early August. Most ornamental brassicas are leafy forms with frilly or bold foliage colored green, white, burgundy, and pink. In warmer areas, they will grow well all winter, eventually bolting and flowering with tall spikes of yellow flowers when temperatures warm up in spring.

Showy ornamental cabbages like *Brassica oleracea* 'Nagoya Red' bring color and texture to the winter garden and can be harvested to provide a lovely garnish for the dinner plate or splash of color in a salad.

Brugmansia

Angel's trumpet

BLOOM PERIOD: June to September
SIZE: 4–15 ft. tall
HARDINESS: Zones 8–10

Angel's trumpets, mostly *Brugmansia suaveolens* and hybrids, are subtropical shrubs or trees with huge tubular flowers. The intensely fragrant, pendant trumpets range from white to yellow, peach, and pink. Angel's trumpet responds well to moisture and fertilization and will grow quickly when pushed with plenty of both. In warm areas, angel's trumpets will die to the ground in winter and return the following year, flowering again when the stems reach 3–4 ft. In cooler regions, lift plants in fall and bring indoors or mulch well outdoors in zone 7 gardens. All parts of *Brugmansia* plants are extremely toxic.

In warm gardens *Brugmansia* 'Jamaican Yellow' will sprout from the ground each year and grow to over 8 ft. by autumn.

Caladium

Caladium, angel wings

BLOOM PERIOD: Non-flowering
SIZE: 14–30 in. tall
HARDINESS: Zones 9–11

Caladium bicolor is a subtropical tuber with colorful heart- to arrow-shaped leaves. The foliar color is typically a pattern of green, white, pink, and red. Caladiums can burn in full sun unless given plenty of moisture and are typically best in bright shade. They can be slow to get started in spring and so are often best started indoors in early spring and planted out after the danger of frost is past. In fall, dig the tubers, dry them on a natural surface like wood, and store in a cool, dark place in wood shavings or sphagnum moss.

Recent breeding has brought a wide variety of bright colors to caladiums, like the chartreuse and red of *Caladium* 'Yellow Blossom'.

Calibrachoa, million bells

BLOOM PERIOD: May to September

SIZE: 2–6 in. tall

HARDINESS: Zones 9–11

☀ ☼ 🦌 🐝▸

Million bells is a group of hybrids of *Calibrachoa* which some authorities do not recognize as distinct from the genus *Petunia*. In any case they are low, spreading, subtropical perennials grown as annuals for hanging baskets, cascading out of pots, or as a colorful groundcover around taller perennials. Plants grown in sunny spots will have hundreds of small petunia-like blossoms in an amazing array of colors and will not suffer a decline during the heat of summer as many petunias will. Plant calibrachoa after danger of frost in spring. Plants may return after winter in warm zone 8 gardens but not reliably.

Resembling miniature petunias, calibrachoas provide season-long, intense color for annual beds, containers, and hanging baskets.

Ornamental pepper

BLOOM PERIOD: May to September

SIZE: 12–36 in. tall

HARDINESS: Annual

☀ ☼

Ornamental peppers, *Capsicum annuum* varieties, are grown for their small, showy orange, red, or purple edible fruit. Typically, the ornamental varieties are extremely hot, but some varieties, like 'Chilly Chili', are sweet. Many forms will have upright facing clusters of fruit in various stages of maturity in colors from yellow to orange and bright red. Some selections have purple leaves occasionally splashed with white as well. Grow ornamental and edible peppers in a loose soil in full sun for best production.

Most ornamental peppers, like *Capsicum annuum* 'Explosive Ignite', retain their heat but hold fruit upright instead of below the foliage.

Catharanthus

Vinca, Madagascar periwinkle

BLOOM PERIOD: **May to September**

SIZE: **8–14 in. tall**

HARDINESS: **Zones 10–11**

 ☀ ◐ 🦌

Catharanthus roseus or vinca, not to be confused with the genus *Vinca*, is a woody based, shrubby plant in its native Madagascar and other dry, tropical areas where it has escaped cultivation. In temperate gardens it grows as a long-blooming, heat- and drought-tolerant flowering annual. Deep green leaves with a white midrib are topped by masses of white, pink, lavender, or rose flowers often with a darker eye. The several prostrate selections can be grown over the edges of containers. Vinca needs full sun and well-drained soil; it tolerates drought conditions once well rooted.

Catharanthus roseus is ideal for growing in well-drained locations where it will flourish and produce pinwheel flowers all summer long.

Cosmos

Cosmos

BLOOM PERIOD: **May to October**

SIZE: **14–60 in. tall**

HARDINESS: **Annual**

 ☀ ◐ 🐝

Cosmos are annuals in the aster family with dissected foliage and daisy-like, yellow to orange flowers in *Cosmos sulphureus*, or white, pink, and rose flowers in *C. bipinnatus*. Cosmos grow easily from seed sown indoors in spring or outdoors shortly before the first frost-free date. Cosmos can slow down in summer but will rebound in fall. On the other hand, if the spring stand seems to have succumbed to the heat, sow a new crop in August for a bright fall show. Plants will often self-sow and return year after year, mingling with perennial plants in unexpected combinations. Do not overfertilize, especially the taller *C. sulphureus*, as plants can flop.

Butterflies love the bright orange and yellow flowers of *Cosmos sulphureus*.

Duranta

Pigeon berry, golden dewdrop

BLOOM PERIOD: June to September
SIZE: 2–6 ft. tall or more in tropical areas
HARDINESS: Zones 10–11

Duranta erecta or pigeon berry is a glossy-leaved tropical shrub with racemes of small blue to white flowers. In late summer or fall in warm gardens, showy yellow-orange fruits form, but they rarely do in cooler, temperate areas. Gold-leaved or gold-variegated forms are often grown for their foliage as much as the flowers in annual displays or as centerpieces in containers. To bring them indoors for the winter, place in a bright window. Mature plants will often form sharp spines.

Duranta erecta 'Goldleaf' is grown in annual displays more for its foliage than its flowers.

Gomphrena

Globe amaranth

BLOOM PERIOD: May to September
SIZE: 12–24 in. tall
HARDINESS: Annual

Globe amaranth is typically represented in gardens by magenta, ball-shaped flower clusters—these are actually bracts surrounding the tiny and insignificant true flowers—of *Gomphrena globosa*. Additional colors from pink to red, orange, and white are available from hybrids with other species like the orange-flowered *G. haageana*. Plant out after frost and pinch stems back once or twice early in the season for bushier plants. The straw-textured bracts last for a long period and can be cut and used for dry flower arrangements. Best color comes from harvesting newly opened flowers and drying them in a dark space.

The straw-textured bracts of gomphrenas last a long time in the garden or can be cut and dried for indoor arrangements.

Ipomoea

Morning glory, sweet potato vine
BLOOM PERIOD: June to September
SIZE: 5–15 ft. tall
HARDINESS: Zones 9–11

Ipomoea is a genus of mostly vines with trumpet-shaped flowers and often bold, heart-shaped leaves. Morning glory, *I. purpurea*, is typically purple but can include white, pink, and red and is a quick-growing annual vine. Other tropical species can be grown as annuals and extend the color range. For example, candy corn vine, *I. lobata*, bears spikes of dark orange to yellow, tubular flowers instead of the typical wide-flared trumpets of morning glories. Sweet potato vines grown as ornamentals, *I. batatas*, have chartreuse, purple, or variegated foliage and rarely flower, although new forms have increased summer flowering. Grow all in full sun to part shade. Morning glories need a supporting structure while sweet potatoes can grow as an annual groundcover or cascading from containers.

Ornamental sweet potato vines come in a wide variety of foliage colors, from chartreuse to bronze to burgundy, and make a quick groundcover.

Musa

Banana
BLOOM PERIOD: August to September
SIZE: 4–15 ft. tall
HARDINESS: Zones 7–11, depending on species

Few plants can create a tropical feel as easily as bananas. The hardiest species, *Musa basjoo*, is reliable to zone 7 where it can quickly form large clumps to 15 ft. tall. While most bananas will not form fruit in temperate gardens, the hardy pink banana, *M. velutina* will reliably bear small pink-skinned bananas in zone 8 gardens. Other tropical bananas can be grown in containers and moved indoors or dug and stored in a cool, dark spot for the winter. Bananas respond well to irrigation and fertilizer.

The surprisingly hardy *Musa basjoo* has a bold texture that will quickly provide impact if given plenty of water and fertilizer, elevating an ordinary garden to extraordinary. RIGHT The pink-fruited banana, *Musa velutina*, will reliably set small pink bananas in a season through much of the Southeast.

Pelargonium

Geranium

BLOOM PERIOD: **May to September**

SIZE: **12–24 in. tall**

HARDINESS: **Zones 10–11**

☀ ☀ ☀ 🦌 ✂

Geraniums, not to be confused with the genus *Geranium*, are a group of subtropical perennials grown as annuals with showy red, white, or pink flowers. Most geraniums are hybrids best grown in full sun to light shade. The rounded, lobed foliage often has some burgundy shading. They flower best if the clusters of flowers are removed promptly when they begin to fade. Ivy geraniums have glossier foliage and a lax habit that makes them suitable for hanging baskets. Scented geraniums are grown for their aromatic foliage which mimics lemon, coconut, and other fragrances, but the flowers are somewhat insignificant.

Several colorfully leaved and variegated selections like *Pelargonium* 'Crystal Palace Gem' combine showy flowers and foliage.

Petunia

Petunia

BLOOM PERIOD: May to September
SIZE: 8–14 in. tall
HARDINESS: Zones 10–11

Petunias are widely grown for their showy tubular flowers in just about every shade imaginable. They grow as spreading plants in most soils so long as the soil is well drained. Petunias can become leggy and decline during the heat of the summer—cut them back hard to stimulate new growth and flowering for the rest of the season. Petunias' cascading habit and preference for well-drained soils make them ideal for hanging baskets and containers.

Petunias offer a wide range of color options, from pastel to vivid pinks, red, and purple.

Plectranthus

Swedish ivy, Cuban oregano

BLOOM PERIOD: August to September
SIZE: 12–28 in. tall
HARDINESS: Zones 10–11

Swedish ivy is widely grown as a houseplant but it makes an excellent shade-tolerant foliage plant in the garden. The white-edged *Plectranthus australis* 'Variegatus' makes a mound of rounded, scalloped foliage brightening up shaded spots. Somewhat different is the silver-leaved *P. argentatus*, which makes large, vigorous mounds of foliage. It is quite tolerant of sun but can grow in partly shaded spots as well. Although most forms are grown for their foliage, 'Mona Lavender' is a hybrid with spikes of showy lavender flowers. *Plectranthus* plants root easily from cuttings stuck in moist soil in a bright spot away from direct sun.

The silver foliage, large size, and bold texture of *Plectranthus argentatus* make it a great backdrop for other annuals or a tropical specimen in a bed or container.

Portulaca

Moss rose, purslane

BLOOM PERIOD: June to September
SIZE: 2–6 in. tall
HARDINESS: Annual

Moss rose, *Portulaca grandiflora*, lives up to its name, forming a low mat of cylindrical, succulent, moss-like foliage topped with bright flowers in shades of scarlet, fuchsia, yellow, orange, and white. Purslane, *P. oleracea*, can be a lawn weed, where its flat, succulent leaves and small yellow flowers are a nuisance, but the large-flowered hybrids with brightly colored blooms make good summer annuals. Both moss rose and purslane's flowers stay closed on cloudy days but shine bright on even the hottest summer days. Plant in well-drained soils or as low-maintenance hanging baskets.

Few plants can match the dazzling display of moss rose's richly saturated flower color, but it requires very well-drained soil.

Scaevola

Fan flower

BLOOM PERIOD: June to September
SIZE: 8–18 in. tall
HARDINESS: Zones 10–11

This tender perennial thrives in the Southeast's hot and humid climate in full sun to part shade, where it makes a mound of foliage with clusters of fan-shaped blue to lavender flowers. Although scaevolas are found in quite a few subtropical and tropical regions around the world, the Australian *Scaevola aemula* is the only species widely grown as an annual. Plant in a well-drained to moist spot in the garden or cascading from a container or hanging basket.

The asymmetric flowers of genus *Scaevola* give rise to its common name of fan flower.

Solanum

Naranjilla, bed of nails, Jerusalem cherry

BLOOM PERIOD: June to August

SIZE: 2–6 ft. tall

HARDINESS: Zones 8–11

Solanum is a large genus which includes edibles like eggplant, but several species are grown strictly as ornamentals in temperate gardens. The spiny *S. quitoense*, or naranjilla, has large, lobed foliage with purple spines. Its orange fruit is used for juice in South America. Another spiny foliage plant, *S. pyracathum*, has yellow-orange thorns all over and small orange fruit. Somewhat hardier than the others is Jerusalem cherry, *S. pseudocapsicum*, with masses of bright orange-red fruits among the dark evergreen foliage. It is hardy to zone 8 gardens where it makes a small subshrub. In southern gardens it can become a nuisance weed.

The dramatic foliage of *Solanum quitoense* always elicits comment from visitors, and the orange fruits can be used for naranjilla juice with the addition of significant quantities of sugar.

Solenostemon

Coleus

BLOOM PERIOD: August to September

SIZE: 20–30 in. tall

HARDINESS: Zones 10–11

Solenostemon scutellarioides, better known as coleus, is among the most popular annuals for shade gardens. Coleus makes an upright plant with foliage in a dazzling array of colors, including green, chartreuse, lime, burgundy, gold, and orange. It is often multicolored and sometimes deeply lobed. Some coleus are seed strains but most are propagated by cuttings. They need adequate moisture during the heat of the summer or will wilt, and they can be grown in full sun with irrigation. Pinch the growing tips out when young to develop bushier plants.

Coleus brightens shady spots and provides incredibly vivid foliage color that makes a striking addition to containers and perennial and annual beds.

Strobilanthes

Persian shield

BLOOM PERIOD: **Insignificant**
SIZE: **2–3 ft. tall**
HARDINESS: **Zones 10–11**

Persian shield, *Strobilanthes dyerianus*, is a dramatic mounding foliage plant for sun or shade, growing to 3 ft. tall and 4 ft. wide. The foliage is silvery with a purple cast which is especially noticeable on new growth and in shade. Flowers rarely appear unless overwintered indoors as a houseplant. Persian shield prefers a relatively rich soil with consistent moisture all season long. It is excellent planted en masse or as a specimen potted plant.

The iridescent foliage of Persian shield makes it a valuable and noteworthy addition to containers and borders.

Tagetes

Marigold

BLOOM PERIOD: **May to September**

SIZE: **8–40 in. tall**

HARDINESS: **Annual**

☀ ☼ 🦌 🐝▸

Annual marigolds are usually named African marigolds (*Tagetes erecta*) or French marigolds, (*T. patula*), despite the fact that both species originate in Central America. The former are typically tall with large 2- to 4-in. flowers, while the latter are smaller in all respects. The cheery warm colors of marigolds are well known, and hybrids between the species have brought large flowers to compact plants—the best of both worlds. Marigolds should be deadheaded regularly to keep them blooming freely. They are especially useful planted as borders around vegetable gardens, where the strongly aromatic foliage deters rabbits and other rodents.

Large flowers in bright colors make African marigolds showy annuals.

Talinum

Jewels of Opar, flameflower

BLOOM PERIOD: May to September

SIZE: 12–24 in. tall

HARDINESS: Zones 9–11

☀ ◐ ☼ ◉

Jewels of Opar, *Talinum paniculatum*, is a tender perennial with succulent foliage and shallow roots. It is topped with airy panicles of tiny hot pink flowers which form showy red fruits over a long season. The chartreuse-leaved cultivars 'Kingwood Gold' and 'Limon' or white-edged 'Variegatum' are often grown for increased ornamental value. Jewels of Opar will continue popping up from seed for years after they are planted, often in the cracks of pavers and other inhospitable spots. They are easy to pull where not wanted and often make memorable pairings when they appear among other plants.

Bright foliage topped with red fruits make *Talinum paniculatum* 'Kingwood Gold' a lovely garden plant, but beware the seeds that can pop up for years to come. RIGHT The large-leaved and panicle-flowered *Tibouchina heteromalla* is less commonly encountered but is well worth seeking out for tropical displays.

Tibouchina

Princess flower, glory bush

BLOOM PERIOD: June to August

SIZE: 3–6 ft. tall

HARDINESS: Zones 9–11

☀ ☼

Tibouchina urvilleana is the species most commonly encountered in this showy genus of woody subtropical plants. It makes a 4- to 6-ft. plant in a season, with felted, distinctly veined leaves and a spectacular display of vivid violet flowers off and on throughout the summer. Other species include *T. heteromalla*, with large, silvery, downy foliage and pyramidal panicles of large flowers, and *T. granulosa*, with dark green, long, narrow leaves and similar flowers. All can be grown as shrubby plants or trained as trees. Dig up and bring indoors to a sunny spot in winter.

Bulbs

Bulbs are among the easiest and most reliable plants for southeastern gardens and can be installed among other perennials, around shrubs, and below trees. The term bulb covers a host of different growth forms from true bulbs like onions and daffodils to other forms of underground storage organs or geophytes—geo meaning ground and phyte, lover—such as tubers, tuberous roots, corms, and rhizomes, which are thickened horizontal roots. In many cases, plants have developed these underground storage organs to protect against difficult environmental conditions like drought; in fact, many bulbs are found in desert, dry mountain, and Mediterranean climates.

Some generalities about bulbs will help with success for the vast majority of garden geophytes. Most will appreciate good drainage and a loose soil and many prefer full sun. Since many smaller bulbs are winter flowering or spring ephemerals, plant them under deciduous trees and shrubs where they will receive sunlight while actively growing. Plant spring-flowering bulbs in fall and early winter, and they will emerge and flower the following spring. Summer bulbs are often planted in spring,

Bulbs are at their best when planted in masses and drifts to welcome spring back to the garden.

especially those planned for single-season displays, although summer bulbs which are reliably hardy can be planted in fall when dormant. Almost any geophyte can be planted from a container when in active growth. Plant most bulbs about three times as deep as their diameter, allowing for several layers of different-sized bulbs in one spot and a more intricate display of bloom. When the top or bottom of a bulb is difficult to determine, plant the bulb on its side. It will right itself over time.

Allow bulb foliage to begin dying back before cutting the leaves off, but you have no need to wait until the leaves are completely dead. Established clumps of bulbs may stop flowering over time for a variety of reasons. They may simply need some fertilizer to bulk up for the following year. In other cases the bulbs need to be dug and separated as they begin to crowd each other. In many instances, bulbs which prefer more sun begin to be shaded out by trees and shrubs which have grown up over the years. The only solution here is to move the bulbs or remove trees. Generally, geophytes can be fertilized after they finish flowering to help build reserves for the following season. Many spring bulbs are at their best when planted in masses and an investment in several hundred or even thousand bulbs can pay off for decades as the carpet of spring flowers signals the end of winter each year.

Agapanthus

Agapanthus, lily-of-the-Nile

BLOOM PERIOD: June to September

SIZE: 12–40 in. tall

HARDINESS: Zones 7–11

☀ ☀ 🐝▸

Agapanthus is a perennial with thick, fleshy roots and strappy, grass-like leaves arising from the base. Flower stalks emerge in early to late summer bearing a rounded umbel of showy tubular flowers. Agapanthus is typically blue but white forms are also available. All are butterfly magnets. They tend to hybridize freely, and most found in gardens are complex hybrids. Agapanthus is notorious for thriving when overcrowded and should not be divided as frequently as many other bulbs. Several variegated forms are also available.

The rounded blue flower clusters of *Agapanthus* selections combine well with grasses and summer perennials.

Allium

Ornamental onion

BLOOM PERIOD: April to September, depending on selection

SIZE: 4–60 in. tall

HARDINESS: Zones 6–10

☀ 🦌

The ornamental onions are a variable group ranging from diminutive rock garden species to towering hybrids in colors from white to pink, blue, and yellow. The 12-in. *Allium christophii* always elicits comment with its large round clusters of starry, violet, long-stalked flowers over wide leaves. Taller species and hybrids such as the 45-in. *A. rosenbachianum* have smooth, bare flower stems topped with round clusters of deep purple flowers, perfect for dotting through a perennial border. Newer hybrids like 'Millennium' and 'Pink Feathers' bring masses of long-blooming flowers and deserve a spot in every garden.

The large heads of the star-shaped flowers of *Allium christophii* can be allowed to dry in the garden or be brought indoors where they are favorites in dried arrangements. RIGHT The thick-textured foliage, large size, and vertical habit make *Alocasia* 'Portadora' an excellent exclamation point in annual color beds.

Alocasia, upright elephant ear

BLOOM PERIOD: Insignificant

SIZE: 18–96 in. tall

HARDINESS: Zones 7–11

The alocasias are distinguished from the colocasias mainly by their upright to somewhat horizontal leaf arrangement. The 6-ft.-tall *Alocasia macrorrhizos* makes a dramatic specimen with huge upright leaves and is even showier in the form 'Variegata'. The 8-ft. hybrid between *A. odora* and *A. portei* called 'Porta-dora' boasts immense, wavy-margined leaves. These selections will appreciate a thick layer of mulch in winter at the northern end of their range. Several tropical species and selections (such as 'Sarian', an *A. zebrina* and *A. micholitziana* hybrid) add white veins and can be grown in the warmest areas of the Southeast or in containers and annual beds.

Amorphophallus

Voodoo lily, devil's tongue

BLOOM PERIOD: April to May

SIZE: 2–5 ft. tall

HARDINESS: Zones 7–11

This group of mostly subtropical species includes the massive *Amorphophallus titanum* which grows to 15 ft. and sports the largest inflorescence of any plant. Although this species is not hardy in the Southeast, several others grow well outdoors including *A. konjac* with dark burgundy, foetid, Jack-in-the-pulpit-type flowers in spring followed by stout, 4-ft.-tall leaf stalks topped with cut-leaf, umbrella-like leaves. *Amorphophallus bulbifer* is a bit smaller with cute pink flowers. The corms of voodoo lilies can be quite large, and happy plants will offset to form nice patches. More species are available for adventurous gardeners.

The speckled leaf stalk of *Amorphophallus konjac* supports the shredded umbrella-like leaf for a dramatic, tropical effect.

LEFT Despite the plant's common name of devil's tongue, spring flowers of *Amorphophallus bulbifer* are quite beautiful, even if they smell like rancid meat.

Arisaema

Arisaema, cobra lily, Jack-in-the-pulpit

BLOOM PERIOD: March to May

SIZE: 18–30 in. tall

HARDINESS: Zones 6–11

☀ ☁ 🦌 ◉

Cobra lilies are intriguing plants for the shade garden, where the strange flowers and lovely foliage add season-long interest. The native *Arisaema triphyllum* has a hooded flower beneath its three-part leaves. The showier Japanese trifoliate species *A. ringens* has huge, glossy leaves above the flowers that give justice to the name cobra lily. Other Asian species are worth growing for their foliage as well, especially the umbrella-spoke foliage of *A. taiwanense*. *Arisaema sikokianum* is a species grown primarily for its dramatic flowers with their purple-black spathe (pulpit) surrounding the snowy white spadix (Jack). All species of *Arisaema* can form stalks of showy orange-red fruits in late summer to fall.

The showy flowers of this form of *Arisaema sikokianum* are highlighted by foliage with silvery markings. RIGHT *Arisaema ringens* has perhaps the glossiest foliage of any cobra lily and is one of the best growers, forming large, showy clumps.

Arum, lords and ladies

BLOOM PERIOD: **March to May**

SIZE: **12 in. tall**

HARDINESS: **Zones 5–11**

Arums are ideal plants for the space-challenged garden since their leaves emerge in fall as other plants are going dormant, allowing for gardeners to plant arums and summer perennials in nearly the same hole. The common Italian arum, *Arum italicum*, has silver-veined, arrow-shaped leaves emerging in fall followed by white flower spathes at ground level in spring as the foliage goes dormant. Naked stalks of bright orange-red fruits follow in summer. Italian arum has been named as an invasive species in some parts of the Southeast, so check with your local extension agent for the plant's status in your area before planting. Less well known and less cold tolerant are *A. dioscorides* and *A. concinnatum*, which have solid green leaves and burgundy coloring to the spathes in midspring.

The foliage of *Arum italicum* is a welcome addition to the winter landscape, especially when heavily marked with silver like this form. LEFT The showy fruit stalks of *Arum concinnatum* and others are bright lights in the summer shade garden.

Chionodoxa

Glory-of-the-snow

BLOOM PERIOD: February to April

SIZE: 6–10 in. tall

HARDINESS: Zones 4–9

Glory-of-the-snow is one of the first bulbs to bloom in late winter, producing small flower stalks topped with clusters of 5 to 12 mostly blue, 1-in. flowers. *Chionodoxa forbesii* is the largest of the group, sometimes growing to 10 in. tall with pale blue, white-eyed flowers, or pale pink in 'Pink Giant'. Similar but smaller is *C. luciliae*, while *C. sardensis* has pure caerulean blue flowers with no trace of white. All species are best in a well-drained location. They are ideal planted at the base of deciduous shrubs or around late-emerging perennials.

The early, clear blue flowers of *Chionodoxa forbesii* are welcome harbingers of spring.

Colocasia

Elephant ear, taro

BLOOM PERIOD: Insignificant

SIZE: 3–6 ft. tall

HARDINESS: Zones 7–11

Elephant ears are a southern garden mainstay mostly represented by *Colocasia esculenta*, which is the taro of culinary use in the South Pacific and tropical Asia. Huge, heart-shaped leaves are held on sturdy stalks. Breeding efforts have led to a wide variety of ornamental forms with a range of characteristics like red stems, black leaves, cupped foliage, variegation, or some combination of these attributes. They grow quickly in moist, fertile soils. For the wow factor, few plants can compete with the fairly tender *C. gigantea* Thailand Giant seed strain, with its massive leaves rising to 9 ft. or taller.

Colocasia esculenta 'Black Magic' was an early dark-leaved form of elephant ear.

Crinum

Crinum lily, swamp lily

BLOOM PERIOD: **May to September**

SIZE: **2–4 ft. tall**

HARDINESS: **Zones 7–11**

☀ ☼ 🦌 🐝▸ ◉

Crinum lilies are easy, long-lived bulbs for southern gardens where they will thrive on neglect. The strappy foliage is topped by bare stems of five to twelve large, tubular, pink to white, lily-like flowers. The hybrid *Crinum ×powellii* is one of the hardiest, growing well into zone 6. 'Alamo Village', a hybrid of unknown origin, has been grown for years in the South where the burgundy buds open to reveal spidery, white flowers. Our native southern species, *C. americanum*, is found growing in swampy spots but is fine in average garden soil. Warmer gardens can grow the purple-leaved *C. procerum* hybrid, 'Sangria', with its deep pink flowers.

The selection *Crinum* 'Carnival' has bright pink flowers with heavy-textured, recurved petals.

Crocus

Crocus

BLOOM PERIOD: **January to March**

SIZE: **8 in. tall**

HARDINESS: **Zones 5–8**

☀ ☼

Crocuses are one of the true harbingers of spring, with some species starting to flower as early as January. The small single flowers emerge in white, purple, and gold tones for a bright winter display. The best species for growing in the Southeast include *Crocus tommasinianus*, *C. vernus*, *C. sieberi*, and *C. flavus*. All grow well in average, well-drained soils with plenty of sun. They are ideal for planting around deciduous shrubs like butterfly bush or at the base of shrubs you have cut back. They are also fun planted in lawns, but don't cut the grass until the crocus foliage begins to die back.

The feathery purple highlights on the flowers of *Crocus vernus* 'King of the Striped' encourage you to stop and appreciate the subtle beauty even on a cold winter day.

Cyclamen

Cyclamen, Persian violet, sowbread

BLOOM PERIOD: October to March

SIZE: 6 in. tall

HARDINESS: Zones 7–10

☀ ◐ ☼ 🅂 🦌

Cyclamen is well known as a potted florist's plant, but several species are suited for southeastern gardens, where they go summer dormant, reemerging in fall to flower and grow. All will prefer a spot that is well drained. Most commonly encountered is *Cyclamen hederifolium*, which often has exceptionally showy silver markings on the foliage. Pink or white flowers with strongly reflexed petals usually emerge before the leaves in fall. The smaller *C. coum* bears attractive rounded leaves and late winter flowers. They are best planted around deciduous trees, which remove excess summer water during cyclamen dormancy.

The foliage of *Cyclamen hederifolium* appears after the fall flowers but can be amazingly marked on the best forms.
BOTTOM The winter flowers of *Cyclamen coum* appear with rounded foliage and come in all shades of pink.

Dahlia

Dahlia

BLOOM PERIOD: May to October
SIZE: 1–4 ft. tall
HARDINESS: Zones 7–10

Dahlias have been hybridized for years, leading to more than 20,000 named selections. Many are grown for their intricate flowers, which are shown at exhibitions. The best garden plants are often the shorter single-flowered selections which do not need staking and will flower in spring and again in fall with sporadic summer blooms. The purple-leaved Bishop series has proved to be exceptional in the garden. The pinnate foliage of dahlias can be attractive and is especially showy on the tree dahlia, *Dahlia imperialis*, which can grow to 10 ft. in temperate gardens and 30 ft. in its native Central America.

Dichelostemma

Firecracker flower, ookow

BLOOM PERIOD: April to May
SIZE: 30 in. tall
HARDINESS: Zones 7–9

This western U.S. genus is not a bulb but a corm, or vertical, swollen underground stem, that produces narrow, grassy foliage and tall, skinny flower stalks topped with umbels of tubular flowers. The brilliant red tubes of *Dichelostemma ida-maia*, or firecracker flower, are tipped with greenish-yellow and attract hummingbirds and butterflies. The somewhat heavier-flowering *D. congestum*, with violet to pink flowers, is usually represented in gardens by the rose-colored 'Pink Diamond'. Individual plants can look a bit sparse and are best either massed or intermingled with grasses and other perennials.

BOTTOM Dahlias come in almost every color and flower form imaginable, but the single-flowered types with dark foliage like *Dahlia* 'Knockout' provide welcome color even as late as October. RIGHT The long-tubed red flowers of *Dichelostemma ida-maia* provide a yellow bulls-eye for the hummingbirds that frequent them.

Eucomis

Pineapple lily

BLOOM PERIOD: June to August
SIZE: 10–36 in. tall
HARDINESS: Zones 7–9

The South African pineapple lilies are a group of strap-leaved bulbs with spikes of tightly packed white to burgundy flowers topped with a tuft of leaves for a pineapple effect. Plants range from the late-emerging dwarf *Eucomis vandermerwei*, which requires perfect drainage, to the tall *E. pole-evansii*. Most garden plants are hybrids or selections of *E. autumnalis* or *E. comosa*. Several cultivars like *E. comosa* 'Sparkling Burgundy' have burgundy foliage and flowers while others have speckled foliage. *Eucomis* 'Reuben' has green leaves and pink flowers for a pleasing contrast. The dwarf Mini Tuft series is excellent for smaller gardens and containers.

Galanthus

Snowdrops

BLOOM PERIOD: December to February
SIZE: 6 in. tall
HARDINESS: Zones 6–9

Snowdrops emerge from late fall through winter, bearing single white flowers with three longish, narrow petals surrounding three shorter, green-tipped petals. Galanthophiles, as snowdrop aficionados are known, collect many forms with slight differences in flowers and will be happy to point out the minutiae at length. Snowdrops, especially *Galanthus nivalis* and *G. elwesii* grow well in the Southeast and will naturalize in a woodland setting over many years, creating an unforgettable carpet of white under deciduous trees.

The intricate winter flowers of *Galanthus elwesii* var. *monostictus* can be appreciated up close or massed in a woodland garden. LEFT The pink flowers of *Eucomis* 'Reuben' are welcome additions to the summer garden and will last for weeks as cut stems in flower arrangements.

Gladiolus

Gladiolus, glads

BLOOM PERIOD: June to November
SIZE: 1–4 ft. tall
HARDINESS: Zones 7–10

Glads are often represented in gardens by the florist's hybrids which boast spikes of large flowers above lanceolate leaves. Many of these tender forms are planted in spring and dug up after flowering. They can be planted in succession every couple of weeks to extend bloom period as long as the corms have about 90 days of warmth to get to flowering size. The hardier *Gladiolus dalenii*, *G. murielae*, and *G. byzantinus* have given rise to selections which are hardy into zone 6, such as the late-blooming *G. dalenii* 'Halloweenie' with orange-red and yellow blossoms in late October through November.

Gloriosa

Gloriosa lily

BLOOM PERIOD: June to September
SIZE: 7 ft. tall with support
HARDINESS: Zones 7–10

This restrained, tuberous-rooted, vining plant makes a showy display climbing over shrubs or on small trellises. Long stems arise in spring with narrow lily-like leaves that curl into clinging tendrils at their tips. Beginning in early summer, *Gloriosa superba* sends up a succession of showy flowers with reflexed, wavy-margined, red petals. The form 'Rothschildiana' has the largest flowers, which are bright yellow at the base and up the margins. Several yellow forms, including 'Lutea', are also available and are especially showy when planted with the red form. Cut the stems to the ground after frost.

Few plants have the wow factor of *Gloriosa superba* 'Rothschildiana' with its brilliant flowers and reflexed petals.
LEFT The flowers of *Gladiolus dalenii* 'Halloweenie' are quite frost tolerant and often continue until late November.

Hippeastrum

Amaryllis

BLOOM PERIOD: **April to May**

SIZE: **18 in. tall**

HARDINESS: **Zones 7–10**

Amaryllises are best known as bulbs for winter forcing, but they make excellent garden plants in warm southern gardens. Flowers range from white to red with every shade in between. Among the hardiest, with reports of success into zone 6, is the 200-year-old hybrid *Hippeastrum ×johnsonii* with brilliant red flowers highlighted by a white streak down the center of each petal. Double-flowered hybrids like 'Aphrodite' and butterfly types such as 'Jungle Star' are often more tender and best in zone 8 and warmer. Provide excellent drainage for increased winter survivability.

The still-striking old hybrid amaryllis, *Hippeastrum ×johnsonii.*

Iris

Iris

BLOOM PERIOD: **March to May primarily**
SIZE: **6–36 in. tall**
HARDINESS: **Zones 4–9, depending on species**

  ☀ ☀ ◉

Irises have been grown and hybridized for centuries and now come in a great range of forms that fit in various garden niches, from water to rock gardens. Irises for average garden soils include the native dwarf crested iris, *Iris cristata*, with pale blue spring flowers, which spreads to form mats of spiky foliage. A species which should be more widely grown is the winter-flowering *I. unguicularis*, with flowers from November to March nestled in the evergreen foliage. The bearded iris of *I. germanica* descent are among the most widely grown. For the longest flower show, grow the remontant, or reblooming, cultivars. 'Again and Again' is one selection that flowers from April to November.

Irises can be found for difficult garden spots such as permanently or seasonally boggy areas. The copper iris, *Iris fulva*, with its unusual metallic flowers, and *I. virginica* are two natives which grow well in wet locations. Japanese iris, *I. ensata*, is available in a range of colors and adds elegance to pond edges. Roof iris, *I. tectorum*, is well-suited for dry spots including under trees, although flowering is decreased in shade.

Bearded irises like *Iris* 'Golden Panther' come in a huge range of colors; one can be found to complement any color scheme.

Iris unguicularis provides welcome flowers during the heart of winter in zone 7 gardens.

Lilium

Lily

BLOOM PERIOD: **May to August**

SIZE: **2–6 ft. tall**

HARDINESS: **Zones 5–8**

The true lilies are some of the showiest species available for cool temperate regions where the vertical stems and vibrant colors brighten midspring and summer gardens. Many species, including the native *Lilium philadalphicum* and Asian *L. lancifolium*, are bright orange or yellow with dark spotting on the recurved petals. Other species that grow well in the Southeast have long-tubed flowers instead of the recurved petals. The purple-flushed, white flowers of *L. regale* and *L. formosanum* are exceptionally fragrant. They are best in a sunny spot in rich soil where they multiply quickly.

Lilies have been hybridized for years to create a range of sizes, colors, and flower forms for the garden. Among the most exciting developments has been crossing the fragrant Asiatic-type lilies with the heavy-textured, trumpet-flowered forms, resulting in so-called orienpet lilies which possess both the intense fragrance of one parent and the large flowers of the other. Orienpets are typically stouter stemmed and tougher than either parent.

The double flowers of *Lilium lancifolium* 'Flore Pleno' make a brilliant statement in the midsummer garden.

The very tall, large-flowered *Lilium formosanum* reliably flowers in late summer, perfuming the garden with a sweet fragrance. LEFT Orienpet lilies like *Lilium* 'Scheherazade' have tall, strong stems, thick-textured flowers, and intense fragrance.

Lycoris

Lycoris, surprise lilies, naked ladies

BLOOM PERIOD: July to September

SIZE: 24 in. tall

HARDINESS: Zones 6–10

The surprise lilies put out grassy foliage in fall or spring, which dies back to the ground before the naked stems emerge topped with a cluster of showy, narrow-petaled flowers. The exceptionally hardy, peachy pink *L. squamigera* is grown throughout northern gardens but does not perform well in high heat. Better forms for the Southeast include the red *L. radiata*, gold *L. chinensis*, white *L. albiflora*, and the pink flowers with electric-blue tips of *L. ×haywardii*. All are easy in sun to light shade and most will multiply quickly in loose, fertile soil, creating a bright summer display.

Few plants draw as much attention as a mature clump of *Lycoris ×haywardii* with its stalks of showy pink flowers tipped with blue.

Muscari

Grape hyacinth

BLOOM PERIOD: February to March

SIZE: 8 in. tall

HARDINESS: Zones 5–9

Grape hyacinth, generally represented by *Muscari armeniacum* in gardens, is an easy late winter flowering bulb. The foliage emerges in fall and is followed by spikes of small, bell-shaped, azure (occasionally white), fragrant flowers. Other similar species include *M. aucheri*, *M. azurea*, and *M. botryoides*. Grow all of these in full sun to part shade where they will naturalize over time. Less common but quite beautiful and deserving a space in a rock garden or along a path is *M. macrocarpum*, whose flower spikes start purple-brown before becoming gold.

The blue winter flowers of *Muscari armeniacum* 'Christmas Pearl' are a welcome relief from the cold and when planted in masses are breathtaking.

Narcissus

Daffodil, jonquil

BLOOM PERIOD: January to April
SIZE: 8–16 in. tall
HARDINESS: Zones 5–9

Daffodils are well-known garden bulbs for sunny, rich soils. Some forms, such as the true jonquil, *Narcissus jonquilla*, are intensely fragrant while many of the large-flowered hybrids have no fragrance at all. All are cheery garden plants, ideal for adding early color to the garden. Many of the small species, like *N. fernandesii*, with fine foliage and bright gold flowers, bring a different texture than the typical hybrids. If old patches of daffodils stop flowering heavily, divide and replant in a sunny spot.

The small flowers and fine foliage of the small wild-type daffodils are not as common as the large hybrids, but many, like *Narcissus jonquilla*, make wonderful garden plants.

Oxalis

Sorrel, shamrock

BLOOM PERIOD: April to June
SIZE: 8 in. tall
HARDINESS: Zones 7–9

The clumping forms of sorrel make outstanding garden plants where they form tight mounds or slowly spreading mats of clover-like leaves topped in spring with small white or pink flowers. Many cultivars of *Oxalis triangularis* have showy variegated or purple foliage. Another species, *O. tetraphylla*, sometimes listed as *O. deppei*, with four-leaf-clover leaves, is known for the purple-centered foliage of the selection 'Iron Cross'. It is easy in sun to part shade but may go summer dormant in gardens of the Deep South. Much different is the tiny *O. palmifrons* for the rock garden, with finely divided leaves and relatively large flowers.

The burgundy foliage of some forms of *Oxalis triangularis* provides color throughout the season, rendering the white flowers almost superfluous.

Rhodophiala

Oxblood lily

BLOOM PERIOD: **August to September**

SIZE: **16 in. tall**

HARDINESS: **Zones 7–10**

Oxblood lily, *Rhodophiala bifida*, is an easy amaryllis relative with brilliant red flowers highlighted by yellow stamens appearing in clusters atop naked stems in late summer. As the flowers open, the foliage starts to grow and stays evergreen through the winter before dying out in spring. In a rich, well-drained soil, it will naturalize over time. Pink forms can be found occasionally.

The oxblood lily begins flowering just as the leaves emerge in late summer. TOP RIGHT Among the earliest bulbs to appear in the new year is the sky-blue *Scilla bifolia*. BOTTOM RIGHT Unlike the typical small winter flowers of most squill, *Scilla peruviana* is a robust, spring-flowering bulb.

Scilla

Squill

BLOOM PERIOD: **January to March**

SIZE: **6 in. tall**

HARDINESS: **Zones 4–9**

The small, early-flowering squills, best represented by *Scilla bifolia*, with outward-facing flowers, and *S. siberica*, with downward-facing blossoms, are at their best when planted out in masses in turf, woodlands, or bare flower beds. Both species have selections from the typical blue to white and pink. They are easy in a loose soil and will naturalize over time. The much larger *S. peruviana* grows to 18 in. and has broad heads of azure flowers opening from blue-black buds in late spring. Despite its name, it is native to the Mediterranean region and is best relegated to zone 7 and warmer gardens.

Sinningia

Hardy gloxinia

BLOOM PERIOD: **May to September**
SIZE: **3 ft. tall**
HARDINESS: **Zones 7–10**

☀ ☀ 🐝▸

Sinningia tubiflora from South America forms large potato-like tubers which spread, creating mats of silvery, felted foliage topped for a long period with tall spikes of long-tubed, creamy white flowers.

Somewhat taller is the reddish flowered *S. sellovii* which also makes an excellent garden plant. Hybrids with these species and others have given rise to a number of hardy cultivars like 'Scarlet O'Hara' and 'Bananas Foster' which thrive in loose, well-drained soil and full sun to light shade. All of the long-tubed selections are among the best hummingbird plants.

The selection aptly called 'Lovely' is an apple blossom–colored form of the tough *Sinningia tubiflora*.

Sprekelia

Aztec lily

BLOOM PERIOD: May, occasionally again in October

SIZE: 14 in. tall

HARDINESS: Zones 7–10

This exotic Mexican bulb looks like it has no business growing in temperate gardens, but in a sunny spot with well-drained soil *Sprekelia formosissima* thrives. The large, 6-in., brilliant red flowers with three clustered lower petals and three widely spaced upper ones appear among the grassy leaves in May and sometimes again in fall. The selection 'Karwinskii' has white-edged petals but is a bit less cold hardy. Mulch it well toward the northern end of its range for increased winter hardiness.

Trillium

Trillium, wakerobin

BLOOM PERIOD: March to May

SIZE: 6–20 in. tall

HARDINESS: Zones 5–9

Our native trilliums are among the most cherished of the Southeast's woodland wildflowers, with three leaves often mottled with silver and three-part flowers from pure white to yellow, pink, and burgundy. The classic is *Trillium grandiflorum*, a relatively tall species with a pure white, occasionally pink, outward-facing flower. Similar in appearance but with a burgundy-red flower is *T. erectum*. Slightly smaller with a burgundy upward-facing flower is the mottled-leaf *T. cuneatum* and several similar species which will form tight clumps in the garden. On the small side is the diminutive *T. pusillum*, with white flowers aging to pink.

The mottled foliage of *Trillium cuneatum* is attractive in a woodland setting and forms nice clumps. LEFT Few hardy bulbs match the exotic appearance of *Sprekelia formosissima*, which often will flower twice in a year.

Tulipa

Tulip

BLOOM PERIOD: **March to April**
SIZE: **6–22 in. tall**
HARDINESS: **Zones 5–9**

Tulips are one of the classic garden bulbs much loved in northern gardens. Unfortunately, many of the hybrids are not suitable for culture in the South due to a lack of chilling during the winter. Prechilled bulbs planted in fall do well but should be considered annuals and removed in spring after flowering and more planted the following autumn. In cooler areas of the Southeast, they can be kept in the ground where they will often perennialize. Where they do not receive enough chilling, the hybrids will either flower on very short stalks at ground level or not flower at all.

A good option for warm climate gardens are some of the species tulips. Perhaps the best for average garden spots is *Tulipa clusiana* or lady tulip, a favorite of Thomas Jefferson. Carmine outer petals open to show the creamy white interior, or gold interior of *T. clusiana* var. *chrysantha*. Lady tulip will naturalize, flowering reliably year after year. In well-drained soils, the diminutive *T. bakeri* and *T. batalinii* make very good garden plants. The tongue-twisting *T. vvedenskyi* 'Tangerine Beauty' with large, full flowers over wide leaves has proved to be an excellent southern substitute for the hybrids.

The gold form of lady tulip, *Tulipa clusiana* var. *chrysantha*, is one of the best for the Southeast, where it multiplies rapidly and puts on a reliable flower show each year. BOTTOM The satiny orange flowers of *Tulipa vvedenskyi* 'Tangerine Beauty' provide a spot of richly saturated color in the spring landscape and will return and flower every season.

Zantedeschia

Calla lily

BLOOM PERIOD: April to June, often again in September

SIZE: 20–48 in. tall

HARDINESS: Zones 7–10

Calla lilies are much in demand as cut flowers but also make excellent garden specimens. Most prefer a moist soil and can be grown at pond edges or in containers in water features, but they also perform well in average soils. The arrow-shaped leaves are spotted with translucent white spots in several species and their hybrids. A thick-textured spathe in shades of white to orange, gold, pink, and near black curls around the spadix of tiny flowers. The large species, *Zantedeschia aethiopica* and *Z. elliotiana*, make dramatic specimens while many of the small hybrids mingle well in the perennial garden.

Zephyranthes

Rain lily, Atamasco lily

BLOOM PERIOD: April to October

SIZE: 6–10 in. tall

HARDINESS: Zones 7–11

Rain lilies are small bulbs native to the southeastern United States across to the Southwest and through Mexico to South America. The crocus-like, summer-flowering plants are mostly native to sunny, dry areas and have adapted to flower after rain events. In the wet Southeast, they will flower over an extended period, often starting in midspring and continuing on and off through fall. The late-season southeastern native Atamasco lily, *Zephyranthes atamasco*, is a woodland species with relatively large white flowers preferring light shade and moist soils. Other species and hybrids flower mostly in shades of white, yellow, and pink in sunnier situations.

LEFT While the traditional garden calla lilies have white spathes, new hybrids such as *Zantedeschia* 'Sunshine' have expanded and intensified the colors available. RIGHT The southwestern rain lilies and their hybrids, like *Zephyranthes* 'Capricorn', come in a wide range of colors. They open their flowers after a rain, a rarity in their native habitat but a regular occurrence during summers in our region.

Grasses

Grasses and grass-like plants are often the unsung heroes of the garden, providing a textural contrast to the more plentiful broadleaf specimens that make up the bulk of the landscape. Different varieties can be found for shady spots, damp areas, or sunny locations where they are often planted en masse. While grasses are considered some of the toughest workhorses in the garden, many provide bright color and elegant flowering as well as the texture for which they are often used.

Like many horticulturists, I learned to differentiate true grasses (family Poaceae) from the sedges (*Carex*) and rushes (*Juncus*) with the old saying, "Sedges have edges, rushes are round, grasses have knees down to the ground." The saying holds mostly true, although as with many things in life, the more you learn, the more you learn there is to learn. I am personally enamored especially with the sedges and have trouble imagining myself gardening in the shade without my arsenal of *Carex* plants, both variegated and green.

For those garden designers who actually plant in masses, unlike the drifts of one typically found in my garden, grasses should be used freely as they are tough, low care, and beautiful in sweeps and drifts. Grasses can be especially useful in tough urban settings, as green infrastructure like bioswales, and as lawn alternatives.

Few plants add texture and movement to the garden in quite the same way as grasses swaying in the wind.

Bluestem

BLOOM PERIOD: **August to October**

SIZE: **2–4 ft. tall (to 7 ft. in flower)**

HARDINESS: **Zones 4–9**

Bluestem is a group of showy, warm season grasses for native landscapes. Big bluestem, *Andropogon gerardii*, grows well throughout much of the Southeast. It makes a tight clump of blue-green foliage, often tipped red in fall. Fall color can be spectacular. The slightly less hardy southern species *A. glomeratus*, or bushy bluestem, prefers a damper soil and is worth a spot in rain gardens or other wet areas for the showy fall flowers that develop into seedheads enjoyed by songbirds.

The southern bushy bluestem is as showy with dry seedheads as it is in active growth.

Arundo

Giant reed grass

BLOOM PERIOD: **September**

SIZE: **8–12 ft. tall**

HARDINESS: **Zones 7–10**

☀ ☀ ☀

Giant reed grass, *Arundo donax*, has a reputation as a garden thug due to its large size and vigorous clumping habit. The species grows to 12 ft. with pale green leaves on jointed stalks. The old variegated selection, 'Variegata', sometimes listed as *A. donax* var. *versicolor*, emerges pure white before becoming edged and striped with cream and ultimately turning entirely green in the heat of summer. 'Peppermint Stick' is similar but keeps its variegated color all summer long, and 'Golden Chain' has creamy yellow variegation and grows to about 9 ft. All will take dry soils or grow as marginal pond plants.

The brilliant white streaks on *Arundo donax* 'Peppermint Stick' last all summer, unlike the older forms of variegated giant reed grass which fade with the heat.

Bambusa

Clumping bamboo

BLOOM PERIOD: **Non-flowering**

SIZE: **10–15 ft. tall**

HARDINESS: **Zones 7–11**

☀ ◑ 🦌 🌲

Clumping bamboo, *Bambusa multiplex*, makes a dense mass of tall, woody stems bearing ferny branchlets. The quick-growing stems make a strong statement in the landscape without the thuggish tendencies of spreading bamboos. The gold-stemmed 'Alphonse Karr' adds bright color to the garden. Smaller gardens may be best served growing the 6-ft. 'Tiny Fern' with its fine texture and restrained size. Stems of clumping bamboo should be left alone unless damaged by cold. Established plants will survive single digit temperatures but will be killed to the ground. New shoots are edible when peeled and blanched.

The bright yellow stems with irregular green striping of *Bambusa multiplex* 'Alphonse Karr' make a bold statement as a large clump.

Calamagrostis

Feather reed grass

BLOOM PERIOD: **June to September**

SIZE: **2–3 ft. tall (to 6 ft. in flower)**

HARDINESS: **Zones 4–9**

☀ ◑ ☼ 🐐 📍

The early-blooming hybrid feather reed grass, *Calamagrostis* ×*acutiflora*, is a popular landscape plant for sunny spots, especially the very upright form, 'Karl Foerster'. It tolerates most conditions including heavy clay. Several variegated forms of this hybrid are available, including the gold-striped 'El Dorado' and the white-edged 'Avalanche'. The species *C. brachytricha* is an excellent garden addition, especially when planted in masses, even in relatively shady spots. The airy, pink late summer flower plumes turn tawny in fall. All are quite deer resistant.

The white edged foliage of *Calamagrostis* ×*acutiflora* 'Avalanche' provides a bright vertical accent useful for massing or using as a specimen with flowering perennials.

Carex

Sedge

BLOOM PERIOD: **Insignificant**
SIZE: **6–18 in. tall**
HARDINESS: **Zones 5–10**

☀ ● 🦌 🌲 🔺 ◉

The sedges are a large group of plants found all over the world. They are typically quite shade tolerant and very easy in the landscape. Native species like *Carex pennsylvanica*, *C. eburnea*, and *C. muskingumensis* make fine-textured foils in woodland gardens for other perennials. The variegated *C. muskingumensis* 'Oehme' is especially good for brightening shade. These sedges can be used as low-input lawns or groundcovers in shady spots. While Europe does not have as many species as North America or Asia, the brilliant gold-foliaged *C. elata* 'Bowles Golden' is among the showiest sedges, especially in damp locales.

The Asian species are also quite adaptable and showy with numerous variegated forms. The similar broad-leaved *Carex ciliatomarginata* and *C. siderosticha* have bright white and gold variegated forms that will spread to form low patches. Brilliantly white-edged *C. phyllocephala* 'Sparkler' is among the most distinctive of perennials. Much finer textured are the clumping forms of *C. oshimensis*, including the excellent all-gold 'Everillo' and white-variegated 'Everest'. New Zealand is home to many fine sedges as well, including *C. testacea* with vividly orange winter foliage and the bronze-foliaged *C. buchananii*, known as dead sedge, which does not do this fine plant justice.

The brilliant gold foliage of *Carex elata* 'Bowles Golden' can be planted in masses as a tall groundcover or used for year-round color in a perennial border.
BOTTOM *Carex phyllocephala* 'Sparkler' never fails to elicit comment with its bold color and unusual form.

Chasmanthium

River oats, sea oats

BLOOM PERIOD: June to August

SIZE: 40 in. tall

HARDINESS: Zones 5–10

☀ ☁ 🦌 📍

The native river oats, also called sea oats, is one of the few true grasses that thrives in sun or shade. The northern species, *Chasmanthium latifolium*, is most commonly cultivated with clumps of upright stems bearing narrow leaves and topped by oat-like flowers and seedheads. The flowers and seeds are highly prized for cut flower arrangements. Northern river oats will seed freely in almost any soil and so is especially good for erosion control and natural settings. A variegated form, 'River Mist', is a striking, easy-to-grow addition to the garden.

Cortaderia

Pampas grass

BLOOM PERIOD: August to October

SIZE: 6 ft. tall (to 9 ft. in flower)

HARDINESS: Zones 7–10

☀ ☼ 🦌

Few grasses pack the punch that a mature clump of the South American pampas grass, *Cortaderia selloana*, does. Arching, strappy foliage reaches 6 ft. or more in height, topped in late summer by dense silvery flowerheads that dry for a long-lasting display. In the Deep South, plants are evergreen but are generally best cut back to the ground in late winter. Several white and gold variegated forms are available and generally stay smaller than the species, as does the much hardier dwarf form, 'Pumila'. In some areas, pampas grass has escaped cultivation and become a nuisance.

The gold-striped leaves of *Cortaderia selloana* 'Aureolineata' make the already imposing form of pampas grass an even more striking specimen, especially when topped with its feathery plumes. LEFT The seedheads of river oats are beautiful whether left out in the garden or cut and brought indoors.

Papyrus, umbrella plant

BLOOM PERIOD: Insignificant

SIZE: 12 in. tall or 6 ft. tall, depending on species

HARDINESS: Zones 7–10

The hardy papyrus is a showy, tropical-looking plant for the landscape, with upright stems topped by a whorl of foliage. Short *Cyperus albostriatus* 'Nanus' and white-striped 'Variegatus' make low, spreading groundcovers in damp to surprisingly dry soils. Much taller is the towering *C. alternifolius*, whose smooth stems are topped by strappy leaves making a long-lived, spreading clump in average garden soils. The true papyrus, *C. papyrus*, is also a tall plant, topped with thread-like leaves, best in permanently wet soils or shallow ponds. It is subtropical but can be grown into zone 8 gardens if planted in well-drained soil.

The tall stalks of *Cyperus alternifolius* topped by whorls of flat, grassy blades thrive in average to dry garden soils.

AGGRESSIVE VS. INVASIVE

The term *invasive* is used quite a bit when talking about garden plants, and people often have misconceptions about what the term means. Many plants are aggressive growers and will spread quickly in a cultivated landscape. These garden thugs will swamp and smother more delicate plants and can become a nuisance to get out of the garden. This rapid growth and vigorous habit does not make the plant invasive, however. What is an invasive plant, then? Many people and groups have different definitions. To some it means any plant that could escape from a cultivated area and survive in the wild. This is an overly broad interpretation to me and could include nearly any plant we grow in our gardens today.

My definition of an invasive plant is any plant that:

1) escapes from cultivation,
2) naturalizes in native ecosystems, and
3) displaces native plants.

In other words, it should not just have the potential to escape but have been proved to escape in a given area. It must also naturalize and not just continue to exist as a single specimen or clump. Also note that it should be in a functioning native ecosystem. Many people see a non-native tree growing alongside a highway and think of it as a terrible invasive plant, but in reality no plants are native to highway roadside cuts. If that same kind of tree pops up in intact, natural ecosystems then it is indeed an issue. If a plant never escapes beyond the unnatural man-made habitat, it really is not a problem.

Eragrostis

Love grass

BLOOM PERIOD: June to July

SIZE: 10–36 in. tall

HARDINESS: Zones 6–10

☀ ☀ ☀ ⚕ ♀

The native purple love grass, *Eragrostis spectabilis*, is a low-growing, clumping grass good for naturalizing in exposed spaces. It can even be used as a turf replacement where foot traffic is minimal. The South American relative, *E. curvula* or weeping love grass, grows three times as tall with narrow, light green foliage that provides a great deal of movement as a breeze blows through it. It is best planted in masses and can be used for stabilizing slopes. All love grasses tend to self-sow and are best planted where they can spread.

Floating above the low foliage, the airy mauve flower panicles of *Eragrostis spectabilis* are followed by seedheads which slowly become tan.

Fargesia

Clumping bamboo

BLOOM PERIOD: Non-flowering

SIZE: 6–12 ft. tall

HARDINESS: Zones 6–9

☀ ◑ ⚕ 🌲

The bamboos in cultivation in this group have proved to be good clumping forms best grown in the middle regions of the Southeast where the weather is neither too cold nor too hot. They form dense clumps with arching canes for a graceful effect. *Fargesia rufa* is a relatively small-statured species to 6 ft. Much larger is *F. murielae*, with tall stalks clothed in narrow leaves. Several similar species are available. All should be grown in sun to part shade and tolerate any kind of soil. Cut stems to the ground if they are damaged during the winter.

The foliage of *Fargesia rufa* is a favorite of pandas in their native habitat in China.

Hakonechloa

Hakone grass

BLOOM PERIOD: August to September

SIZE: 18 in. tall

HARDINESS: Zones 4–7

Hakone grass is a warm-season, fully deciduous grass, losing its gracefully arching stems in late fall. The wild form is rarely seen in cultivation; the variegated types are more typical. *Hakonechloa macra* 'Aureola' and 'Albostriata' are streaked with gold and white respectively and provide a soft summer texture in the shade garden. A somewhat more restrained plant is 'Beni Kaze', with red-tipped, green foliage whose color intensifies in fall. The brilliant 'All Gold' lives up to its name but can be painfully slow in cultivation. Plant all in moist, well-drained soil in a cool, shady spot.

The bright foliage of *Hakonechloa macra* 'All Gold' is the perfect foil for other plants like this burgundy-patterned Asian mayapple.

Juncus

Rush

BLOOM PERIOD: Insignificant

SIZE: 10–36 in. tall

HARDINESS: Zones 5–10

The round, pointed leaves of rushes are easy to distinguish from most other plants. The native *Juncus effusus* makes an excellent textural accent with deep green, pencil-thin foliage in a spiky clump. For added garden interest, several spiral-foliaged forms exist, like the diminutive 'Corkscrew' or more upright 'Unicorn'. *Juncus inflexus*, hailing from Europe to Asia and Africa, is a taller plant reaching over 3 ft., with glaucus blue foliage. The rigidly upright 'Blue Arrows' is one of the very finest forms. All rushes prefer boggy soils but will also grow in average soils with regular irrigation.

The blue-green, round stems of *Juncus inflexus* 'Blue Arrows' provide a vertical accent, especially in spots that tend to stay damp.

Melinis

Ruby grass

BLOOM PERIOD: May to July

SIZE: 18 in. tall

HARDINESS: Zones 8–10

Melinis nerviglumis is a silver-blue-foliaged clumping grass from southern Africa. It is topped in spring through much of the summer with soft pink flowerheads for a dazzling display, easily as showy as most other garden perennials. The pink flowers turn soft tan-buff in late summer and fall. Although not hardy through much of the Southeast, it is quick enough to be grown as an annual. Seed sown in mid- to late winter will be large enough to plant out and make a showy display by spring. Best in a well-drained soil, established plants will tolerate significant drought.

Silvery blue foliage and pink flowerheads make *Melinis nerviglumis* well worth a permanent place in the garden.

Miscanthus

Maiden grass, miscanthus

BLOOM PERIOD: July to September

SIZE: 4–8 ft. tall

HARDINESS: Zones 5–9

Maiden grass, *Miscanthus sinensis*, is virtually synonymous with ornamental grass in many minds. The narrow foliage, growing in graceful, arching clumps, is topped in summer with showy flowers rising 1–2 ft. above the foliage. There are quite a few garden-worthy selections, from variegated cultivars to dwarf or giant types. All are very drought tolerant and show well with other sun-loving perennials. Miscanthus can seed around and has escaped along roadways in areas of the Southeast.

Few grasses provide the elegance and display of maiden grass, and now several sterile forms are available, such as *Miscanthus sinensis* 'NCMS1', usually sold as My Fair Maiden.

RIGHT The dried heads of maiden grass provide winter interest and seed for birds if left until early spring.

Muhlenbergia

Muhly grass, sweetgrass

BLOOM PERIOD: September to October

SIZE: 30–52 in. tall

HARDINESS: Zones 6–10

No plant garners more attention than a mass of pink muhly grass, *Muhlenbergia capillaris*, in full flower in late summer. Thin ribbons of blue-green foliage are topped with airy clouds of soft rose-pink turning soft khaki in fall. 'Pink Flamingos' is an outstanding hybrid between pink muhly and the southwestern *M. lindheimeri*, making a tall clump to 5 ft. in flower. For a different texture, the somewhat less hardy *M. dumosa* mimics a clump of bamboo 4 ft. tall and wide. All muhly grasses are quite drought tolerant and easy in the landscape. Plant in masses for best display.

Panicum

Switchgrass, panic grass

BLOOM PERIOD: August to September

SIZE: 3–5 ft. tall

HARDINESS: Zones 4–9

Switchgrass makes upright to arching clumps of strappy foliage. Selected forms of *Panicum virgatum* such as 'Shenandoah' are heavily tinted with red, especially as weather cools in the fall. The extra large 'Thundercloud', which can grow to 8 ft. tall, can be used as a hedging plant in place of large shrubs. Less often seen but well worth a place in the garden is sand switchgrass, *P. amarum*. Especially nice is the silvery blue foliage of 'Dewey Blue'. All switchgrasses are drought tolerant when established and are best mixed with prairie perennials like rudbeckia and coneflower or planted in masses. Songbirds appreciate the seedheads.

Many selections of switchgrass, such as *Panicum virgatum* 'Shenandoah', develop red highlights as summer progresses into fall. LEFT The haze of flowers above pink muhly grass is among the highlights of the late summer garden.

Pennisetum

Fountain grass

BLOOM PERIOD: June to September
SIZE: 1–6 ft. tall
HARDINESS: Zones 6–9

☀ ☼ ☀ 🦌

Fountain grasses make tidy clumps of narrow to wide strappy leaves topped from midsummer to fall with bottlebrush flowers. The two hardiest forms commonly grown in gardens are *Pennisetum alopecuroides* and *P. orientale*. Selections of both range from 1 ft. to over 6 ft. Both make excellent textural contrasts in perennial borders or easy-care plants for massing. Less hardy are some of the purple-leaved complex hybrids like 'Princess Caroline' or 'Black Stockings', which are best grown as annuals or in gardens that are zone 8 or warmer. Cut back fountain grass to about 10 in. in late winter.

The compact *Pennisetum alopecuroides* 'Cassian's Choice' makes a fine specimen for smaller gardens.

Saccharum

Sugar cane

BLOOM PERIOD: September to November
SIZE: 10–12 ft. tall
HARDINESS: Zones 6–10

☀ ☼ 🦌

Hardy sugar cane, *Saccharum arundinaceum*, is not for the faint of heart. Huge tropical-looking clumps of gray-green foliage with a distinct white midrib grow to 10 ft., topped with showy rose-pink flower plumes. The foliage and flowers age to gold-tan over the winter. Hardy sugar cane can seed around quite a bit in Deep South gardens but the late flowering prevents this issue north of zone 7. The true sugar cane, *S. officinarum*, is rarely grown as an ornamental, but some purple varieties are grown as annuals and can top 12 ft. with plenty of moisture and fertility.

Hardy sugar cane makes a huge plant and is only for the largest of gardens.

Schizachyrium

Little bluestem

BLOOM PERIOD: August to October

SIZE: 2–4 ft. tall

HARDINESS: Zones 3–9

Little bluestem, *Schizachyrium scoparium*, is a native, warm-season, clumping grass with silvery blue foliage often taking on burgundy tones as the weather cools in fall. Tan flower plumes top the colorful foliage in late summer through fall. The dwarf form 'The Blues' is among the showiest, with powder-blue foliage in tight low clumps. Some taller forms can flop if grown with high fertility but 'Standing Ovation' is a 4-ft. selection with very sturdy stems and great color. Cut back to 6 in. in late winter and divide the clumps every three to four years.

Schizachyrium scoparium 'Standing Ovation' does not flop and the blue foliage takes on purple and burgundy tints as the weather cools.

Sorghastrum

Indian grass

BLOOM PERIOD: July to September
SIZE: 3 ft. tall (to 6 ft. in flower)
HARDINESS: Zones 4–9

☀ ☼ 🐐 📍

The warm-season, clumping *Sorghastrum nutans* makes a tough plant for prairies and wildlife gardens, with low, 3-ft. clumps of light green foliage topped in late summer by 6-ft. tan flower plumes. The silver-blue-foliaged forms like 'Sioux Blue' or 'Indian Steel' are better plants for integrating into traditional landscapes. The low clumps of foliage work well with almost any other sun-loving perennial, especially meadow plants like black-eyed Susan or purple coneflower. The tall seedheads should be left for winter interest and songbird food before cutting back in late winter.

Sporobolus

Prairie dropseed, sacaton

BLOOM PERIOD: June to August
SIZE: 2–5 ft. tall
HARDINESS: Zones 4–9

☀ ☼ ☼ 🅂 🐐

Prairie dropseed, *Sporobolus heterolepis*, is a small, very fine-textured, native clumping grass. The arching foliage turns coppery in fall before fading to light tan. Airy, midsummer flower panicles form a haze over the foliage, later turning to seedheads favored by songbirds. Excellent for using near the front of a perennial border or as a no-mow lawn substitute. Less well known is the large sacaton, *Sporobolus wrightii*, a southwestern species that grows to 5 ft. in dry to wet spots. In areas where *Miscanthus* seeds around, sacaton can be used as a good substitute.

Sporobolus wrightii is a tall option for wet or dry spots. LEFT A close-up view shows the beautiful flowers of *Sorghastrum nutans*.

Perennials

Technically, a perennial is a plant which will return and flower year after year. By this definition, all trees and shrubs are perennials as are many plants we grow as annuals. In practice, when gardeners speak of perennials they generally mean hardy, herbaceous, non-woody plants which will return and flower every year.

Herbaceous perennials are the paint which gardeners use to create their living canvases, providing an infinite array of color, shade, and texture. Because they live longer than one season, perennials are among the best values in the garden. Whether you need a lacy, ferny texture or huge, bold foliage, brilliant color or subdued pastels, there is a perennial for you. Don't be afraid to experiment with different plants in different places. Gardening is all about experimenting and that means sometimes you will succeed and sometimes you will fail.

Plant your herbaceous plants in well-amended beds for the best growth and spread. Many will appreciate being divided every three to four years to keep vigor, and undivided plants will often begin to decline or die out in the center. As with many things in life, we like easy classifications—this plant is a sun perennial, this one is for shade—but in reality, plants rarely fall neatly into these designations. Numerous plants will grow wonderfully in shade but may never flower well unless given more light. A plant which requires some shade to survive your bright coastal garden with sandy soils may need full sun in an upland garden in order to thrive.

Perennials provide not only color to the garden but also texture and movement.

Acanthus

Bear's breeches

BLOOM PERIOD: **May to June**
SIZE: **30–54 in. tall**
HARDINESS: **Zones 6–8**

☀ ◑ 🦌 🌲

Bear's breeches are much loved for their large clumps of tropical-looking foliage and tall spikes of white flowers with dusky purple hoods. *Acanthus mollis* with its broad, lobed leaves is the most commonly encountered species and is best grown with some shade in southern gardens. Variegated selections like 'Tasmanian Angel' and 'Whitewater' have white-splashed foliage and typically pink flowers. Hybrids between *A. mollis* and *A. hungaricus*, like 'Summer Beauty' and 'Morning Candle', are more heat tolerant, making them better suited for southern gardens. Deep South gardeners can try the unusual *A. sennii*, with spiny leaves on sprawling stems and late season, deep red-orange flowers.

'Morning Candle' is among the more heat tolerant of the large-leaved selections of bear's breeches.

Adiantum

Maidenhair fern

BLOOM PERIOD: **Non-flowering**
SIZE: **10–20 in. tall**
HARDINESS: **Zones 7–9**

◑ ● 🦌 📍

The native maidenhair ferns are among the most elegant perennials for shade, with light green fronds on thin black stems, technically called rachises. The southern species, *Adiantum capillus-veneris*, makes a low patch with unbranched fronds to about 12 in. tall. It is best grown in a loose, moderately moist soil in zone 7 or warmer. The northern *A. pedatum* is slightly taller, with distinct horseshoe-shaped, branched fronds which mingle well with other shade perennials like hostas and Asian mayapples. The northern maidenhair fern can be grown successfully in even the highest, coldest regions of the Southeast.

Adiantum pedatum makes a tough but delicate-looking companion for other shade plants.

Agastache

Anise hyssop, hummingbird mint

BLOOM PERIOD: June to September

SIZE: 18–40 in. tall

HARDINESS: Zones 7–10

These mint family perennials are mostly native to the dry Southwest and grow best in well-drained, open locations. Flower color ranges from pale blue to pink, orange, and yellow. *Agastache foeniculum* is the most tolerant of humid conditions, and the hybrid 'Blue Boa' is a heavy flowering form that is especially good. Other species and selections can be short-lived perennials in the Southeast but are show-stopping, long-blooming butterfly and hummingbird magnets, making them well worth their place in the garden. Favorites include the orange *A. rupestris* and its hybrids, like the pink 'Desert Sunrise'. The aromatic foliage is a strong deer deterrent.

Agastache 'Blue Boa' is tolerant of high humidity and one of the most reliable anise hyssops for southern gardens, with a long season of bloom and sturdy stems. RIGHT Flowers come in a wide range of colors, from the bright pink of *Agastache* 'Raspberry Summer' to soft orange and yellow.

Alstroemeria

Peruvian lily, princess lily

BLOOM PERIOD: June to September
SIZE: 12–30 in. tall
HARDINESS: Zones 7–9

Alstroemeria is widely grown for cut flowers but makes an outstanding garden plant as well. The species *A. psittacina*, most widely known in its white-edged form, 'Variegata', grows in light shade as a spreading plant with unusual red trumpet flowers tipped green in spring and early summer before going semi-dormant as the summer heats up. Hybrid selections such as the gold 'Sweet Laura' and pink 'Tessa' are more typical clump-forming plants, flowering in early summer often through early fall. The intricately speckled and striped flowers are produced in abundance when plants are grown in a well-drained, organically rich soil.

The flowers of most Peruvian lilies like *Alstroemeria* 'Tessa' can be intricately speckled and colored.

Amsonia

Bluestar

BLOOM PERIOD: April to May
SIZE: 18–30 in. tall
HARDINESS: Zones 5–10

Few perennials are as reliable as bluestar, which makes clumps of upright stems with lance-shaped or thread-like leaves topped in spring with clusters of pale blue flowers. The queen of the group, *Amsonia hubrichtii*, from Arkansas, bears fine foliage that turns rich gold in fall, rivaling any woody plant for autumn display. Another fine-leaved form, 'Georgia Pancake', is a selection of *A. ciliata* whose prostrate stems make a low mat. The darkest blue selection available, 'Blue Ice', a hybrid between *A. tabernaemontana* and an unknown parent, makes a tidy mound of glossy willow-like leaves. Grow all bluestars in average to well-drained soil.

'Blue Ice' shows how bluestar's sky-blue spring flowers on long-lived perennial mounds make the plant so invaluable to gardens.

Asarum

Wild ginger

BLOOM PERIOD: March to May

SIZE: 3–10 in. tall

HARDINESS: Zones 6–10

Wild gingers make mostly evergreen groundcovers or low clumps with heart or arrow-shaped foliage for woodland gardens. The spreading *Asarum splendens* lightens the shade with silvery patterning on its matte leaves, while the native *A. shuttleworthii* 'Calloway' spreads slowly to form dense mats of small, silver-veined, glossy foliage. The deciduous *A. canadense* is ideal for native gardens growing around ferns. Both the clumping *A. delavayi* and the patterned *A. kumangeanum* have large, glossy leaves and provide year-round interest. Grow all asarums in rich, organic soil for best performance.

Asarum delavayi makes a nice clump of large, glossy, heart-shaped leaves.

Asclepias

Butterfly weed, milkweed

BLOOM PERIOD: May to July

SIZE: 24–40 in. tall

HARDINESS: Zones 4–9

The monarch butterfly relies on the many species of *Asclepias* for larval food and nectar. The drought-tolerant *A. tuberosa* requires a well-drained, sunny spot where the upright stems are topped by clusters of vibrant orange flowers. It can be difficult to establish in the garden but is worth the effort. You will have an easier time with the taller, coarser milkweeds like *A. incarnata* or *A. speciosa* with stout stems, broad leaves, and pale pink flowers. Deep South gardeners can grow the showy South African *A. curassavica* with its willow-like leaves and all-summer show of red and yellow flowers.

Asclepias tuberosa and other milkweeds are must-haves for the sunny habitat garden, where they provide nectar for pollinators and are the host plant for monarch caterpillars.

Asparagus

Asparagus

BLOOM PERIOD: **May to June**
SIZE: **30–54 in. tall**
HARDINESS: **Zones 5–9**

☀ ☼ ☼ 🦌

Asparagus officinalis is a well-known perennial vegetable whose young shoots are harvested in early spring. Asparagus can also be a beautiful ornamental addition to other types of gardens. In the South, the harvest period can be short before the shoots quickly grow past the edible stage, forming showy masses of tall, feathery stems. Many other species of asparagus are suitable for gardens, such as the wiry stemmed, clumping *A. denudatus* and the sprawling, feathery *A. microraphis*. All prefer sunny, well-drained gardens, dying back to the ground in winter in all but the mildest locations. Small white flowers give rise to bright red fruits in late summer.

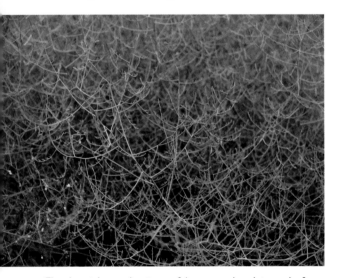

The almost-bare, wiry stems of *Asparagus denudatus* make for an unusual texture in the ornamental garden.

Aspidistra

Cast-iron plant

BLOOM PERIOD: **May to July**
SIZE: **18–30 in. tall**
HARDINESS: **Zones 7–10**

☼ ☁ ☼ 🦌 🌲

Cast-iron plant is a popular houseplant due to its tolerance for low light and periodic drought, characteristics which also make it a great landscape plant. The upright, lanceolate foliage, often streaked or spotted with white or yellow, adds interest to the garden year round. *Aspidistra elatior* is the species commonly grown although others are available. Forms like 'Ippin', with white streaking, and 'Amanogawa', with creamy yellow streaking and spots, light up the shade. The white-tipped 'Asahi' is among the most dramatic foliage plants for shade gardens. For best performance, cut old foliage to the ground after the new leaves have emerged and grown to half their ultimate height.

The striking foliage of *Aspidistra elatior* 'Asahi' brightens up a dim spot even in dry shade with root competition.

Aster

Aster

BLOOM PERIOD: September to November
SIZE: 12–48 in. tall
HARDINESS: Zones 5–9

☀ 🐝 📍

Well known for their cheery fall show, asters make up a large group which has recently been split into several different genera, including *Symphyotrichum*. The classic clumping species *S. novae-angliae*, or New England aster, comes in colors from white to pink to purple, in shades from pastel to bright. The Asian *Aster ageratoides* is a spreading species topped in fall with masses of flowers. Other *Aster* species range from tall stalked to low and mounding, all with the typical daisy flowers in an array of sizes and shades. Most prefer a well-drained soil in sun, are quite drought tolerant, and attract butterflies.

The display put on by New England asters is always a highlight of autumn.

Athyrium

Lady fern, painted fern

BLOOM PERIOD: Non-flowering
SIZE: 18–30 in. tall
HARDINESS: Zones 4–9

☀ ☁ 🦌 📍

Athyriums are ideal for providing texture and color in the garden. The lady fern, *Athyrium filix-femina* from the United States and Europe, has long been popular, and many forms have been selected through the years. Most are quite easy, making 18- to 26-in. clumps of lacy foliage. Japanese painted ferns, *A. niponicum*, newly classified as *Anisocampium niponicum*, add burgundy and silver tones to the typical green palette found in the fern family. These combine beautifully with heucheras and bleeding hearts as well as other woodland plants. They are best in shade with a rich, well-drained soil.

Our native lady fern makes a soft-textured, apple-green presence in woodland settings.

Baptisia

Baptisia, wild indigo

BLOOM PERIOD: April to May

SIZE: 18–48 in. tall

HARDINESS: Zones 5–10

☀ ☼ ☀ 🐝 📍

Baptisias are among the most reliable of native perennials, forming rounded clumps of green foliage topped with spikes of pea flowers that are followed by inflated seed pods. Once established they are long-lived, no-care plants. The blue-flowered *Baptisia australis* is most commonly encountered along with white *B. alba* and yellow *B. sphaerocarpa*. Recent breeding between species has led to a wider range of flower color. Quite different is *B. arachnifera*, grown more for its silver leaves than the small yellow flowers. The stems of baptisias will abscise, or detach, at ground level in fall and blow around the garden like tumbleweeds.

Recent breeding with baptisias has opened the door to new flower colors. RIGHT The red stalks of *Beschorneria septentrionalis* add to the flower display.

Beschorneria

False agave, amole

BLOOM PERIOD: April to May

SIZE: 24 in. tall (to 5 ft. in flower)

HARDINESS: Zones 8–11

☀ ☼ ☀ 🦌 🌲

These agave look-alikes grow as rosettes of strappy evergreen leaves but are pliable and not spiny. *Beschorneria septentrionalis*, with narrow, glossy foliage, puts up a tall, red flower spike bearing green-tipped, scarlet, bell-like flowers in spring. Slightly more tender is the broader-leaved *B. yuccoides*. Alien-looking, stout flower stalks drip with numerous green-tinged flowers over much of the spring. The variegated form 'Flamingo Glow' has a broad yellow band down the center of each leaf. Grow false agave in well-drained soil for best results.

Bletilla

Japanese ground orchid

BLOOM PERIOD: April to May

SIZE: 24 in. tall

HARDINESS: Zones 6–10

The pleated, iris-like leaves and delicate flowers of *Bletilla striata* belie the tough nature and ease of cultivation of this essential shade perennial. The typically lavender, occasionally white flowers are reminiscent of tiny cattleya orchids for an exotic garden look. Individual plants will quickly form showy spreading clumps in humus-rich soil. There are several white-margined selections that add interest after the flowers fade. The Japanese selection 'Ogon' ups the ante with solid chartreuse-gold foliage. A relatively new species to cultivation, *B. ochracea* grows a bit taller and bears creamy yellow flowers.

Bletilla striata looks tender and exotic but is actually a very easy shade garden plant.

Calanthe

Hardy calanthe orchid

BLOOM PERIOD: April to May

SIZE: 14 in. tall

HARDINESS: Zones 7–9

Calanthes bear wide, pleated leaves arising from underground pseudobulbs. They are often evergreen in warm gardens of zone 8 and points south, and the 1-ft. flower stalks bear delicate orchid flowers. The bright yellow flowers of *Calanthe sieboldii* are among the showiest of the group, but others like *C. discolor* and the hybrid seed strain *Calanthe* 'Kozu Spice' bear bicolor flowers in shades of pink, red, tan, yellow, and white. While calanthes can be expensive, they are relatively tough if given good soil and will become prized garden specimens as the clumps enlarge and bear dozens of flower stalks.

Calanthe 'Kozu Spice' is typically bicolor and makes an easy garden plant.

Callirhoe

Winecups

BLOOM PERIOD: April to June
SIZE: 8 in. tall
HARDINESS: Zones 6–10

☀ ☀ ☀ ⦿

Callirhoe involucrata, or winecups, spreads its finely dissected foliage from a basal rosette to weave around other plants. It displays its rose-colored, poppy-like flowers in spring and early summer. White forms such as 'Logan Calhoun' and the pastel-colored, extra-lacy *C. involucrata* var. *tenuissima* give more color variety to this western species. The southeastern *C. bushii* is similar but tends to grow somewhat taller, allowing its flowers to mingle with other spring bloomers. Plant in a sunny, well-drained spot.

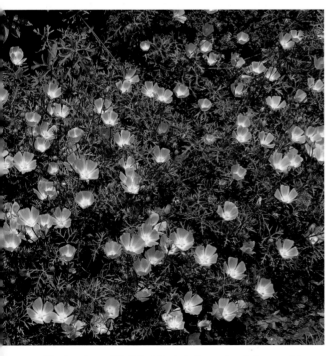

The lacy-leaved *Callirhoe involucrata* var. *tenuissima* provides soft color and fine texture.

Campanula

Bellflower

BLOOM PERIOD: May to July
SIZE: 8–24 in. tall
HARDINESS: Zones 4–8

☀ ◖

Bellflowers range from tiny alpine plants to upright, vigorous perennials, but many prefer cool climates. Perhaps the easiest for our region is the vigorously spreading *Campanula punctata*, which makes a mat of foliage topped in early summer with arching pale flowers heavily spotted with rose on the inside. The clumping hybrid 'Sarastro' brings the same large flowers but in a gorgeous blue hue, making it an even better garden plant. The low, spreading *C. poscharskyana*, with thousands of starry blue flowers over an extended period, is ideal for weaving around the base of small shrubs.

The large flowers of *Campanula punctata* 'Cherry Bells' look equally good in sun or part shade.

Canna

Canna lily

BLOOM PERIOD: June to October
SIZE: 4–6 ft. tall
HARDINESS: Zones 7–10

☀ ☀ 🐝▶

Few plants can add a tropical feel like cannas. Upright stalks of broad waxy foliage are topped by brilliant flowers in shades ranging from white to gold, pink, red, and orange. Many selections are grown more for their foliage than for the hummingbird-attracting flowers. *Canna* 'Bengal Tiger', with gold-striped leaves, and 'Australia', with deep burgundy foliage, are favorites. Cannas can grow in damp soils and pond edges. Leaf roller worms can disfigure plants and are hard to treat, but affected plants can be cut to the ground and allowed to resprout. Cannas spread by thick underground rhizomes which can be dug and stored over winter in cold climates.

Many canna lilies such as *Canna* 'Phasion' have boldly variegated foliage and brilliant flowers, making them pop in the landscape. RIGHT Garden mum colors run from soft pastels like *Chrysanthemum* 'Gethsemane Moonlight' to bold brights and provide reliable late season color in the landscape.

Chrysanthemum

Garden mum

BLOOM PERIOD: October to November
SIZE: 15–36 in. tall
HARDINESS: Zones 5–9

☀

Typical garden mums are hybrids between several species and have been cultivated for centuries. The flower color is virtually unlimited with most selections growing as upright clumps or spreading perennials. Many of the selections that are sold in fall as heavily pinched mounds of color for seasonal color make weak garden plants, but some selections, like the bright pink *Chrysanthemum* 'Miss Gloria's Thanksgiving Day' and the soft yellow 'Gethsemane Moonlight', are among the most reliable perennials. Plant them in almost any garden soil in full sun. Plants can be cut back halfway to the ground in early July to keep them more compact and less prone to flopping.

Clinopodium

Calamint

BLOOM PERIOD: May to June or August to October

SIZE: 12–30 in. tall

HARDINESS: Zones 7–10

☀ ☼ 🐇 ⚙ 🐝 📍

This group of mint relatives is widespread around the world, including two natives of the southeastern United States, *Clinopodium coccineum* and *C. ashei*. The former bears tubular, large-lipped, orange-red flowers on sparse, semi-woody stems in late summer, which are adored by hummingbirds. The latter is mounding with numerous pink flowers in spring. Most calamints prefer sunny, very well-drained soils, but the European *C. grandiflorum*, with large pink flowers, will tolerate semi-shaded spots as well. The aromatic foliage is a deterrent to deer and rabbits.

Native *Clinopodium coccineum* needs well-drained soil. Its long-tubed flowers are irresistible to hummingbirds.

Coreopsis

Coreopsis, tickseed, calliopsis

BLOOM PERIOD: May to October, depending on species

SIZE: 10–36 in. tall

HARDINESS: Zones 5–9

☀ 🐝 📍

Coreopsis is a New World genus with mostly yellow daisy flowers. Not surprisingly, some of the best garden plants for the South are our own native southeastern species. The fine texture of some species, like the popular *C. verticillata*, makes it a worthwhile garden plant even when out of bloom. Other species have a somewhat coarser texture but the cheery yellow flowers are always welcome in the garden, especially for butterflies. Breeding has expanded the color palette to include reds, oranges, and pinks. Among the best of these selections for hardiness has been the pink *C.* 'Heaven's Gate'. Grow in sun and well-drained soil.

The selection *Coreopsis* 'Creme Brulee' provides a soft, buttery yellow bloom, as opposed to the typical gold of most coreopsis.

Curcuma

Hidden cone ginger, pine-cone ginger

BLOOM PERIOD: August to October
SIZE: 2–6 ft. tall
HARDINESS: Zones 8–11

This group of subtropical plants bears stems of upright, broad, canna-like foliage sometimes marked with burgundy or edged with white, like the popular *Curcuma petiolata* 'Emperor'. The flowers emerge relatively low to the ground and are often hidden by the foliage. The true flowers are small but are typically held by a colorful, fleshy, cone-like structure or are topped by bright pink or white bracts. They are best grown in relatively rich soils with summer moisture, especially in sunny spots. Mulch well in winter in colder areas or dig the fleshy rhizomes and store in a cool, dark spot.

Cynara

Cardoon, globe artichoke

BLOOM PERIOD: June to July
SIZE: 30–48 in. tall (to 6 ft. in flower)
HARDINESS: Zones 5–9

Few plants can match the display of the thistle relative, *Cynara cardunculus*, with its 3-ft. mounds of impressive silvery leaves. In summer, tall flower stalks bearing huge buds open to reveal the lavender flowers. After flowering, cardoons will die to the ground and disappear for about four weeks before reemerging. The edible artichoke is *C. cardunculus* Scolymus Group, whose flower buds should be harvested as they emerge, before they open. It is a showy plant suitable for a sunny, well-drained spot in the ornamental garden.

Edible artichoke can be planted as a specimen perennial where it makes an impression even before it flowers. LEFT The small yellow flowers of *Curcuma* 'Raspberry' are held in a waxy-textured structure which lasts long after the plant has finished blooming.

Cypripedium

Lady slipper

BLOOM PERIOD: May to June

SIZE: 12–24 in. tall

HARDINESS: Zones 4–8

Seeing a well-grown clump of lady slipper orchids in flower is a breathtaking experience. Our native lady slippers such as the yellow *Cypripedium parviflorum* have a reputation for being difficult. This stems from the improper practice of wild collecting which typically ends with a dead plant. Container-grown plants from reputable nurseries should be planted in a compost-rich soil in light shade. Roots will grow horizontally through the top compost layer and should not be disturbed. In recent years a host of hybrids have been introduced which are spectacular garden plants.

Cyrtomium

Holly fern

BLOOM PERIOD: Non-flowering

SIZE: 12–24 in. tall

HARDINESS: Zones 7–10

The glossy evergreen foliage of holly fern makes it a welcome addition to woodland gardens, where it provides year-round interest. The broad pinnae, or leaflets, of the common *Cyrtomium falcatum* add a bold texture to the garden quite unlike the lacy feel most ferns give. The somewhat finer and hardier *C. fortunei* makes a more upright specimen. All holly ferns are avoided by deer and are excellent in masses or scattered throughout a shade garden in loose, organic soils. Occasionally remove old fronds to keep the plant looking fresh.

The glossy foliage of *Cyrtomium falcatum* sparkles even in shade and is unpalatable to deer. LEFT New hybrids like *Cypripedium* 'Philipp' are spectacular woodland specimens and should be placed where they can be appreciated.

Dicentra

Bleeding heart

BLOOM PERIOD: April to May

SIZE: 12–24 in. tall

HARDINESS: Zones 4–8

Bleeding hearts are classic shade garden plants, most commonly represented by the Asian *Dicentra spectabilis*, now classified in the genus *Lamprocapnos*. It has lacy foliage and arching flower stalks bearing delicate heart-shaped blossoms in spring. This species will go summer dormant, so take care to avoid damage when planting other perennials nearby in fall. For added impact, the dark red *D. spectabilis* 'Valentine' or bright-foliaged 'Gold Heart' can be grown. Our native bleeding heart, *D. eximia*, doesn't go dormant early and is smaller in all aspects with lacy blue-green foliage. The form 'Dolly Sods' is among the best, with all-season flowering and great sun tolerance.

The selection *Dicentra spectabilis* 'Valentine' has some of the deepest color of all bleeding hearts. RIGHT New species of *Disporopsis* are being found in Asia, which will expand the range of these excellent woodland plants.

Disporopsis

Evergreen Solomon's seal

BLOOM PERIOD: April to June

SIZE: 10–20 in. tall

HARDINESS: Zones 6–10

This spreading evergreen perennial for shade gardens can be used tucked around shrubs and small trees. *Disporopsis pernyi* is most commonly found in cultivation where the arching stalks of ovate to lanceolate leaves bear white flowers in spring. It is exceptionally tough and can grow in the deepest shade. The more rounded leaves of *D. aspersa* provide a different texture but are just as tough and the flowers have a citrusy sweet fragrance. The flowers of both species are followed by round, blue-black fruit. Expect a 2- to 3-ft. clump in five to eight years.

Disporum

Fairy bells

BLOOM PERIOD: **April to May**
SIZE: **10–54 in. tall**
HARDINESS: **Zones 6–9**

Fairy bells is a shade perennial with upright stems bearing clusters of terminal flowers in spring. Among the easiest to grow is the yellow-flowered *Disporum flavens*, whose blossoms emerge as the stems are still shooting upward in April. Also easy is the smaller, narrow-leaved *D. sessile*, which is usually encountered in its variegated form. The taller species like *D. cantoniense* need the support of a shrub to grow up through. Grow all species in rich soil in partial shade. *Disporum sessile* can be used as a deciduous groundcover to good effect.

Dryopteris

Fern

BLOOM PERIOD: **Non-flowering**
SIZE: **2–3 ft. tall**
HARDINESS: **Zones 6–10**

This widespread group of ferns typically makes clumps of elegant, deer-resistant foliage. The autumn fern, *Dryopteris erythrosora*, is an evergreen species whose new growth emerges in spring with a coppery orange color. Among the most handsome of all ferns is the cycad-like *D. crassirhizoma* and the large and lush *D. wallichiana*, which has an unusual wild distribution split between Asia and Mexico. Our native male fern, *D. filix-mas*, prefers cooler temps than those found in the Deep South but makes a lovely fine texture in cool, damp spots, especially when one of the many crested or dissected forms is used.

Many forms of *Dryopteris filix-mas* have been selected, including varieties with crested fronds. LEFT Terminal clusters of gold flowers emerge from the unfurling foliage of *Disporum flavens*.

Echinacea

Coneflower

BLOOM PERIOD: May to July

SIZE: 18–36 in. tall

HARDINESS: Zones 4–9

Perhaps no other plant has seen so much advancement through breeding in recent years as coneflower. The drooping purple-pink petals surrounding a cone of orange that characterize the garden staple *Echinacea purpurea* have been hybridized with the yellow *E. paradoxa*, giving rise to a host of gold, orange, red, and pink forms, often with larger or doubled flowers. Coneflowers are quite drought tolerant, but reward rich soils and regular summer moisture with more flowers; deadhead to lengthen the flowering season. The summer blooms draw butterflies, and the seedheads from the single-flowered forms can be left for birds at the end of the season.

Echinacea purpurea is among the best perennials for wildlife gardens, with nectar-rich flowers for butterflies and seeds for a range of songbirds. BOTTOM Saturated reds and oranges such as those in *Echinacea* 'Tangerine Dream' have expanded the range of coneflowers available to gardeners.

Epimedium

Fairy-wings, bishop's cap

BLOOM PERIOD: **March to April**

SIZE: **8–30 in. tall**

HARDINESS: **Zones 5–9**

☀ ☁ ☀ 🦌 🌲

Epimediums are Asian woodland perennials with panicles of airy flowers held on wiry stems above foliage that is semi-evergreen to deciduous. The flowers range from tiny stars to relatively large blossoms, all with a distinctive four-spurred shape in colors from white to yellow, pink, and purple, often in bicolors. The foliage in many forms emerges with burgundy edges or speckling before becoming solid green. Cut foliage to the ground before the spring flowers emerge. Selections include both running and clumping types, and all are great in dry shade but perform best in rich, moist soil.

The long-spurred flowers of *Epimedium grandiflorum* 'Dark Beauty' are bicolored and the foliage emerges with purple tones.

Eupatorium

Joe-pye weed

BLOOM PERIOD: **August to October**

SIZE: **4–7 ft. tall**

HARDINESS: **Zones 5–9**

☀ ☀ 🐝 📍

Native Joe-pye weeds are tall perennials for the back of the border where the large leafy clumps are topped in late summer with huge heads of mauve or occasionally white flowers. Several similar species, newly classified as *Eutrochium*, are native to the South, including *Eupatorium purpureum*, with solid stems tinged purple at the leaf nodes, *E. fistulosum*, with hollow purple stems, *E. maculatum*, with flat-topped flowerheads, and *E. dubium*, with distinctly three-nerved leaves. Grow in moist, rich soil in sun to part shade. Cut back halfway in early summer to control height and to keep from flopping.

Eupatorium fistulosum 'Selection' is a large, showy perennial perfect for making a late-season garden statement.

Farfugium

Leopard plant

BLOOM PERIOD: October to November
SIZE: 18–24 in. tall
HARDINESS: Zones 7–9

Farfugium japonicum is a reliable evergreen perennial for adding a bold textural element to the garden. The typical gold-spotted form, 'Aureomaculatum', gives rise to the common name and will come mostly true from seed. Other interesting forms include the huge glossy-foliaged 'Giganteum' and the thin white-margined 'Kinkan'. For those who prefer a less-restrained look, 'Kaimon Dake' emerges with white leaves lightly speckled green that gradually become solid green. There are several crested, contorted selections like 'Lunar Landing'. Golden daisy flowers late in the season add to the charm of these tough plants.

The huge, glossy green leaves of *Farfugium japonicum* 'Giganteum' make a bold statement, especially when topped by gold daisy flowers.

Gaillardia

Blanket flower

BLOOM PERIOD: July to October
SIZE: 12–24 in. tall
HARDINESS: Zones 5–9

Blanket flowers are butterfly-attracting, easy, long-blooming plants for sunny, well-drained gardens where the gold, orange, and red petals surround the central ball of yellow or burgundy. New introductions are often bicolors, doubles, or have tubular petals over a tight mound of matte foliage. The Texas *Gaillardia aestivalis* var. *winkleri* is a more open plant with white to pale lavender petals around a burgundy center and grows well in even the driest garden. The selection 'Grape Sensation' is a dark-petaled form that pops in the garden as it weaves through other drought-tolerant plants like yucca and agave.

The purple-flowered Gaillardia *aestivalis* var. *winkleri* 'Grape Sensation' needs well-drained soil to thrive.

Geranium

Geranium, crane's bill

BLOOM PERIOD: **June to October**

SIZE: **6–24 in. tall**

HARDINESS: **Zones 4–9**

The hardy perennial species of true geraniums have perhaps suffered by being confused with the annual zonal and bedding geraniums which are a completely different animal (see *Pelargonium* in the annuals and tropicals section). True geraniums have rounded and lobed or dissected foliage with generally five-petaled flowers in shades of white, pink, and blue which butterflies enjoy. Selections like *Geranium* 'Ann Thompson' and 'Espresso' add season-long foliar color. Most are very easy in any garden setting and many also have excellent fall color. The native *G. maculatum* tolerates shadier conditions than most of the Eurasian species.

The flowers of many perennial geraniums like *Geranium* 'Ballerina' have petals with a darker eye and veins. RIGHT The fragrant terminal spikes of *Hedychium* 'Slim's Orange' are appreciated by hummingbirds and people alike.

Hedychium

Flowering ginger

BLOOM PERIOD: **July to October**

SIZE: **3–7 ft. tall**

HARDINESS: **Zones 7–11**

Who doesn't love the tropical look that a clump of flowering ginger provides? Upright, fleshy stalks with corn-like foliage topped in mid- to late summer with heads of fragrant white, yellow, or orange flowers provide a vertical accent to the garden and attract hummingbirds. Many selections have somewhat open flowerheads with extended tubular flowers, but others like the aptly named *Hedychium densiflorum* have tighter spikes. In full sun they grow quickly and flower heavily, but the foliage can look a bit tired. Plants are perhaps best in a moist spot with some afternoon shade.

Helleborus

Hellebore, Lenten rose, Christmas rose

BLOOM PERIOD: December to March

SIZE: 10–20 in. tall

HARDINESS: Zones 5–9

Hellebores are prized for their evergreen foliage, winter flowers, and deer resistance, in addition to the ability to thrive in dry shade. The species can be broadly split into two groups: the stemmed, or caulescent, and the unstemmed, or acaulescent. *Helleborus foetidus* is the most common of the former. The pale green flowers form atop the finely divided, palmate leaves. The old flowers can be removed after flowering or the stems can be cut to the ground. If the flowers on most hellebores are allowed to go to seed, they will sow freely in the garden, creating an evergreen carpet.

The acaulescent forms most often seen are the hybrids known simply as *Helleborus ×hybridus*. Recent improvements in breeding and production have opened the door to a variety of colors from slate-black to yellow, rose, and white, often with picotee or spotted petals. The broad, palmately compound leaves provide great texture all year. Other hybrids such as *H. ×sternii* and *H. ×ericsmithii* add improved foliage effects with silver veins and burgundy tints. For best floral display, many of the stemless forms will benefit from removal of the old foliage before flowering starts.

The few variegated selections available, like *Helleborus ×sternii* 'Fire and Ice', add interest throughout the year. BOTTOM Hellebore breeding has greatly increased the variety of flower color and form in the hybrids.

Hemerocallis

Daylily

BLOOM PERIOD: **May to August**
SIZE: **2–4 ft. tall**
HARDINESS: **Zones 4–9**

Daylilies are easy, low-care, reliable perennials with strappy foliage topped in summer with large, lily-like flowers usually in shades of yellow, orange, or red, often with a contrasting throat. Daylilies have been the subject of much breeding and the color range and diversity of flower forms is amazing. The narrow-petaled spider flower types are especially distinct. Other breeders are creating reblooming cultivars which greatly extend the flowering season. Extra-tall selections rising to as much as 6 ft. can be found for the back of the border.

The spider-flowered daylilies like *Hemerocallis* 'Nona's Garnet Spider' have a finer texture with their strappy petals.

Heuchera

Coral bells, heuchera

BLOOM PERIOD: April to June or August to
September
SIZE: 8–20 in. tall
HARDINESS: Zones 4–8

The coral bell hybrids are legion and have proved to be of mixed performance in the Southeast. The hybrids with our native *Heuchera americana* and *H. villosa* are generally better candidates for high heat and humidity. Coral bells make a low mound of rounded, lobed foliage of gold, purple, amber, or other color, often with silvered veins. They are best in a moist, well-drained spot in light shade. Heucheras will not tolerate tree leaves left on their crowns in fall. Over time their stems can become exposed and they should be dug and replanted with the stems below ground.

While many selections are chosen for their foliage, the flowers of some heucheras live up to the name coral bells, like those of *Heuchera* 'Paris'.

Hosta

Hosta, plantain lily

BLOOM PERIOD: **June to August**

SIZE: **4–36 in. tall**

HARDINESS: **Zones 3–8**

Hostas are iconic shade perennials making clumps of showy foliage all summer long. The leaves are often broad and corrugated but can also be quite narrow and strappy. Hostas range from tiny plants suitable for a woodland rockery to huge clumps that serve the purpose of a shrub during summer. The white or lavender summer flowers on spikes held above the foliage can be quite showy and are attractive to hummingbirds. *Hosta plantaginea* and its hybrids are very fragrant in flower. They are all best in a relatively moist, rich soil and are very susceptible to deer, voles, and slugs.

Hosta 'Rainbow's End' is just one option among many hundreds of variegated selections. BOTTOM The silvery blue foliage of *Hosta* 'Halcyon' has made it a popular garden perennial for shade.

Kniphofia

Red-hot poker

BLOOM PERIOD: **May to July**

SIZE: **20–48 in. tall**

HARDINESS: **Zones 7–10**

Red-hot poker forms a clump of thick-textured strappy foliage topped in summer with spikes of tightly clustered tubular flowers that humming-birds appreciate. In many selections the unopened flowers are orange-red, opening to yellow from the bottom up for a two-toned effect, giving rise to the common name. Other forms are all yellow, orange, or red and in some instances caramel colored. Most newer selections are relatively small but some species can grow to almost 8 ft. in flower. Kniphofias are quite drought tolerant but will grow surprisingly well in moist soil, as evidenced by some species that grow in seeps and marshes.

The typical flower color for red-hot pokers like *Kniphofia uvaria* 'Lola' gives rise to its common name. BOTTOM Selections like *Kniphofia* 'Sunningdale Yellow' add color and a vertical texture to the landscape.

135

Liriope, monkey grass

BLOOM PERIOD: June to August

SIZE: 12–24 in. tall

HARDINESS: Zones 6–10

Liriopes grow throughout the Southeast, where the quickly spreading species *Liriope spicata* is widely planted as a groundcover. The dark green, grass-like foliage is admirably suited for growing under trees in this way. The non-spreading *L. muscari* is better suited for gardens where it makes a tight clump of strappy leaves with spikes of lavender (occasionally white) flowers in summer. The foliage is especially showy on the all-gold 'Pee Dee Ingot' and the white-flushed 'Okina'. Other species are slowly entering the market, such as *L. platyphylla*, that has flower stalks rising to 3 ft. over 18-in. clumps.

While liriopes are typically known for their green, grass-like foliage, *Liriope muscari* 'Pee Dee Ingot' has bright gold leaves.

Manfreda, deciduous agave

BLOOM PERIOD: May to June

SIZE: 12 in. tall (to 4 ft. in flower)

HARDINESS: Zones 7–10

Manfreda is a soft-textured, deciduous agave relative forming a small rosette of almost succulent silvery blue foliage that is often spotted with burgundy. A tall flower stalk rises to 4 ft. or more in early summer, with cream to burgundy flowers. The native *Manfreda virginica* has solid silver leaves but other southwestern species, such as *M. undulata* and its selection 'Chocolate Chip', can be quite heavily spotted. Some hybrids like 'Helen Wynans' are vigorous spreaders. New hybrids have been made with true agaves, named as the new genus ×*Mangave*, and we can look forward to evergreen, spotted agaves soon. They are all best in sunny, well-drained spots.

×*Mangave* 'Macho Mocha' is a *Manfreda-Agave* hybrid with stiff silvery blue leaves heavily spotted with burgundy.

Nepeta

Catmint

BLOOM PERIOD: April to June, then sporadically through summer
SIZE: 10–24 in. tall
HARDINESS: Zones 5–9

The catmints form tight clumps of aromatic green to silver-grey foliage topped in late spring with lavender, occasionally white or pink, flowers. Flowering will often continue sporadically through summer, especially in cooler climates. If the spent blooms are sheared off after flowering a late summer rebloom will usually be assured. They are easy-care plants if given plenty of sun and a well-drained, somewhat lean soil.

Nepeta 'Joanna Reed' is a reliable clump-forming perennial for a sunny spot.

Ophiopogon

Mondo grass

BLOOM PERIOD: June
SIZE: 3–24 in. tall
HARDINESS: Zones 7–10

Mondo grass is often confused with liriope with which it is closely related. Most mondos are clumpers or very slow spreaders, making them easy to use in the garden. *Ophiopogon japonicus* makes a 10-in. clump of fine foliage, but its dwarf form 'Gyoku Ryu' is even more commonly encountered. Black-foliaged *O. planiscapus* 'Kokuryu' is also widely grown, though often under the incorrect names 'Nigrescens' or 'Arabicus'. The stiff, curling foliage of *O. umbraticola* is quite different in the shade garden. Flowers of mondo grass are usually held low to the foliage so the white or lavender flowers are not very showy.

The black mondo grass *O. planiscapus* 'Kokuryu' can be used to make memorable color combinations.

Osmunda

Cinnamon fern, royal fern

BLOOM PERIOD: **Non-flowering**

SIZE: **3 ft. tall**

HARDINESS: **Zones 4–9**

Among our finest native ferns, newly classified in the genus *Osmundastrum*, are the deciduous cinnamon fern, *Osmunda cinnamomea* (or *Osmundastrum cinnamomeum* as it is now known), and the royal fern, *O. regalis*. The latter is found in Europe as well, and a closely related species, *O. japonica*, occurs in China and Japan. All have relatively bold-textured, pale green fronds arising from tight clumps. They are easy in average to moist garden soils in some shade. Like all ferns, they are mostly deer proof. The cinnamon fern is noted for its fertile, rusty orange fronds which rise above the foliage in spring, like giant sticks of incense.

An ancient clump of royal fern, *Osmunda regalis*, emerging in spring with fresh, lime-green foliage.

Paeonia

Peony

BLOOM PERIOD: **April to May**

SIZE: **18–48 in. tall**

HARDINESS: **Zones 4–8**

Peonies can be frustrating for the southern gardener. Most grow quite well in the South but if the temperatures get high during the spring bloom, they can come in and out of flower in a matter of days. Some species peonies like the pale pink *Paeonia lactiflora* perform quite well, as do the smaller woodland plants, white *P. japonica* and pink *P. obovata*. Some of the best herbaceous peonies for the South include old hybrid cultivars like 'Krinkled White' from the 1920s. *Paeonia* 'Bartzella' is an example of the new intersectional hybrids between the tree and herbaceous peonies which are proving to be exceptional garden plants.

Paeonia 'Bartzella' is an intersectional or Itoh hybrid peony, one of the hybrids between tree and herbaceous peonies.

Penstemon

Penstemon, beardtongue

BLOOM PERIOD: April to June
SIZE: 12–30 in. tall
HARDINESS: Zones 5–10

Penstemons are found only in North America, typically in exposed, well-drained spots or open sandy woodlands. In general, they are clumping plants with upright stems of tubular to bell-shaped outward-facing flowers of white, blue, pink, or orange. They are excellent hummingbird and butterfly attractors and extremely showy when well grown. Many hybrids, like *Penstemon ×mexicali* and selections, have been made for more deeply saturated or larger flowers, and these forms can compete with any other perennial in the late spring garden. Plant beardtongue in a bright spot with excellent drainage.

Penstemon ×*mexicali* 'Red Rocks' is just one of the wide variety of flower colors and sizes available; all are excellent pollinator plants.

Perovskia

Russian sage

BLOOM PERIOD: August to October
SIZE: 2–3 ft. tall
HARDINESS: Zones 5–9

This exceptionally heat- and drought-tolerant perennial makes an upright clump of semi-woody stems bearing dissected ferny silver foliage. In late summer it is topped with cool blue to lavender flowers. The silver stems can provide some winter interest but should be cut back by early spring. While the species *Perovskia atriplicifolia* is widely grown, several dwarf forms like 'Little Spire' and 'Lacey Blue' are becoming popular for edging and smaller gardens. Russian sage must have full sun and very well-drained soil especially during winter. The aromatic foliage deters deer while the flowers are visited by butterflies.

Russian sage, as in *Perovskia atriplicifolia* 'Little Spire', is a tough, reliable perennial for any sunny dry spot.

Phlomis

Jerusalem sage, candela, phlomis

BLOOM PERIOD: April to June

SIZE: 20–36 in. tall

HARDINESS: Zones 7–10

Phlomis is generally represented in southeastern gardens by the evergreen subshrub *P. fruticosa* (Jerusalem sage). The silver, felted leaves are attractive year round and the whorls of bright gold flowers around the stems in spring are outstanding. The Spanish *P. lychnitis* is similar but smaller in all respects, as is the lavender-flowered *P. italica*. These need full sun and well-drained soil. Several herbaceous species have large, arrow-shaped green leaves bearing yellow or purple whorls of flowers as in *P. russelliana* and *P. maximowiczii* respectively. The herbaceous plants are more tolerant of average soils and light shade.

Phlomis fruticosa makes an evergreen subshrub with fuzzy, silvery leaves and bright yellow flowers.

Phlox

Phlox

BLOOM PERIOD: April to May or June to September

SIZE: 3–36 in. tall

HARDINESS: Zones 4–8

Phlox flowers are butterfly magnets with their pinwheels of white, pink, and lavender typically appearing in spring. The fragrant *Phlox divaricata* and *P. stolonifera*, including the selection 'Weesie Smith', tolerate light shade. This has been one of my favorite perennial groundcovers, quickly spreading to 6 ft. across in three years and topped with lavender spring flowers. *Phlox pilosa* is a noteworthy native species producing bright pink flowers. The moss phloxes, *P. subulata* and *P. nivalis*, have needle-like evergreen foliage and are solid sheets of color in spring. Tall, summer-flowering border phlox, *P. paniculata*, is topped with white, pink, or lavender flowers. Look for mildew-resistant forms like 'David' for best performance in the South.

The bubblegum-pink *Phlox pilosa* is one of many outstanding native species which should be more widely grown. RIGHT *Phlox subulata*, moss phlox, makes an excellent groundcover in sunny to partly shaded spots with cheery spring flowers.

Podophyllum

Mayapple

BLOOM PERIOD: **March to May**
SIZE: **12–30 in. tall**
HARDINESS: **Zones 6–10**

Our native mayapple, *Podophyllum peltatum*, is of limited use in gardens as the spreading plants go dormant by early summer. The Asian species stay up all summer, forming clumps instead of spreading. *Podophyllum pleianthum* can grow to 30 in. with leaves that have the look and feel of green '60s pleather cut into stars with pinking shears. *Podophyllum delavayi* and *P. difforme* and their hybrids are patterned with burgundy. All species grow like small umbrellas and bear their flowers below the foliage—single white for our native and clusters of burgundy blossoms on the Asian types.

The showy flowers of *Podophyllum pleianthum* are carried beneath their large plastic-textured leaves.

Polygonatum

Solomon's seal

BLOOM PERIOD: **April to May**
SIZE: **8–60 in. tall**
HARDINESS: **Zones 5–10**

Solomon's seal is a deciduous perennial with upright stems rising from underground rhizomes. The typically arching branches bear small, white, bell-shaped flowers followed by blue-black fruit from August to October. The 24-in. *Polygonatum odoratum* is common in gardens, often in variegated forms like 'Double Stuff'. More subtle, but still showy, is the red-stemmed 'Jingui'. Spreading *P. humile* makes an 8-in. deciduous groundcover. On the other end of the scale is the 5-ft., narrow-leaved *P. kingianum*, with unusual orange to red flowers. New species and selections are rapidly coming into cultivation, adding to the diversity of this woodland perennial.

Whorls of orange to red flowers circle the tall stems of *Polygonatum kingianum*. RIGHT *Polygonatum odoratum* 'Variegatum' provides excellent fall color rivaling the autumn tints of trees and shrubs.

Polystichum

Christmas fern, tassel fern, shield fern

BLOOM PERIOD: Non-flowering
SIZE: 12–24 in. tall
HARDINESS: Zones 5–8

Polystichum ferns are found in North America, Europe, and across Asia. Our native Christmas fern, *P. acrostichoides*, sends dark green fronds vertically, letting them gradually droop to the ground as they age. The Korean *P. polyblepharum* is shorter with wider fronds that are dark green and highlighted by an orange to black rachis, which is the midrib of a fern frond. Perhaps my favorite garden fern is Makino's shield fern, *P. makinoi*, which makes a cycad-like specimen to 24 in. tall and wide. Any polystichum is well worth a spot in the woodland garden and like all ferns will be virtually deer proof.

The glossy fronds and dark rachis of Korean tassel fern, *Polystichum polyblepharum*, stand out in the garden.

Pyrrosia

Tongue fern

BLOOM PERIOD: Non-flowering
SIZE: 12 in. tall
HARDINESS: Zones 7–11

Few evergreen ferns are as distinct as the tongue fern, *Pyrrosia lingua*, with creeping rhizomes that send up individual, decidedly un-ferny fronds with a texture of thick leather and tan, felted backs. Happy plants can make a sizable patch to 2 ft. across in five years. The variegated 'Ogon Nishiki' adds a touch of color to the shade garden, and several forms have toothed edges like 'Hiryu'. Other species include the three- and five-lobed *P. hastata* and *P. polydactyla*, respectively, which tend to clump more than spread. All three species grow best on steep slopes rather than flatland.

The leather-textured fronds of tongue fern are brightened by chartreuse striping on *Pyrrosia lingua* 'Ogon Nishiki'.

Rohdea

Sacred lily

BLOOM PERIOD: **May to June**

SIZE: **8–24 in. tall**

HARDINESS: **Zones 6–10**

Rohdea japonica is highly prized in Japan, where hundreds of selections of this evergreen, rosette-forming perennial offer different variegation patterns, crested and contorted foliage types, and a range of sizes. In the garden, sacred lily thrives even in deep, dry shade. Short spikes of white flowers are not showy but are followed by bright red fruit from November to February. Plants are slow to grow and are consequently expensive in the trade, but they are easy and long lived, so worth the investment. The larger *R. chinensis* growing to 30 in. has showy orange flowers on low pinecone-like spikes before the red fruit.

Rohdea japonica growing with carex and hostas in a shade garden.

Rudbeckia

Black-eyed Susan, brown coneflower, rudbeckia

BLOOM PERIOD: **June to August**

SIZE: **18–72 in. tall**

HARDINESS: **Zones 4–9**

Perennial rudbeckias draw butterflies with their brown-eyed, gold flowers in mid- to late summer. The classic species is *Rudbeckia fulgida*, epitomized by the compact, floriferous 'Goldsturm' which has large flowers above a mostly evergreen rosette. Somewhat different is giant black-eyed Susan, *R. maxima*, with large, ovate, blue-green basal leaves topped by towering 8-ft. flower stalks. The chartreuse-leaved selection 'Golda Emanis' provides an extra burst of color. Other species can be found in the trade, including *R. hirta*, which tends to grow as an annual or biennial. Grow all in open, sunny spots. Old seedheads can be left to provide food for songbirds.

Huge, glaucous, silver-blue leaves are topped by towering flower stalks on *Rudbeckia maxima*, sometimes known as the elephant-ear rudbeckia. LEFT Displaying smaller flowers than are common in this genus, *Rudbeckia triloba* makes up the difference with sheer numbers.

Ruellia

Ruellia, false petunia

BLOOM PERIOD: **July to September**

SIZE: **8–48 in. tall**

HARDINESS: **Zones 7–10**

Ruellias are represented in gardens mostly by *Ruellia simplex*, sometimes listed as the synonym *R. brittoniana*, often in one of its dwarf forms, such as the 8-in. 'Katie' or the 24-in., pink-flowered 'Chi Chi'. The species can be 4 ft. or taller, with narrow leaves topped with tubular lavender flowers. 'Black Beauty', a dark-leaved hybrid, is among the most striking of perennials. The red-flowered South American *R. elegans* is somewhat tender, but 'Ragin' Cajun' is hardy to zone 7. Grow all in sun and well-drained, rich soil. In subtropical areas, avoid ruellias as they can be overly vigorous.

Ruellia simplex 'Katie' is a long-blooming, easy perennial for planting in masses or edging a garden.

Salvia

Sage

BLOOM PERIOD: **April to October**

SIZE: **12–40 in. tall**

HARDINESS: **Zones 7–10**

☀ ☼ ☼ 🦌 🌲 🔺 🐝▸

The sages are a large group ranging from annuals to edible herbs to showy garden perennials. *Salvia officinalis*, culinary sage, has evergreen, gray foliage on semi-woody stems. Colorful-leaved forms like gold-edged 'Icterina' or 'Tricolor' can be used for cooking and year-round interest in the garden. Other subshrubs include *S. greggii* and *S. microphylla*, which form twiggy, semi-evergreen plants with small leaves and masses of white to pink to red flowers blooming heaviest in spring and fall but also sporadically through summer. Trim plants back after the heavy spring bloom to keep plants denser. Grow all in sun and well-drained soil.

Most flowering sages are herbaceous sun lovers with flowers in any color imaginable. Among the best is the tall, fall-blooming *Salvia guaranitica*, with blue flowers on top of spreading 48-in. stems. Some of the most floriferous types come from the shorter, rosette-forming *S. ×sylvestris*. The pink 'Eveline' is outstanding, as is the old favorite 'Mainacht'. Less commonly grown are the Asian woodland species. Among these, the very hardy *S. koyamae*, with yellow flowers, and *S. glabrescens*, with purple to pink blooms rising above large triangular flowers, are easy in light shade and moister soils than typical for sage.

Salvia greggii makes a shrubby, semi-evergreen plant with flowers in a huge range of colors, like the bright pink of 'Lipstick'. RIGHT The reliable *Salvia ×sylvestris* 'Eveline' has quickly become a favorite for its masses of flowers, which combine well with other perennials.

149

Sempervivum

Hens and chicks, cats and kittens, houseleek

BLOOM PERIOD: **Sporadic**

SIZE: **3 in. tall**

HARDINESS: **Zones 4–8**

Hens and chicks are small, succulent, rosette-forming plants which develop offsets, giving rise to the common names. Many selections have been made over time, producing a diversity of foliage colors in the light green, silver, and burgundy palette. Short spikes of pink or white star-like flowers form occasionally, often due to stress or overcrowding. *Sempervivum arachnoideum* is covered in cobweb-like hairs. All sempervivums need well-drained soils in sun. In the deeper South, they prefer some afternoon shade. Hens and chicks make great plants in containers, where they provide year-round color and texture.

Hens and chicks prefer well-drained soil, and once growing happily the "chicks" can be separated from the "hens" to plant elsewhere or share with fellow gardeners.

Spigelia

Pinkroot

BLOOM PERIOD: May
SIZE: 24 in. tall
HARDINESS: Zones 5–9

If not the most striking eastern U.S. wildflower, pink-root is certainly in the running. *Spigelia marilandica* offers deep green foliage topped in late spring with the most incredible scarlet-red tubular flowers, highlighted by bright yellow interiors. Grow this in a moist, sunny to partially shaded site where you and the hummingbirds can appreciate it. The much rarer *S. gentianoides* requires a sunny, well-drained garden spot to thrive.

TOP *Spigelia gentianoides* creates a beautiful pink mound, but requires sun and good drainage. RIGHT Hummingbirds are as attracted to the bright red and gold flowers of pinkroot as gardeners are. BOTTOM The bright flowers and tidy habit of pinkroot make it one of the showiest native plants for southeastern gardens.

Stokesia

Stokes' aster

BLOOM PERIOD: **June to August**

SIZE: **12–24 in. tall**

HARDINESS: **Zones 5–9**

☀ ☼ 🐝▸ 📍

Stokes' aster, *Stokesia laevis*, is a southeastern native that forms a rosette of smooth green foliage topped for much of the summer with frilly daisies. The form 'Peachie's Pick' is especially floriferous, making it one of the finest for perennial gardens. White selections like 'Alba' and yellow ones like 'Mary Gregory' can be found, along with the typical lavender to blue color of the species. Swallowtail butterflies are especially attracted to them. Stokes' aster will grow well in most garden soils, including damp spots in full sun.

Titanotrichum

Gold false foxglove

BLOOM PERIOD: **September to October**

SIZE: **20 in. tall**

HARDINESS: **Zones 7–10**

☼ ☁ 🦌 🌱

This African violet relative is a surprisingly hardy woodland garden perennial with dark green, fuzzy, almost succulent foliage. *Titanotrichum oldhamii* makes an upright clump topped in fall, when the rest of the shade garden is going dormant, with richly saturated gold flowers highlighted by a burgundy-red throat. Provide plants with well-drained soil for best winter hardiness. The fuzzy foliage seems to deter deer from browsing on this choice plant.

The richly colored flowers which appear in late summer to fall make *Titanotrichum oldhamii* a valuable addition to the shade garden. LEFT Perhaps the finest Stokes' aster is the universally acclaimed *Stokesia laevis* 'Peachie's Pick' which flowers nearly all summer.

Tricyrtis

Toadlily

BLOOM PERIOD: **August to October**
SIZE: **1–3 ft. tall**
HARDINESS: **Zones 6–9**

Toadlilies are Asian woodland perennials with arching to upright stems clothed with stalkless leaves and bearing terminal or axillary, intricate, mostly either gold or purple-speckled flowers. The easiest to grow is the quickly spreading Taiwan native *Tricyrtis formosana*, which makes large patches topped with heavily spotted white blossoms in late summer. Similar, but even hardier, is the large-leaved *T. ravenii*. The clumping *T. hirta* is the most commonly encountered species. Many species have several variegated cultivars as well. The deep-gold-flowered species *T. macranthopsis* grows on cliffs and is best planted on walls or in containers, where the foliage can cascade. All toadlilies grow well in average to moist soil.

The intricate flower shape and coloration of *Tricyrtis ravenii* and other toadlilies reminds many gardeners of orchid flowers.

Groundcovers

What makes one plant a groundcover instead of a herbaceous perennial or low shrub? Merely the way it is used in the landscape and not necessarily an intrinsic characteristic of the plant. While it is true that most groundcovers will spread relatively rapidly and often root along their stems or leaf nodes, or will send out underground rhizomes, almost any low plant could be used as a groundcover if enough of them are planted. Hence, this list is somewhat arbitrary, although all the plants here are often used as groundcovers. The best choices will spread quickly and densely enough to deter weed seeds from germinating.

When determining a groundcover, consider how the space will be utilized. Groundcovers can be used for stabilizing banks to prevent soil erosion. Some, like the typical suburban lawn, tolerate quite a bit of foot traffic, while others will not survive being walked on at all. Spacing for planting groundcovers is generally the balance between how many plants you are willing to pay for and how quickly you would like the space covered.

Groundcovers are usually planted with the intent that they will be low-input, long-lasting features of the landscape. If a sunny landscape becomes shaded by growing trees over time, the groundcover will need to be replaced with a more shade-tolerant selection. All landscapes should be evaluated periodically, perhaps every five to seven years, to determine if they are still meeting their needed functions.

A dense groundcover like lily-of-the-valley, *Convallaria majalis*, will prevent weeds from growing and define bed space.

Ajania

Pacific daisy, silver and gold chrysanthemum

BLOOM PERIOD: October to November

SIZE: 15 in. tall, 4 ft. wide

HARDINESS: Zones 5–9

☀ ☀ ☀ 🐑 🐝▸

Depending on your choice of reference, this may be listed as *Ajania*, *Chrysanthemum*, or *Dendranthema*, but whatever the name, Pacific daisy, *A. pacifica*, is a great groundcover for a sunny, well-drained spot. Medium green leaves have silver-felted bottoms that curl up at the edges, as though each leaf were rimmed with ice. In autumn, gold button flowers smother the plants and attract butterflies. Pacific daisy starts as a mounding perennial but will spread at a moderate pace via underground rhizomes to make sizable patches. The growth is dense enough to discourage weeds once established but will not tolerate foot traffic.

The silver-edged foliage of *Ajania pacifica* spreads to form a dense, weed-smothering mat.

Ajuga

Bugleweed

BLOOM PERIOD: April to May

SIZE: 3 in. tall, 3 ft. wide

HARDINESS: Zones 3–10

☀ ◑ 🌲

This popular groundcover is typically represented by *Ajuga reptans*, which forms low rosettes of foliage, typically burgundy or variegated with white and pink, in tight, weed-suppressing mats. Short spikes of blue (occasionally pink or white) flowers in spring are held just above the semi-evergreen foliage. Other species, notably *A. pyramidalis*, are not as quick to spread. Plant in sun to part shade, but flowering will be best in full sun. Bugleweed will tolerate light to moderate foot traffic.

The dark-foliaged *Ajuga reptans* 'Binblasca', sold as Black Scallop, provides a contrast for other plants, even in shade.

Ardisia

Marlberry

BLOOM PERIOD: May to June
SIZE: 8–15 in. tall, 3 ft. wide
HARDINESS: Zones 7–11

Ardisia is in large part a genus of shrubby plants, but *A. japonica* is one of the finest groundcovers for warm, shady gardens. Low, woody stems bear dark evergreen, serrate-edged leaves. In spring, small white to pink flowers are mostly obscured by the foliage and followed by relatively large, red fruit from October to January. The small-leaved dwarf cultivar 'Chirimen' is the hardiest form and will stay evergreen through most zone 7 winters. The variegated selections like 'Hakuokan' will usually die to the ground but resprout in spring. Marlberry will tolerate deep shade and spread to form dense mats, but will not take foot traffic.

Ardisia japonica 'Chirimen' is the hardiest form of marlberry and spreads quickly once established.

Chrysogonum

Green and gold

BLOOM PERIOD: May to June
SIZE: 6 in. tall, 30 in. wide
HARDINESS: Zones 5–10

Green and gold, *Chrysogonum virginianum*, is a rosette-forming native perennial found growing in somewhat open, dry woodlands. Mostly evergreen rosettes of foliage will spread to form mats to 30 in. or more. Bright yellow daisies appear in May and then sporadically into summer, especially in cooler climates. The selection 'Eco Laquered Spider' has a bit of purple coloration to the leaf petioles and is exceptionally vigorous, growing to more than 6 ft. across in five years. Unfortunately, it is somewhat shy to flower. Use as a deer-resistant groundcover in dry shade instead of English ivy.

It's easy to see why this native groundcover is known as green and gold.

Convallaria

Lily-of-the-valley

BLOOM PERIOD: April
SIZE: 10 in. tall, 24 in. wide
HARDINESS: Zones 3–8

Although several species can be found, *Convallaria majalis* is the best lily-of-the-valley for use as a groundcover. Upright, broad leaves slowly spread to form a dense, impenetrable mat over time. Sweetly fragrant white flowers in early spring show up especially well against the foliage. Pink and double-flowered forms can also be found. Several variegated cultivars such as 'Albostriata', with creamy white vertical stripes down the leaf, offer variety but will generally be considerably slower growing than the green-leaved forms. Once established, lily-of-the-valley is quite drought tolerant and very long lived. It does not tolerate foot traffic.

Delosperma

Iceplant

BLOOM PERIOD: April to June, occasionally again in fall
SIZE: 3 in. tall, 30 in. wide
HARDINESS: Zones 5–9

Iceplants are a group of mat-forming succulents with showy daisy flowers in spring. Flower color ranges from white to gold, pink, and purple, often with a pale ring around the yellow center. An as-yet-undescribed species for the trade, dubbed Fire Spinner, bears shockingly bright flowers with orange, magenta, pink, and white in concentric circles. Iceplant is a sun-loving, drought-tolerant succulent whose foliage varies from linear leaves to nubbly jelly beans. Delospermas can tolerate very light foot traffic.

Few perennials create the color combination found in the Fire Spinner form of *Delosperma*. LEFT Few groundcovers provide the fragrance and endurance of lily-of-the-valley.

Euphorbia

Spurge, Mrs. Robb's bonnet

BLOOM PERIOD: April to June
SIZE: 18 in. tall, 3 ft. wide
HARDINESS: Zones 6–9

☀ ◑ ☼ 🐐

Euphorbia is a large genus of plants ranging from cactus-like spiny tropicals to woodland weeds, and includes poinsettias among its members. While several species and hybrids, including *E. characias*, make excellent clumping perennials for sunny, well-drained spots, others, most notably *E. amygdaloides*, are spreading plants. This species, especially *E. amygdaloides* subsp. *robbiae*, is an evergreen groundcover tolerant of even deep, dry shade. The glossy black-green leaves are topped in spring by chartreuse flowers which last for months. Cut back the flowering stems in mid- to late summer to keep plants looking fresh. The milky sap of all spurges can irritate skin.

Few groundcovers are as easy and reliable in shade as *Euphorbia amygdaloides* subsp. *robbiae*.

Isotoma

Star creeper

BLOOM PERIOD: April to June
SIZE: 2 in. tall, 30 in. wide
HARDINESS: Zones 5–9

☀ ◑

The Australian native star creeper, *Isotoma fluviatilis*, sometimes listed under the synonymous genus *Laurentia*, makes a low mat of tiny green leaves topped in spring with little blue flowers. It tolerates light shade, making it an ideal plant for weaving around stepping stones in a woodland garden. In dry soils it can be slow to spread, but in moist spots it is vigorous and dense, especially when grown in a sunny location. Star creeper tolerates moderate foot traffic.

Sky-blue flowers give star creeper its common name.

Juniperus

Juniper

BLOOM PERIOD: Non-flowering
SIZE: 12 in. tall, 4 ft. wide
HARDINESS: Zones 5–9

☀ ☼ 🦌 🌲 📍

Junipers are a large group of trees, shrubs, and groundcovering conifers found around the world. While all groups are important landscape plants, the groundcovers are the most widely planted, particulary *Juniper procumbens*, *J. horizontalis*, and *J. conferta*. All three are low, vigorous spreaders suitable for well-drained soils in full sun, although *J. conferta*, or shore juniper, tolerates light shade. Many selections of each are available, often displaying different shades of green to silvery blue and even gold. They are highly susceptible to fungal problems if grown in poorly drained soils.

Juniperus horizontalis 'Mother Lode' makes a screaming statement as a groundcover. BOTTOM The silver needles of *Juniperus horizontalis* 'Icee Blue' make it stand out from the typical green selections.

Lysimachia

Loosestrife, creeping Jenny

BLOOM PERIOD: **June to July**

SIZE: **1–24 in. tall, 30–48 in. wide**

HARDINESS: **Zones 5–9**

Lysimachia or loosestrife, not the invasive *Lythrum*, is a group of herbaceous perennials forming either low, 1- to 3-in. mats or upright, usually spreading plants. Golden creeping Jenny, *L. nummularia* 'Aurea', is a vigorous low groundcover with bright yellow leaves. Less hardy are the *L. congestiflora* cultivars, some with purple or variegated foliage and deep gold flowers. Among the upright species, *L. punctata* and *L. clethroides* are the quickest spreaders, the former with yellow flowers and the latter with curiously curved spikes of small white flowers. All are best in average to moist soils. The creeping species will tolerate moderate foot traffic.

Best in zone 7 and warmer gardens are the purple or variegated selections of *Lysimachia congestiflora*, such as 'Superstition', with deep orange-gold flowers.

Mazus

BLOOM PERIOD: **April to May**

SIZE: **1 in. tall, 28 in. wide**

HARDINESS: **Zones 6–10**

Mazus reptans is a low, creeping, evergreen perennial for partly shaded gardens, where its mats of small rosettes are topped in spring with lavender-blue flowers (white in the cultivar 'Albus'). It is an easy grower in moist to average soils where it can be used between stepping stones or around other perennials. Similar, but a bit less hardy, is *M. radicans* from New Zealand, whose foliage is flecked with brownish spots. Both species will tolerate moderate foot traffic.

Few plants make a better shady groundcover than *Mazus reptans*.

Meehania

Wood mint

BLOOM PERIOD: March to May

SIZE: 5 in. tall, 24 in. wide

HARDINESS: Zones 5–8

The native *Meehania cordata*, found in the higher elevations through the mid-Atlantic states down to North Carolina, makes evergreen patches of bright green, heart-shaped leaves topped in spring by spikes of lavender-blue flowers. *Meehania montis-koyae* is a Japanese wood mint forming low, spreading mats of burgundy-highlighted foliage. In early spring, long, tubular, pink-lavender flowers are held low to the foliage. Both species prefer slightly moist soils but will tolerate drier spots. In warm areas, the Japanese species can go summer dormant, especially in dry soils. Neither tolerates foot traffic.

Meehania montis-koyae bears comparatively large flowers and attractively marked foliage across tight mats.

Muehlenbeckia

Wire vine

BLOOM PERIOD: Insignificant

SIZE: 1 in. tall, 5 ft. wide

HARDINESS: Zones 8–11

Muehlenbeckia is a Southern Hemisphere group, forming wiry-stemmed shrubs and vines. The vine *M. complexa* is often grown in containers or over topiary forms, but it makes a very vigorous ground-cover in warm gardens, where the thin black stems bear glossy, round leaves. An even smaller version, *M. axillaris*, is slightly less vigorous with tinier foliage. Wire vine's flowers appear in spring but are inconspicuous at best. They are quite drought tolerant once established and will tolerate foot traffic.

Muehlenbeckia complexa makes a tough, easy care groundcover.

Onoclea

Sensitive fern

BLOOM PERIOD: Non-flowering
SIZE: 22 in. tall, 40 in. wide
HARDINESS: Zones 3–9

Sensitive fern, *Onoclea sensibilis*, is a rapidly spreading fern equally at home in damp, nearly boggy soils and quite dry locations. The bold fern fronds emerge bluish-green before becoming light green. In late summer, separate fertile fronds shoot up vertically, turning cinnamon-brown in fall and winter. The foliage will die back after frost, leaving the spikes of spore-bearing fertile fronds to mark its place in the garden. Like all ferns it is almost completely deer proof. Does not tolerate foot traffic.

Sensitive fern makes an attractive deer-proof groundcover for natural areas. RIGHT *Pachysandra procumbens* has attractively mottled foliage and interesting bottlebrush flowers.

Pachysandra

Pachysandra

BLOOM PERIOD: March to April
SIZE: 10 in. tall, 3 ft. wide
HARDINESS: Zones 3–9

Pachysandras are a much-used groundcover for shade, especially the Asian *Pachysandra terminalis*, which forms a spreading mat of dark green, whorled foliage topped in spring with small spikes of white flowers. Several white-edged forms are available which brighten the shade. The best cultivar for Deep South gardens is the heat- and humidity-tolerant 'Green Sheen', with high-gloss foliage. The Asian *P. axillaris* is another spreading groundcover with whitish veins. Our native *P. procumbens*, with green spring leaves that become silver splotched, is an outstanding clumping woodland perennial.

Rubus

Creeping raspberry

BLOOM PERIOD: Insignificant

SIZE: 6 in. tall, 40 in. wide

HARDINESS: Zones 7–10

☀ ◑ ⚠

Rubus is a genus best known for our native brambles with arching stems and edible blackberries and raspberries, but the Chinese *R. rolfei*, which is often mislabeled as *R. calycinum* or *R. pentalobus*, is an outstanding groundcover. This species makes a vigorous mat of rounded, highly textured foliage spreading by above-ground stems which will root at their nodes. Mostly inconspicuous white flowers give rise to orange raspberries if multiple clones are grown. The foliage is semi-evergreen, turning plum-purple in all but the coldest winters. *Rubus rolfei* 'Emerald Carpet' is commonly grown but needs another form to produce fruit. Creeping raspberry tolerates foot traffic.

Rubus rolfei 'Emerald Carpet' makes a vigorous groundcover for sun to shade.

Sarcococca

Sweetbox

BLOOM PERIOD: January to March

SIZE: 18–30 in. tall, 3 ft. wide

HARDINESS: Zones 6–9

☀ ● ☀ 🦌 🌲 ⚙

Sweetboxes are generally Asian shrubs with evergreen foliage and fragrant winter flowers. *Sarcococca hookeriana* is a spreading form usually seen in its small variety, *S. hookeriana* var. *humilis*. It makes a slowly expanding mass of upright, arching stems with glossy, lanceolate leaves and somewhat inconspicuous but intensely fragrant flowers starting as early as January. In sunnier gardens, the foliage can go off color and become somewhat yellowish. It is happiest in part sun and rich, moist, well-drained soils, but will tolerate drought once established. Sweetbox does not tolerate foot traffic.

The fragrant flowers of *Sarcococca hookeriana* var. *humilis* are among the joys of the winter garden.

Saxifraga

Strawberry begonia, saxifrage

BLOOM PERIOD: May to June

SIZE: 6 in. tall, 3 ft. wide

HARDINESS: Zones 6–10

Saxifrages are much-loved plants, especially in rock gardens, but few grow well in the heat and humidity of the southeastern summer. The Chinese *Saxifraga stolonifera*, or strawberry begonia, is one of the few that thrives in the South, where it forms rosettes of rounded leaves often highlighted with silvery veins and purple backs. Long, strawberry-like runners spread from the rosettes, then root and form new plants, ultimately creating a dense mat of showy foliage topped in spring by 12-in. spikes of airy white flowers. 'Maroon Beauty' has purple-highlighted foliage and pink-tinged flowers. Saxifrage tolerates light foot traffic.

Attractive foliage and flowers make strawberry begonia a showy groundcover for shade.

Sedum

Stonecrop, sedum

BLOOM PERIOD: January to March

SIZE: 2–20 in. tall, 3 ft. wide

HARDINESS: Zones 5–9

Sedums are among the most popular succulents for sunny, dry spots. The clumping forms like *Sedum sieboldii*, *Sedum* 'Autumn Joy', and the many hybrids are excellent perennials that flower in late summer. The groundcovering species form low, spreading mats with white, yellow, or pink flowers. Perhaps the quickest spreader is *S. emarginatum* 'Eco-Mt. Emei' which can fill large spaces quickly, while the round succulent leaves of *S. tetractinum* provide a fun texture in the garden. Several colorful or variegated forms are available, especially in *S. spurium*. Sedums tolerate moderate to light foot traffic, depending on species.

Sedum 'Angelina' has gold, needle-like foliage that turns flaming orange in winter. RIGHT *Sedum sieboldii* is a clump-forming succulent that can be used as a groundcover if planted in masses.

Thyme

BLOOM PERIOD: May to July

SIZE: 1–8 in. tall, 30 in. wide

HARDINESS: Zones 5–9

☀ ☼ 🦌 🌲

Thymes are mostly spreading, evergreen, mat-forming plants with aromatic foliage and small white to pink flowers in late spring. Drought tolerance and an herb scent make *Thymus caespititius* and other thymes good for growing around stepping stones. The culinary herb *T. vulgaris* is common in herb gardens but is a welcome addition to any landscape. The citrus-scented cultivars of *T. ×citriodorus* can help repel mosquitoes if planted around sitting areas or when rubbed on exposed skin. Several gold forms offer a spot of color, such as *T. pulegioides* 'Goldentime'.

Its tiny evergreen foliage, herb scent, and lovely flowers make *Thymus caespititius* useful for planting around sunny stepping stones. RIGHT Gold-foliaged thyme selections such as *Thymus pulegioides* 'Goldentime' provide a bright contrast to other plants.

Verbena

BLOOM PERIOD: March to October

SIZE: 8 in. tall, 30 in. wide

HARDINESS: Zones 6–9

☀ ☼ ▲ ✿ 🐝 ◉

The creeping verbenas are ideal flowering groundcovers. Most available in the trade are hybrids between native and South American species, best exemplified by the long-blooming *Verbena* 'Homestead Purple'. The aromatic foliage varies from single, deep green leaves to finely dissected, ferny foliage, especially on the forms of *V. tenuisecta*. Clusters of small flowers range from white to brilliant red, purple, and pink and attract butterflies. Verbenas are often sold as annuals because they flower all season, but most are quite hardy. Flowering is heaviest in spring and fall. Best in well-drained spots, they tolerate light foot traffic.

The groundcovering verbenas like *Verbena* 'Royal Chambray' are easy-care, long-flowering selections in a variety of colors.

Veronica

Veronica, speedwell

BLOOM PERIOD: **March to April**
SIZE: **4 in. tall, 30 in. wide**
HARDINESS: **Zones 6–9**

The clumping types like *Veronica spicata* and its hybrids are outstanding garden plants with spikes of blue summer flowers that attract butterflies, but the groundcovering species are often underutilized. The excellent spreading *V. umbrosa* 'Georgia Blue' makes a very low mat of evergreen foliage topped with cheery blue spring flowers. Similar small, tiny-leaved species *V. repens* and *V. prostrata* are even tighter and lower but provide serious impact in their gold-foliaged cultivars like 'Aztec Gold'. They are all best in full sun in moderately well-drained soil and will tolerate light to moderate foot traffic.

Veronica umbrosa 'Georgia Blue' hails from the country of Georgia, not the southern U.S. state, but it grows well throughout the Southeast.

Waldsteinia

Barren strawberry

BLOOM PERIOD: **May to June**
SIZE: **8 in. tall, 30 in. wide**
HARDINESS: **Zones 6–9**

Barren strawberry is found in the eastern United States, Europe, and into Asia. Our native species, *Waldsteinia fragarioides*, has strawberry-like foliage forming vigorous clumps that spread to form dense mats. Bright yellow buttercup flowers appear in late spring among the leaves. Another native, *W. lobata* is similar but does not spread as vigorously, making it more suitable for smaller areas. Both are best in light shade and moist, well-drained soil. They will tolerate a fair amount of drought but will not spread as quickly or densely. They do not take foot traffic.

Waldsteinia lobata is an underutilized native groundcover for sun to shade.

Shrubs

Shrubs are the building blocks of the garden, providing structure between and below the trunks of trees and a sense of permanence around herbaceous perennials. In general, shrubs are multi-stemmed woody plants less than 15 ft. tall, although there is much overlap between larger shrubs and smaller trees.

Generalizing about shrubs is difficult as some are diminutive mounds while others form large specimens and hedges. Ideally, shrubs provide more than one season of interest with some combination of flowers, fall color, showy fruit, attractive stems, or lovely foliage. Choosing the right shrub is important, as too many landscapes are ruined by plants that have outgrown their allotted space or otherwise detract from the garden. Information on plant tags is often generalized for much of the United States, and in the warm Southeast, growth rates and ultimate sizes can be much faster and larger than the tags indicate. I often tell people to assume the size listed on the label is the size the shrub will be in five to seven years.

When selecting shrubs, think carefully about how they will look in the landscape throughout the year. Do you need evergreen foliage to block the view of an air conditioning unit? Are you mostly interested in a bright splash of spring color? Is the shrub for a bird habitat garden where fruit is important? Knowing what is most essential to you will help you choose the right plant when you visit your local garden center.

Along with pops of color throughout the season, shrubs provide a year-round sense of presence in the garden.

Abelia

BLOOM PERIOD: **May to October**

SIZE: **3–6 ft. tall and wide**

HARDINESS: **Zones 6–10**

Abelia is best represented in gardens by the hybrid *A.* ×*grandiflora*, or glossy abelia, and its selections. Glossy abelia is semi-evergreen with small, shiny foliage. The white to pinkish flowers, among the favorites of pollinators, begin to open as early as May in warm areas and continue until frost. Rosy calyces clasp the flowers and remain long after the blossoms fade, lengthening the display. Numerous variegated forms of glossy abelia offer nearly year-round color in the garden. Abelias are quite drought and shade tolerant once established. Other species such as *A. mosanensis* make excellent, pollinator-friendly flowering shrubs for the garden.

Abelia mosanensis displays irresistible two-toned pink flowers.
BOTTOM Many selections of glossy abelia have been made both for variegated foliage and compact size.

Pineapple guava

BLOOM PERIOD: April to June

SIZE: 8–15 ft. tall, 10–12 ft. wide

HARDINESS: Zones 7–10

This lovely fruiting shrub, *Acca sellowiana* or pineapple guava, sometimes classified in the genus *Feijoa*, makes a dense head of dark bluish-green foliage. The foliage emerges with a silvery white fuzz that is retained on the bottoms of mature leaves. Striking pink flowers with red stamens in spring give rise to small, egg-shaped, edible fruit from September to December. Interestingly, the flower petals too are edible, quite sweet and delicious in salads or eaten right off the plant. Pineapple guava is best grown in full sun but will tolerate quite a bit of shade if flowers and fruit are not required. Pineapple guava is tolerant of salt spray and can be attractive pruned into a small tree.

The flower petals of pineapple guava are sweet and can be eaten even where the season isn't long enough for fruit to develop.

ORNAMENTAL EDIBLES

Traditionally the garden has always maintained a separation between strictly ornamental plants and useful plants like edibles and herbs. Early gardeners maintained kitchen gardens, which were often walled off from the rest of the outdoor area. As landscapes have shrunk over the years, maintaining this separation makes less and less sense, especially since so many edibles are attractive in their own right.

Perhaps the easiest to use in the landscape are some of the woody shrubs that bear fruit. Blueberries (*Vaccinium*) are especially lovely garden plants, with pink to white spring flowers and foliage which turns gorgeous colors in fall. Remember to plant at least two or three varieties for the best fruit set. Pomegranates (*Punica granatum*) have glorious bright orange flowers typically, but also come in shades of yellow, pink, and white. The fruit which follows can be almost as showy as the flowers.

Asparagus is a long-lived perennial, and after the early spring harvest, the resulting ferny shoots are lovely and provide interesting texture to the summer garden. The opposite texture can be had with the exceptionally bold foliage of artichokes (*Cynara cardunculus* Scolymus Group). Other annual vegetables like greens, peppers, and eggplant can add interest when tucked into sunny spots among ornamental annuals. Even tomato plants can be grown up, alongside, and through the sunny side of shrubs.

Herbs can also add ornamental interest, from the winter flowers of rosemary (*Rosmarinus officinalis*) to the lovely lavender flowers of chives (*Allium schoenoprasum*), both of which are long-lived perennials. Thyme, oregano, sage, and other culinary herbs are beautiful additions to any sunny, well-drained landscape.

Agave, century plant

BLOOM PERIOD: May to July once mature

SIZE: 10–96 in. tall, 10–120 in. wide (6–25 ft. tall in flower)

HARDINESS: Zones 7–10

☀ ☼ ☀ 🦌 🌲 🐝▸

Agaves are native to the desert Southwest, where they form rosettes of stiff, succulent foliage. Of the large species, *Agave americana* and *A. ovatifolia* are among the best for the Southeast. The former grows to 8 ft. or taller with arching leaves and the latter, known as the whale-tongue agave, has wide, icy-blue foliage. Smaller species like *A. lophantha* fit into any sunny, well-drained garden. The asparagus-like flower stalk erupts from the center of the rosette and can grow to 25 ft. or more, depending on species, and is topped by creamy white, gold, or even pink flowers. Most agaves are monocarpic and the main rosette will die after flowering. Despite the common name of century plant, agaves will generally bloom in 5 to 20 years in the Southeast.

Variegated forms like *Agave lophantha* 'Quadricolor' are often less hardy than the typical species. BOTTOM *Agave ovatifolia* becomes a striking specimen with age.

Japanese aucuba, gold dust plant

BLOOM PERIOD: April to May

SIZE: 5–8 ft. tall, 4–6 ft. wide

HARDINESS: Zones 7–10

☀ ◗ ☼ ♠

Japanese aucuba, *Aucuba japonica*, is the Rodney Dangerfield of plants, it just doesn't get any respect. The ability to grow in deep, dry shade where nothing else survives makes it a workhorse plant. The glossy, evergreen foliage, which is usually heavily spotted with gold, brightens even the shadiest garden nooks. Female selections have the added bonus of half-inch, bright red fruits from November to March. A Japanese cultivar called 'Natso-no-kumo' has a pure white flush of new growth that turns green as summer progresses.

Aucuba japonica 'Natsu-no-kumo' emerges pure white before becoming solid green by midsummer. BOTTOM Among the many gold-speckled selections available, *Aucuba japonica* 'Hosoba Hoshifu' is a standout with long, deep green, glossy leaves heavily spotted with gold.

Butterfly bush

BLOOM PERIOD: June to September

SIZE: 5–12 ft. tall, 4–10 ft. wide

HARDINESS: Zones 5–10

☀ ☀ 🦌 🐝▸

The gray-green foliage topped in summer with spikes of flowers ranging from white to lavender, pink, blue, and purple make butterfly bush, *Buddleja davidii*, an easy choice for adding color to the garden. It is one of the best plants for attracting butterflies and is quite drought tolerant as well. Recent breeding and hybridization has led to dwarf varieties, brighter colors, and reduced seed production. The silver-leaved *B. fallowiana* does not have flowers as showy as the typical species, but the foliage adds interest all season. Grow all butterfly bushes in sunny, well-drained soils and prune before growth begins in spring.

As the common name implies and this *Buddleja davidii* 'Black Knight' shows, butterflies really do flock to these important summer-flowering shrubs.

Boxwood

BLOOM PERIOD: Insignificant

SIZE: 4–20 ft. tall, 4–8 ft. wide, depending on species

HARDINESS: Zones 6–9

☀ ☁ ☀ 🌲

Boxwood needs little introduction, as most gardeners are well aware of the billowy green mounds growing as foundation plants in gardens across the region. The common boxwood, *Buxus sempervirens*, is a larger shrub to nearly 20 ft. tall. It deserves wider recognition for its adaptability to dry shade conditions. Smaller forms such as *B. sempervirens* 'Suffruticosa' or the tiny-leaved *B. sinica* var. *insularis* make better edging plants in formal gardens or small foundation plantings. Underutilized but well worth a garden spot is the relatively long-leaved *B. harlandii*, with its distinctive, upright vase shape and clean, pest-free foliage.

Boxwoods come in a variety of sizes and shapes, from low hedging plants to upright forms like *Buxus sempervirens* 'Graham Blandy'.

Callicarpa

Beautyberry

BLOOM PERIOD: June to July
SIZE: 4–8 ft. tall, 4–6 ft. wide
HARDINESS: Zones 6–10

From September to December, the glossy, almost metallic purple fruits in tight clusters on the Asian beautyberry, *Callicarpa dichotoma*, highlight the gracefully arching shrub, making it perhaps the best garden plant of the genus. The USDA released a white-margined, white-fruited form called 'Duet' which glows in the garden. Our native species, *C. americana*, is a larger, coarser shrub but is ideal for rain gardens and naturalistic settings. Interestingly, birds will devour our native's fruit first before heading to the Asian species and will generally leave the Mexican *C. acuminata* alone. Reports indicate that the crushed leaves of our native species will repel mosquitoes very effectively.

Callistemon

Bottlebrush

BLOOM PERIOD: May to September
SIZE: 8–20 ft. tall and wide
HARDINESS: Zones 8–10

The stiff, evergreen foliage of bottlebrush mimics the conifers from colder gardens. Most species form multi-stemmed shrubs but can also be pruned and staked to a single trunk. One of the hardiest forms, *Callistemon* 'Woodlander's Red', sports red, bottlebrush flowers with long stamens in spring, sporadic summer flowers, and another big display in late summer. Another red-flowered form, *C. brachyandrus*, has rounded, needle-like leaves and gold-tipped, red anthers for a bicolor floral display. All bottlebrushes like full sun and a well-drained soil.

Evergreen foliage and bright flowers make bottlebrushes like this *Callistemon* 'Woodlander's Red' valuable plants for sunny, well-drained gardens. LEFT The Asian beautyberry combines attractive foliage and glossy purple fruits for a stunning fall display.

Calycanthus

Sweetshrub, Carolina allspice, strawberry shrub, sweet bubby

BLOOM PERIOD: April to June

SIZE: 5–9 ft. tall, 5–10 ft. wide

HARDINESS: Zones 6–10

☀ ☁ ❀ ◉

Our Southeast native sweetshrub, *Calycanthus floridus*, makes a large, coarse shrub with 1-in. burgundy flowers and a fruity fragrance. In full sun it will be more compact. A hybrid developed at the JC Raulston Arboretum between our native species and the pink flowered *C. chinensis* gave rise to the glossy-leaved *C. ×raulstonii* 'Hartlage Wine', with increased vigor and very large burgundy flowers. The hybrid 'Aphrodite' is much like 'Hartlage Wine' but has a more restrained habit and better fragrance, while 'Venus' has creamy white flowers over an extended period.

This Southeast native woodland shrub, *Calycanthus floridus*, bears fruity scented flowers in late spring.

Camellia

Camellia

BLOOM PERIOD: September to April, depending on selection

SIZE: 8–15 ft. tall, 5–10 ft. wide

HARDINESS: Zones 7–11

☀ ☁ 🌲

Japanese and sasanqua camellias, *Camellia japonica* and *C. sasanqua* respectively, need little introduction to gardeners. The evergreen foliage and winter flowers are mainstays of southern shade gardens. The named varieties are limitless, with flower colors in every shade of white to red. Less well known are the many small-leaved and small-flowered species like *C. handellii* and *C. lutchuensis* that have a refined habit and are suitable for zone 8 gardens. Gardeners in cooler climes can try the tea oil camellia, *C. oleifera*, which may be a full zone hardier than Japanese camellia. It has white fall flowers and lovely smooth bark.

Camellia japonica 'Pink Icicle' is just one of the many Japanese camellias available to gardeners. RIGHT Small-flowered species like *Camellia lutchuensis* typically have finer foliage and provide a much different texture than typical garden camellias.

Caryopteris

Bluebeard

BLOOM PERIOD: **August to September**
SIZE: **3 ft. tall and wide**
HARDINESS: **Zones 6–9**

Although several species of bluebeard can be found in the trade, none put on the show that the hybrid *Caryopteris* ×*clandonensis* does while retaining a restrained size and tidy appearance. Bluebeard flowers on new growth and should be cut back to about 6 in. in midwinter to keep it clean. Plants make a low mound of blue-gray aromatic foliage topped in late summer by soft blue flowers. Several selections have been made for gold or variegated foliage and different shades of flower color. Grow bluebeard in a sunny, well-drained spot.

Caryopteris ×*clandonensis* 'Longwood Blue' is a tough, drought-tolerant shrub for a sunny spot.

Cephalotaxus

Plum yew

BLOOM PERIOD: **Non-flowering**
SIZE: **5–15 ft. tall, 5–12 ft. wide**
HARDINESS: **Zones 6–10**

Japanese plum yew, *Cephalotaxus harringtonia*, is among the best conifers available for the South. It comes in various shapes and forms from ground-covers to shrubs to small trees. 'Fastigiata' is a very upright form with lustrous dark green needles spirally arranged like bottlebrushes. With age it becomes nearly as wide as tall. A selection called 'Duke Gardens' makes a small mounding shrub perfect for foundation plantings or woodland gardens where the deep green foliage adds year-round texture and structure. The Chinese plum yew, *C. fortunei*, is more often a small tree with lovely red-brown exfoliating bark.

Cephalotaxus harringtonia 'Duke Gardens' is an especially useful and attractive mounded form of plum yew.

Clethra

Summersweet, sweet pepperbush

BLOOM PERIOD: July to August

SIZE: 4–7 ft. tall, 4–6 ft. wide

HARDINESS: Zones 4–9

☀ ☁ ✿ 🐝 ◉

The native summersweet, *Clethra alnifolia*, is a great plant for adding color and fragrance to the late summer garden. Upright stems with medium green leaves are topped by 5-in. spikes of white flowers in July. There are several good dwarfs like 'Crystalina' and 'Sixteen Candles' as well as pink-flowered selections such as 'Ruby Spice'. The cultivar 'Sherry Sue' has the added feature of reddish stems. The Japanese *C. barbinervis* makes a tall shrub with beautiful cinnamon bark in addition to summer flowers. It is likely best in the cooler regions of the Southeast. Summersweet can also be relied upon for a last dash of fall color from October to November.

Pollinators love both the typical white and the pink-flowered summersweets, such as *Clethra alnifolia* 'Ruby Spice'.

Cornus

Redtwig dogwood, shrubby dogwood, redosier

BLOOM PERIOD: April to June

SIZE: 5–12 ft. tall, 6–15 ft. wide

HARDINESS: Zones 4–9

☀ ☼ ☁ ◉

The shrubby dogwoods make multi-stemmed plants with striking bark. The showiest of the native species is *Cornus stolonifera* or redosier. It has red stems, and several variegated forms have been selected, such as 'Hedgerow's Gold'. Yellow-stemmed selections can also be found. The European redtwig dogwood, *C. sanguinea*, has some of the best stem color. The orange-red stems of 'Midwinter Fire' add warm hues to winter landscapes. Clusters of small white flowers in spring give rise to black fruit for *C. sanguinea* and white for *C. stolonifera*. Cut older stems to the ground in spring to encourage new, brighter-colored stems.

Redtwig dogwoods are prized for providing winter interest.

Corylopsis

Winterhazel

BLOOM PERIOD: March
SIZE: 6–12 ft. tall and wide
HARDINESS: Zones 6–8

Winterhazels are rounded, multi-stemmed shrubs with primrose-yellow, late winter flowers. The fragrant winterhazel, *Corylopsis glabrescens*, is one of the hardiest species and often shows good gold fall color in addition to the flowers. A dwarf form, 'March Jewel', is among the finest of small shrubs for the landscape with a low habit and masses of flowers. Among the several very similar species, *C. spicata*, or spike winterhazel, is perhaps the most floriferous, becoming a mass of soft yellow when in flower. Winterhazels are very tough, tolerating both sun and shade with few pests.

Winterhazel's soft yellow flowers brighten the late winter garden.

Cotinus

Smokebush

BLOOM PERIOD: May to June
SIZE: 10–15 ft. tall and wide
HARDINESS: Zones 5–9

The multi-stemmed smokebush, *Cotinus coggygria*, bears rounded, blue-green leaves that turn brilliant colors in fall. Shrubs are covered with an airy mass of small flowers in spring, but the fuzzy flower stems turn pink and last through much of the summer, giving a misty, smoky look to the plant. Plants in landscapes are often purple-leaved selections that are frequently cut to the ground each winter to encourage long shoots with larger leaves and deeper colors. This can be very effective, especially in a mixed border. The selection 'Ancot', usually sold as Golden Spirit, has brilliant gold leaves.

Although many smokebushes are cut back each year to encourage brighter foliage, the flowers on selections like the compact *Cotinus coggygria* 'Little Ruby' can be spectacular.

Smokebushes make invaluable bright accents in the garden, whether in purple or the gold of *Cotinus coggygria* 'Ancot'.

Cycas

Sago palm

BLOOM PERIOD: **Non-flowering**
SIZE: **4–8 ft. tall, 3–8 ft. wide**
HARDINESS: **Zones 8–11**

Sago palm, *Cycas revoluta*, is not a true palm but has a single trunk topped with a ring of long, palm-like fronds to 5 ft. long with glossy green leaflets. It is slow growing but ultimately can form offsets around the base which can be removed or allowed to grow as a clump. Two other cold hardy sago palms, *C. panzhihuaensis* and *C. taitungensis*, are becoming more available. In the cooler end of sago's hardiness zones, mulch well in winter until well established. All sago palms prefer very well-drained soil. Although cycads are quite poisonous, the plastic-like texture and bitter taste generally keep pets away.

The Taiwanese *Cycas taitungensis* is proving to be a hardy palm for warm temperate gardens. RIGHT Sago palms are popular in Deep South gardens where they provide a taste of the tropics.

Cyrilla

Cyrilla, leatherwood, titi

BLOOM PERIOD: June to July

SIZE: 8–12 ft. tall, 4–10 ft. wide (to 25 ft. tall occasionally)

HARDINESS: Zones 6–11

☀ ◑ ☼ 🐿 ⚠ 🐝 📍

The native swamp cyrilla, *Cyrilla racemiflora*, is an evergreen in southern climates but becomes deciduous at its northern limits. It makes a rounded shrub to small tree with leathery, narrow leaves which can turn brilliant orange and red in fall and winter. Very small white flowers held on 6-in. racemes adorn the plant in early summer, attracting thousands of pollinators. It is tolerant of most garden conditions and quite trouble free once established. Cyrilla is a plant whose virtues are praised by gardeners in the know, but it is virtually unknown to the wider gardening public.

Brilliant fall color often lasts through winter on the semi-evergreen *Cyrilla racemiflora*. BOTTOM *Cyrilla racemiflora* has showy flowers that are among the best nectar sources for native pollinators.

Danae

Poet's laurel, Alexandrian laurel

BLOOM PERIOD: Insignificant

SIZE: 2–4 ft. tall, 3–5 ft. wide

HARDINESS: Zones 7–10

☀ ☁ ☼ 🦌 🌲

Danae racemosa, the poet's laurel, is an arching evergreen shrub with branches emerging from the ground, clothed in plastic-textured modified stems called cladophylls which mimic true leaves. It is a trouble-free plant once established, with inconspicuous flowers and orange-red fruits in fall. It is useful in shade gardens where it only needs an occasional pruning back of a stem or two in late winter to remove any damaged material. Flower arrangers prize its cut stems because they will last for weeks in a vase. They are painfully slow from seed but can be divided.

Glossy "leaves" and bright red fruit make the tough *Danae racemosa* an ideal no-care shade garden plant.

Daphne

Daphne

BLOOM PERIOD: January to March

SIZE: 3–6 ft. tall and wide

HARDINESS: Zones 7–9

☀ ☁ 🦌 🌲 ⚙

Daphnes are outstanding garden plants, represented in the South mainly by *Daphne odora* or winter daphne. Plants make a low, dense, evergreen mound of very uniform appearance, topped in winter by white to pale pink flowers whose fragrance drifts around the garden. They are best grown in shady, well-drained spots such as the base of trees to ensure longevity. There are quite a few variegated forms but the green-leaved 'Zuiko Nishiki' is the heaviest flowered form I have encountered. The deciduous, lavender-flowered *D. genkwa*, lilac daphne, is another good choice for cooler southeastern gardens.

The gold-edged *Daphne odora* 'Aureomarginata' provides twelve months of color in addition to the fragrant winter flowers.

Deutzia

BLOOM PERIOD: March to May

SIZE: 4–8 ft. tall, 4–6 ft. wide

HARDINESS: Zones 5–9

The deutzias are a group of flowering shrubs with white to occasionally pink flowers in early spring. When in flower, they are outstanding. The larger selections are often rangy and best suited to sunny shrub borders or the backs of perennial beds. Perhaps most useful is the dwarf *Deutzia gracilis* 'Nikko' which makes a low, wide mound of relatively bright green leaves topped in April with masses of pure white flowers. This form can be very effective in groups as a tall groundcover.

Most deutzias make spectacular specimens when in flower.

Edgeworthia, paperbush

BLOOM PERIOD: February to March

SIZE: 3–6 ft. tall, 3–5 ft. wide

HARDINESS: Zones 7–9

Edgeworthia chrysantha is a deciduous shrub with 4- to 8-in. papery, blue-green leaves held at the ends of stout branches. In fall, flower buds covered with dense, white hairs form at the tip of each branch in tight 1-in. clusters. By late winter the buds open to reveal tubular white flowers with a gold interior and a sweet fragrance. The botanical nomenclature of this genus is quite confused but another form, *E. papyrifera*, has smaller leaves, thinner stems, can grow taller, and has paler, less fragrant flowers. This form tends to not perform as well in the Southeast.

Paperbush can be grown as a multi-stemmed shrub or pruned into a miniature tree like this *Edgeworthia chrysantha* 'Gold Rush'.

Sputnik-like winter flowers on *Fatsia japonica* precede small clusters of black fruit. BOTTOM Variegated forms like *Fatsia japonica* 'Murakumo Nishiki' are slow to propagate, increasing their cost to gardeners.

Fatsia

Japanese fatsia

BLOOM PERIOD: **November to December**

SIZE: **5–10 ft. tall and wide**

HARDINESS: **Zones 7–11**

☼ ☁ ☀ S 🌲

The bold-textured *Fatsia japonica* makes a large evergreen shrub with huge 14-in. leathery, deep green, lobed leaves on stout stems. Round, Sputnik-like flower clusters are held in large panicles at branch tips in late fall and give rise to black fruits in winter. Fatsia makes a dramatic statement in the garden, especially in one of its variegated forms, like the chartreuse-splashed 'Murakumo Nishiki' or the white-veined 'Spider Web'. Established plants are quite tolerant of dense, dry shade and salt spray. The Taiwanese species, *F. polycarpa*, adds texture to warm gardens, with deeply divided foliage and vigorous growth.

Fig

BLOOM PERIOD: **Insignificant**
SIZE: **8–15 ft. tall, 6–10 ft. wide**
HARDINESS: **Zones 7–9**

Common fig, *Ficus carica*, makes a large, bold shrub with thick stems and big, lobed leaves, and is worth growing for its bold texture alone. In addition, it bears delightfully sweet fruit through the latter part of the summer. Some of the best performers in the South include 'Alma', 'Celeste', 'LSU Gold', and 'Brown Turkey'. The last is exceptionally hardy and fruits on new wood, so it can be cut back hard each winter and still bear fruit after resprouting in the spring. Several non-edible figs are available from nurseries, most notably *F. afghanistanica* and climbing fig, *F. pumila*, a dense, evergreen groundcover and climbing vine.

BOTTOM *Ficus pumila* **is widely used throughout the South as a groundcover and to cover walls.** RIGHT **More non-edible figs like** *Ficus afghanistanica* **'Silver Lyre' are increasingly becoming available to southern gardeners.**

Gardenia

Gardenia, cape jasmine

BLOOM PERIOD: May to July

SIZE: 3–6 ft. tall, 3–5 ft. wide

HARDINESS: Zones 7–10

Gardenia, *Gardenia jasminoides*, is synonymous with the South, where its glossy foliage and intensely fragrant white flowers are a mainstay in landscapes. They are best grown in organic, moist, well-drained, acidic soils protected from drying winter winds. Happy specimens will be a source of joy, with heavy flowering in spring and early summer often followed by bright orange fruits. When not sited well, the foliage will turn yellow and several insects, such as whiteflies and scale, can be significant problems. Warm areas can grow the larger selections with fully double, rose-like flowers. In colder areas, the dwarf types with single flowers, like *G. jasminoides* 'Kleim's Hardy', are better choices.

Gardenia jasminoides 'Kleim's Hardy' is low growing with small leaves and single, daisy-like flowers.

Hamamelis

Witchhazel

BLOOM PERIOD: November to March, depending on selection

SIZE: 8–20 ft. tall, 6–15 ft. wide

HARDINESS: Zones 5–8

Witchhazels make large multi-stemmed shrubs or small trees with clean, scallop-edged foliage. The native species, *Hamamelis virginiana* and *H. vernalis*, are nice in woodland gardens where the strappy-petaled, red to yellow flowers are quite welcome in fall and winter. The Asian hybrid *H.* ×*intermedia* is typically the showiest in flower with colors from burgundy to copper and gold in January and February. There are dozens of selections and among the best in the South are *Hamamelis* ×*intermedia* 'Feuerzauber', 'Primavera', and 'Jelena'. Although some witchhazels can have excellent fall color, others retain their dead leaves, obscuring the flower display.

A witchhazel in full bloom, like *Hamamelis* ×*intermedia* 'Aurora', is a welcome winter sight. RIGHT Typical flower color is yellow to coppery orange, but *Hamamelis* 'Amethyst' expands the color palette.

Hibiscus

Hibiscus, shrub althea, rose-of-Sharon, Confederate rose, tree mallow

BLOOM PERIOD: June to August

SIZE: 6–12 ft. tall, 5–8 ft. wide

HARDINESS: Zones 5–10, depending on species

☀ ☼ ◉

The very hardy (to zone 5) rose-of-Sharon, *Hibiscus syriacus*, is the best known of the shrubby hibiscus, with a true trunk and many 3-in. single to double flowers in shades from white to red to blue. It is a tough and drought-tolerant landscape plant once established, although it can seed around the garden. Several species such as the Chinese *H. mutabilis* and our natives *H. coccineus* and *H. militaris*, form multi-stemmed plants, which can be cut to the ground each winter. Their palmately lobed leaves are topped in late summer by large flowers in shades of white to red.

The native wetland *Hibiscus coccineus* can be found in white forms in addition to the typical bright red. RIGHT The flowers on *Hibiscus* 'Peppermint Schnapps' and other mallows can be 10 in. or more in diameter.

Hydrangea

Hydrangea

BLOOM PERIOD: **May to August, depending on species**

SIZE: **4–12 ft. tall and wide**

HARDINESS: **Zones 6–10**

Hydrangeas are a large group of flowering shrubs and vines suited mostly for shady gardens. The native species are among the best shrubs for southeastern woodland gardens, including oakleaf hydrangea, *Hydrangea quercifolia*, a large shrub with flaky-barked stems, large rough-textured leaves, and late-spring panicles of white flowers. Double-flowered forms like 'Snowflake' are especially showy and 'Ruby Slippers' has flowers which turn to deep burgundy as they age. Another native species, *H. arborescens*, has white flowers borne at the tops of the current season's growth; it can be cut to the ground during winter.

Hydrangeas are probably best known by the Asian species *Hydrangea macrophylla*, bigleaf hydrangea. The flowers of this species can be lacecaps with a ring of showy sterile florets around tiny fertile flowers, or mopheads with clusters of sterile florets. Most forms flower on new growth arising from old growth and so should not be cut back hard. Flower color is blue in acid soils, pink in soils with basic pH. Much larger is the panicled hydrangea, *H. paniculata*, with later season white flowers on large shrubs. Panicled hydrangea is more sun tolerant than other species. Among the best for flower show is 'Limelight', with very dense flower panicles.

Flower color among bigleaf hydrangeas changes based on soil acidity, so lime your soil for pink blossoms and add iron to turn them blue. RIGHT Oakleaf hydrangea combines bold foliage, showy flowers, fall color, and attractive bark, making it among the best native shrubs for the Southeast. LEFT *Hydrangea arborescens* 'NCHA1', sold as Invincibelle Spirit, was the first pink mophead introduced from the species.

Holly, winterberry

BLOOM PERIOD: **Insignificant**

SIZE: **4–35 ft. tall, 4–20 ft. wide**

HARDINESS: **Zones 5–10**

Hollies are a variable group ranging from deciduous to evergreen shrubs or trees which are dioecious—having separate male and female sexed plants. Female plants will have red to orange berries from August to January if a male is near enough to pollinate them. The deciduous species, including both the native *Ilex verticillata* and Asian *I. serrata*, are excellent plants for attracting wildlife. Cedar waxwings will flock to the brilliant berries held on bare winter stems. I find it best to plant several different selections in a bright spot to ensure the best show each year.

Many evergreen hollies are pyramidal in shape, especially when young. The native American holly, *Ilex opaca*, has been hybridized with other evergreen species giving rise to a host of often large-growing specimen and hedging plants. Among the best large species for Deep South gardens is the zone-8-hardy Lord's holly, *I. rotunda*, with non-spiny leaves and masses of brilliant red fruit. The smaller evergreen species such as Japanese holly, *I. crenata*, are widely used as a southern replacement for boxwood. Almost all hollies are easy in the landscape and make long-lived garden specimens. A holly can be found for any garden situation from wet to dry, sun to shade, and to fit any need.

Deciduous hollies like *Ilex verticillata* 'Winter Red' add color to the fall landscape and provide food for birds.

Illicium 'Woodland Ruby' is among the best selections of anise.
BOTTOM Like all anise, the gold *Illicium parviflorum* 'Florida Sunshine' is very deer resistant.

Illicium

Anise

BLOOM PERIOD: March to May
SIZE: 6–10 ft. tall, 4–7 ft. wide
HARDINESS: Zones 7–10

☀ ☁ 🦌 🌲 📍

Anise are glossy-leaved, upright, evergreen shrubs making excellent landscape specimens, especially useful in shady conditions. The easiest for all conditions, sun to shade, moist to dry, is the native *Illicium parviflorum*. It has small yellowish flowers and very aromatic foliage. Another native, Florida anise or *I. floridanum*, has glossier leaves and large, red, strappy-petaled flowers. Its extreme dwarf form, 'Swamp Hobbit', makes a tight mound with full-size leaves and flowers. The most notable Asian species is *I. anisatum* with white flowers. Variegated and gold-leaved selections are available, but the showiest flowering form is *I.* 'Woodland Ruby' with large red flowers held on long stalks.

Indigofera

Hardy indigo

BLOOM PERIOD: April to August
SIZE: 1–6 ft. tall, 3–6 ft. wide
HARDINESS: Zones 6–8

The hardy indigos are fine-textured shrubs or suckering subshrubs with small pink (occasionally white) flowers appearing on terminal spikes in spring and sporadically throughout summer. The genus is mostly tropical but several hardy species are available for sunny to dry, shady spots. The Chinese indigo, *Indigofera decora*, is a suckering woody groundcover to 1 ft., topped with pink or white flowers in arching panicles. Slightly larger is *I. kirilowii*, with a finer texture. The white form, 'Angyo Snow' has been especially showy. The larger (to 6-ft.) *I. heterantha* can be cut back each winter to keep it smaller.

Hardy indigos like *Indigofera heterantha* can be cut back each year or allowed to grow as shrubs.

Itea

Sweetspire

BLOOM PERIOD: May to June
SIZE: 3–6 ft. tall, 3–8 ft. wide
HARDINESS: Zones 5–9

Our native sweetspire, *Itea virginica*, is a suckering shrub with arching stems and late spring spikes of white flowers. The clean foliage is spectacular in the fall, especially on the selections 'Henry's Garnet' and 'Saturnalia'. For small gardens, the tiny 'Shirley's Compact' makes an interesting little bun of a plant. Sweetspire occurs naturally in damp woodland areas and will thrive in full sun to shade in moist spots, but is also surprisingly drought tolerant. The suckering habit and versatility make it an ideal candidate for rain gardens. A few Asian species are available but offer no improvement over *I. virginica*.

Few native shrubs are as adaptable as *Itea virginica* 'Henry's Garnet'.

Lespedeza, bush-clover

BLOOM PERIOD: August to September

SIZE: 3–6 ft. tall, 4–8 ft. wide

HARDINESS: Zones 5–8

☀ ☀ ☀

Lespedezas are a group of arching shrubs with three-part leaves and pink to white flowers. *Lespedeza thunbergii* is perhaps the showiest species, with masses of small rose flowers in late summer. A selection of *L. liukiuensis* called 'Little Volcano' has been an excellent performer as well. Many selections will flower in late spring as well as late summer if not cut back in winter, but plants will be cleaner and denser if pruned to the ground when dormant. Lespedezas are best as a large presence at the back of a perennial border or massed on hillsides.

Lespedeza liukiuensis 'Little Volcano' is a striking specimen when in full bloom.

Spicebush

BLOOM PERIOD: March to April

SIZE: 4–12 ft. tall and wide

HARDINESS: Zones 5–9

☀ ◐ 🐀 🐝 ◉

Spicebush is the larval food source for the spicebush swallowtail butterfly and so deserves a spot in habitat gardens. The native *Lindera benzoin* makes a large, somewhat coarse shrub with pale green leaves that follow the small, gold spring flowers. Fall color is often a nice yellow-gold. Male and female plants are needed to develop the small, bright red fruits. Many evergreen and deciduous Asian species make excellent garden plants but are rarely available. The deciduous Japanese spicebush, *L. obtusiloba*, is among the finest plants for fall color with its broadly three-lobed foliage turning shocking gold in fall, while *L. umbellata* 'Togarashi' has softly variegated leaves.

Lindera umbellata 'Togarashi' has chartreuse foliage speckled with darker green, providing a bright spot in light shade.

Loropetalum

Loropetalum, fringe-flower

BLOOM PERIOD: March to April, then sporadically throughout the year

SIZE: 5–12 ft. tall and wide

HARDINESS: Zones 7–10

Loropetalum chinense makes a wide-spreading, vase-shaped, large shrub to small tree with semi-evergreen foliage and white strappy-petaled flowers in spring and then off and on through the rest of the year. In the trade, most selections are burgundy leaved with hot pink flowers. Considerable breeding effort has been made to develop dwarf forms with deeper foliage and flower color that hold up in the heat of the Southeast. The deluge of selections is overwhelming, and size predictions should be met with skepticism as most outgrow their labeled size, although they can be pruned to almost any height.

Loropetalums such as *Loropetalum chinense* 'Zhuzhou Fuchsia' are typically grown as multi-stemmed shrubs but are quite attractive when pruned into a tree.

Mahonia

Mahonia, grape-holly

BLOOM PERIOD: November to February

SIZE: 4–12 ft. tall, 3–6 ft. wide

HARDINESS: Zones 6–9

Mahonias are upright evergreen shrubs with mostly fall and winter gold flowers. The very tall hybrid *Mahonia ×media* is among the showiest in flower with 12-in. terminal spikes of small yellow flowers followed by waxy-coated blue fruits. Two of the best of this group are 'Buckland', with masses of flower spikes, and 'Winter Sun', with very erect spikes. While many mahonias have spiny leaflets, the Mexican *M. gracilis* is softer textured with small spikes of yellow winter flowers held on red stalks. The Asian *M. eurybracteata*, best represented by 'Soft Caress', is finer textured with fall flowers.

Like all the *Mahonia ×media* selections, 'Underway' makes an impressive specimen if allowed to grow tall.

Metapanax

False ginseng

BLOOM PERIOD: **Insignificant**
SIZE: **6–12 ft. tall, 4–8 ft. wide**
HARDINESS: **Zones 7–10**

Delavay's false ginseng, *Metapanax delavayi*, is an interesting evergreen for warm gardens, with palmately compound leaves on a multi-stemmed shrub or small tree. Round clusters of greenish-white flowers in summer give rise to black fruits. The slightly hardier *M. davidii* is similar, but typically smaller and wider with coarse foliage. The leaves are three-lobed on young plants but can become a single leaf on mature specimens. Both species are easy to grow in shady spots. The related *Dendropanax trifidus* is a similar evergreen shrub or tree with an even more bold-textured leaf.

Metapanax davidii makes a bold evergreen for the collector's garden.

Myrica

Waxmyrtle, bayberry

BLOOM PERIOD: **Non-flowering**
SIZE: **4–10 ft. tall and nearly as wide**
HARDINESS: **Zones 6–10**

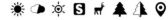

The native species are represented mostly in the nursery industry by the northern bayberry, *Myrica pensylvanica*, and its close relative, southern waxmyrtle, *M. cerifera*. Bayberry is a semi-evergreen to deciduous billowy shrub with deep green leaves, while waxmyrtle is evergreen with smaller olive-green leaves. Both have aromatic foliage especially noticeable in spring. Female plants bear fruits whose waxy coating is used for bayberry candles. They are both tolerant of very poor soils, salt spray, and most other difficult landscape situations, but will thrive in more favorable spots. Several dwarf waxmyrtle selections are available and make excellent landscape plants.

Berries of *Myrica cerifera* are used to make bayberry candles but are also loved by birds.

Nandina, heavenly bamboo

BLOOM PERIOD: May to June
SIZE: 5–8 ft. tall, 3 ft. wide
HARDINESS: Zones 6–10

☀ ☁ 🌲

Nandina domestica is an upright, evergreen shrub with straight, cane-like stems clothed in tri-pinnately compound, blue-green leaves. The foliage emerges reddish and will take on plum to fire-engine tones in winter. Arching panicles of small, white, spring flowers give rise to masses of bright red berries in fall. Many dwarf forms are available in the trade. Among the best are 'Seika' and 'Murasaki', usually sold as Obsession and Flirt, respectively. Nandinas can become leggy at the base, and regular removal of a third of the oldest stems will encourage new growth. They also have a tendency to sucker, forming a colony much wider than 3 ft.

New growth on *Nandina domestica* 'Seika' can be quite striking.

Oleander

BLOOM PERIOD: May to September
SIZE: 8–12 ft. tall and wide
HARDINESS: Zones 8–11

☀ ☀ ☀ S 🦌 🌲 ✿

Oleander, *Nerium oleander*, is a rounded evergreen shrub with deep green lanceolate leaves. Pinwheel flowers in shades of white to red, purple, or yellow are borne over a long season during the hottest part of the year. They are extremely tolerant of drought, heat, and salt spray, making them useful coastal hedges and specimens. There are hundreds of selections, and most are too tender for all but the warmest climates. *Nerium oleander* 'Double Yellow' is a form that has proved to be among the hardiest I've grown, but is still suitable only for zone 7 gardens. All parts of the plant are highly poisonous.

Oleander is often grown as a shrub but may also be pruned into a tree.

Shade Plants	Sun Plants
Ferns	Sweet Potato
Phlox	Petunia
Lily of the Valley	Coneflower
Hydrangia	Creeping Verbenia

Trees	Vines

Shade	Sun	Virginia Creeper
Dogwood	Male Ginko	Trumpet Vine

Nolina

Nolina, beargrass

BLOOM PERIOD: May to June

SIZE: 3–10 ft. tall, 5 ft. wide

HARDINESS: Zones 7–10

☀ ☼ ☼ 🦌 🌲 📍

Beargrass is a group of agave relatives with leathery (but not rigid), strappy leaves forming either a rounded mound or a spherical-headed, trunked plant. They require a sunny, well-drained spot. *Nolina nelsonii* is among the showiest with long, blue-green leaves on a slowly developing trunk to 10 ft. or taller. When mature, it sends up a 5-ft. feathery plume with small creamy flowers that develop into papery, winged fruits. The smaller, hardier (to zone 6), non-trunked *N. lindheimeriana* can be incorporated into a sunny perennial border where the very fine, evergreen foliage provides year-round interest and the 5-ft. spikes of tiny flowers add height in late spring.

Nolina nelsonii provides a striking architectural element in the garden.

Opuntia

Prickly pear, Indian fig, devil's tongue

BLOOM PERIOD: May to June

SIZE: 1–3 ft. tall, 3–6 ft. wide

HARDINESS: Zones 6–10

☀ ☼ ☼ 🦌 🌲 🐝 📍

The southeastern native prickly pear, *Opuntia humifusa*, makes a low, wide mound of flattened, succulent stems or pads with numerous hooked bristles and fewer long spines. In mid- to late spring, yellow flowers are held along the edges of the pads, followed by edible bright burgundy-red fruit. The form 'Sunshine' is especially floriferous. Another selection of prickly pear, *O. cacanapa* 'Ellisiana', with yellow flowers, is more user-friendly due to the lack of spines and bristles on the pads. Other *Opuntia* species are available with red, pink, or white flowers. All forms attract hummingbirds to the garden.

Opuntia cacanapa 'Ellisiana' is a gardener-friendly cultivar with blue-green pads and no spines.

Osmanthus

Osmanthus, false holly, tea-olive, devilwood

BLOOM PERIOD: March to April or
August to October

SIZE: 6–15 ft. tall, 4–10 ft. wide

HARDINESS: Zones 7–10

The hybrid *Osmanthus ×fortunei* is a cross between *O. fragrans* and *O. heterophyllus* and makes a tough, showy plant. BOTTOM The orange-flowered *Osmanthus fragrans* var. *aurantiacus* is intensely fragrant.

Osmanthus is one of the best arguments for living in the South, where the deep green leaves of *Osmanthus fragrans* provide a lovely backdrop for the small but intensely fragrant, white or orange flowers in late summer to fall. In spring, the fragrant flowers of *O. heterophyllus* or false holly are carried among the holly-like to entirely black-green leaves. Several variegated forms are available, most notably 'Goshiki' with heavily speckled foliage. The native devilwood, *O. americanus*, is a rarely encountered open shrub which makes an attractive specimen in a woodland garden.

Pink selections like *Pieris japonica* 'Shojo' add variety to the typically white-flowering species. BOTTOM *Pieris japonica* 'Cavatine' is a dwarf form ideal for shady foundations and woodland gardens.

Pieris

Pieris, andromeda

BLOOM PERIOD: **March to April**
SIZE: **3–8 ft. tall, 3–6 ft. wide**
HARDINESS: **Zones 5–8**

Pieris japonica is an irregularly rounded, evergreen shrub best suited for the cooler areas of the Southeast. On many selections, such as 'Mountain Fire' and 'Red Mill', vivid red new growth emerges as the arching panicles of white, urn-shaped flowers are opening. Dwarf selections like 'Prelude' make low 2- to 3-ft. mounds, typically with shorter flower panicles. Several pink-flowered cultivars are also available. All pieris can be afflicted by lacebugs, which will cause yellowish-brown stippling of the foliage, especially troublesome as the discolored foliage persists for several years.

Pittosporum

BLOOM PERIOD: April to May

SIZE: 5–12 ft. tall, 6–16 ft. wide

HARDINESS: Zones 8–10

☀ ◗ Ⓢ 🌲 ✿

Few of the many species of *Pittosporum* are widely grown in the Southeast. Those that are remain restricted to the Asian species. Most common is *P. tobira*, which makes a mounded, dark, glossy, green-leaved plant. It is often represented in the trade by one of several compact selections such as 'Wheeler's Dwarf', which grows to 3 ft. The fragrant flowers are creamy white aging to pale yellow, and are followed by green fruits which open to reveal brilliant red seeds. Variegated selections such as 'Kansai Sunburst' have white-margined foliage that adds color all year in full sun or dense shade.

Hardy orange, trifoliate orange

BLOOM PERIOD: March to April

SIZE: 8–15 ft. tall, 5–10 ft. wide

HARDINESS: Zones 6–10

☀ ☼ ✿

Hardy orange, *Poncirus trifoliata*, sometimes listed under the syonymous genus *Citrus*, makes a shrub or small tree with jade-green stems, vicious spines, and three-part leaves. White spring flowers are followed in fall by golf ball–sized orange fruits. The fruits are seedy and bitter. I have been told they can be used for marmalade but are better as a twist in a whiskey sour. The plant is quite attractive and unusual in all seasons. The form 'Flying Dragon' has contorted branches and twisted spines and elicits as much comment as any plant in the garden. Plants can seed around the garden unless fallen fruit is raked and composted.

While *Pittosporum tobira* is the most commonly encountered species, many others are available, including the very fine-textured *P. illicioides* var. *angustifolium*. RIGHT The flowers, fruit, and contorted stems of *Poncirus trifoliata* 'Flying Dragon' make it a true four-season plant.

Pomegranate

BLOOM PERIOD: May to July

SIZE: 10–18 ft. tall, 6–12 ft. wide

HARDINESS: Zones 7–10

☀ ☼ ☼ 🦌 🌱

Pomegranates, *Punica granatum*, make medium to large, upright, multi-stemmed shrubs with fleshy flower buds. The buds open to reveal crepe-papery, single or double flowers that are red to orange, yellow, or white, and followed by red to nearly black fruits. They have been grown for the fruit's edible seeds and juice for centuries, figuring prominently in the Greek myth of Persephone and Hades. Among the classics for fruit production is 'Wonderful', with dark orange flowers and juicy red fruits. Dwarf and compact forms have sizes as small as 3 ft., and cultivars such as 'State Fair' are excellent shrubs for containers and smaller landscapes. Pomegranates are perfect choices for adding edibles to ornamental landscapes.

Dwarf pomegranates like *Punica granatum* 'State Fair' provide bright flowers and fruit at a much smaller scale.

Indian hawthorn

BLOOM PERIOD: April to May

SIZE: 4–10 ft. tall and wide

HARDINESS: Zones 7–10

☀ ☼ ☼ 🅂 🌲

Indian hawthorn is mostly represented in landscapes by *Raphiolepis umbellata* and its hybrid with *R. indica*. It forms a medium to large mounded shrub with deep green, leathery leaves. White or pink spring flowers are followed by blue-black fruits in fall, which last well into winter. Indian hawthorn is drought and salt tolerant and is widely used in coastal landscapes. Many forms are highly susceptible to leaf spot and are best grown in full sun with good air circulation. 'Conia', usually sold as Olivia, is a compact form with good leaf spot resistance, and 'Spg-3-003', commonly sold as Redbird, flushes in spring with bright red-burgundy new growth.

Compact *Rhaphiolepis indica* 'Conia', or Olivia as it is more widely known, has proved to have outstanding disease resistance.

Rhapidophyllum

Needle palm

BLOOM PERIOD: May
SIZE: 6–10 ft. tall and wide
HARDINESS: Zones 6–10

Rhapidophyllum hystrix or needle palm is a short-trunked, clumping palm with large, rounded, palmately compound leaves. It received its common name from the 6- to 10-in. sharp spines that develop around the leaf sheaths and upper trunk. Needle palms grow throughout the Southeast in full sun to deep shade, often in moist bottomlands, but they are quite adaptable to soil. They are among the hardiest of all palms but should be grown with some protection in cooler climes until well established.

Needle palm is among the hardiest palms and will slowly form a stout trunk. RIGHT The foliage of the yak-type rhododendrons is spectacular, even long after the flowers have faded.

Rhododendron

Rhododendron, azalea

BLOOM PERIOD: April to May
SIZE: 3–12 ft. tall and wide
HARDINESS: Zones 5–10

Rhododendron is a large and well-known group. Plants commonly known as rhododendrons are typically evergreen shrubs with showy spring flowers. Many can be difficult to grow in the Deep South, where the high heat and humidity lead to fungal problems like root rot. Among the best for the South are hybrids with *R. makinoi* or the so called yak-types, *R. degronianum* subsp. *yakushimanum*. These cultivars have foliage which emerges covered in silvery or tan hairs and are generally low growing. In cooler areas, there is a wide selection of cultivars, many derived from *R. fortunei* and the natives, *R. catawbiense* and *R. maximum*.

The plants known as azaleas are generally smaller than many of the leathery-leaved species. Azaleas are best known in the South for the overwhelming spring floral display of the Asian satsuki and southern indica selections that are among the most popular landscape plants throughout the region. The native deciduous azaleas and their progeny, like the Aromi and Exbury hybrids, can be shockingly bright, bringing yellow, orange, and red into the more typical white, pink, and purple of other rhododendrons. All rhododendrons will appreciate some shade from afternoon sun and a moist, well-drained soil for long-term survival.

If planted in a moist, well-drained, acidic soil, *Rhododendron fortunei* and its hybrids grow well through much of the Southeast. RIGHT Deciduous azaleas like *Rhododendron* 'Mandarin Lights' provide saturated colors for the jewelbox garden.

Rose

BLOOM PERIOD: April to October
SIZE: 3–6 ft. tall, 2–6 ft. wide
HARDINESS: Zones 5–10

Roses are such a large and diverse group and have been cultivated and hybridized for so long that it is difficult to state anything with authority about the group as a whole. They range from groundcovers to shrubs to vigorous vines, and the wild species can grow much larger than the typical landscape rose. Many are highly susceptible to a variety of diseases and insects. Among my favorites, which have stood the test of time with reasonable disease resistance, are *Rosa* 'Nearly Wild', a low, wide shrub growing to 3 ft. tall and 4 ft. wide with single pink flowers, and 'Seafoam', with a similar size and creamy white double flowers.

Rosa 'Nearly Wild' bears large, single, pink flowers on a tough, landscape-ready shrub.

Schefflera

Hardy schefflera

BLOOM PERIOD: August to September
SIZE: 6–15 ft. tall, 4–10 ft. wide
HARDINESS: Zones 8–10

Hardy scheffleras provide a distinctly tropical texture to the garden with large, evergreen, palmately compound leaves. Among the hardiest is *Schefflera delavayi*. New growth on this species is covered in tan hairs before becoming glossy. It makes a broad, multi-stemmed shrub with small, white, late-summer flowers followed by black fruit. Other species include *S. taiwaniana* and *S. gracilis*. All are best under high shade and may need to be protected from cold spells when young.

Schefflera delavayi has been a reliable performer in the South where it appreciates the high shade of pine trees.

Serissa

Japanese snow rose, serissa, yellow-rim

BLOOM PERIOD: April to May

SIZE: 2–4 ft. tall, 3–5 ft. wide

HARDINESS: Zones 7–10

Serissa japonica, Japanese snow rose, sometimes listed as *S. foetida*, is often found as a bonsai specimen but makes an outstanding low garden shrub with small leaves that are often edged with white where the margins roll up. In spring, it flowers heavily with small white to pink flowers and then sporadically throughout the year. It is generally a mounding plant, although the very hardy 'Sapporo' is stiffly upright. In cold winters it can lose most of its leaves, but it is useful as a low hedge or structural element in a perennial border, or for growing in tough dry shade conditions.

Japanese snow rose is a tough, underused shrub with showy flowers and foliage.

Spiraea

Spiraea

BLOOM PERIOD: March to June

SIZE: 2–5 ft. tall, 3–6 ft. wide

HARDINESS: Zones 4–9

Spiraea is a large group including native species which have been used sparingly at best in landscapes. Most garden spiraeas are *S. japonica* or its hybrid, *S. ×bumalda*, which form low mounds topped in midspring with flat clusters of white to pink flowers. The foliage on some of the forms such as 'Gold Mound' is yellow to chartreuse and new growth is often reddish. Prune these species before growth starts in the spring. *Spiraea thunbergii* has narrow leaves and late winter flowers. The gold-leaved 'Ogon' is especially attractive and has intense fall color. Prune this species after flowering if necessary.

Many spiraeas, like *Spirea japonica* 'Candlelight', have spectacular fall color in addition to bright foliage and showy flowers.

Stachyurus, spiketail

BLOOM PERIOD: February to March

SIZE: 6–15 ft. tall, 8–20 ft. wide

HARDINESS: Zones 6–10

Stachyurus praecox is an unusual, multi-stemmed, arching shrub with long, drooping racemes of pale yellow flowers. The effect is something like a 1970s-era bead curtain. Several variegated forms are available, most notably the white-edged 'Sterling Silver' and 'Carolina Parakeet' with a subtle chartreuse center to the foliage. Stachyurus performs well in full sun or shade preferring a moist, well-drained soil. Though *S. praecox* is the most effective species in the garden, the willow leaf spiketail, *S. salicifolius*, adds great summer texture, but it is not as showy in flower and is only reliable in zone 8 and warmer.

The willow leaf spiketail, *Stachyurus salicifolius*, offers great summer texture in the warmer parts of our region.

Ternstroemia, false cleyera

BLOOM PERIOD: April to May

SIZE: 8–15 ft. tall, 6–10 ft. wide

HARDINESS: Zones 7–10

Ternstroemia gymnanthera is a tough evergreen shrub in the camellia family, with an upright oval form. New growth emerges burgundy before turning glossy green. In the fall, the leaves become plum-purple, especially when sited in full sun. Small, creamy white flowers in spring give rise to 1-in. red fruits in autumn. The selection 'Burnished Gold' has leaves which emerge coppery before turning bronze-gold and then finally deep green. *Ternstroemia* has often been confused with the similar but larger-leaved *Cleyera* but makes a much better landscape subject, suitable for hedging or wherever a tough evergreen is needed.

Ternstroemia gymnanthera is often used as a hedge. The flowers are easily overlooked, but the fruit shines against the foliage.

Vaccinium

Blueberry

BLOOM PERIOD: **March to May**

SIZE: **3–7 ft. tall, 3–5 ft. wide**

HARDINESS: **Zones 5–10**

Many types of *Vaccinium* are available, from cranberries to non-fruiting evergreen species—the native *V. darrowii*, for example, does not produce edible fruits. In general, however, the best plants for the Southeast are the rabbit-eye and southern highbush blueberries. These fruiting blueberries perform well in acidic, well-drained soils. Several selections that have withstood the test of time include *V.* 'Tifblue', 'Climax', and 'Premier', but others are widely available. Try planting several varieties to ensure good fruiting. The ornamental qualities of blueberries are underappreciated. The white to pink spring flowers, blue-green foliage, and spectacular fall color all make blueberries worthy garden plants.

The native *Vaccinium darrowii* is a beautiful evergreen for sunny, well-drained spots.

Viburnum, arrowwood

BLOOM PERIOD: March to May

SIZE: 3–12 ft. tall, 3–10 ft. wide

HARDINESS: Zones 5–10

☀ ◖ ✿ ♣ ⌂ ◉

Viburnums are among the Southeast's most important landscape plants, with showy spring flowers and fruit. Deciduous viburnums like *Viburnum plicatum* generally flower before the foliage, and mature specimens can be absolutely breathtaking. Some selections such as 'Mohawk' fill the late winter garden with an intoxicating spicy-sweet fragrance. Many of these viburnums have bright red to blue-black fruit as well. The forms known as cranberry-bush viburnums, *V. opulus* and *V. trilobum*, are grown as much for their fruit as their flowers. They are quite shade tolerant but will flower and perform best in a sunny spot.

Evergreen and semi-evergreen viburnums add interest to the garden throughout the year. The native *Viburnum nudum* has nice white flowers, but really shines in late summer when the developing fruit turns from white to pink to pale blue, and finally to blue-black. Less well known is the small Asian *V. propinquum*, with deep green, narrow foliage and white flowers followed by black fruit. The southeastern native *V. obovatum* is a somewhat rangy shrub, but dwarf forms like 'Raulston Hardy' and 'Compactum' are tight mounds of mostly evergreen small leaves with a mass of spring flowers. This species has proved to be exceptionally drought tolerant and will often flower sporadically through the year.

Viburnum obovatum 'Raulston Hardy' is a reliable native for sun or shade. RIGHT *Viburnum plicatum* is among the finest flowering shrubs.

Weigela

Weigela

BLOOM PERIOD: **April to May**

SIZE: **4–8 ft. tall and wide**

HARDINESS: **Zones 6–9**

☀ ☀ 🐝▸

Weigelas are somewhat old-fashioned shrubs, forming arching mounds of foliage with exceptionally showy tubular, mostly pink, spring flowers. *Weigela florida* and its hybrids have been the subject of much breeding work, giving rise to dwarf forms, purple, gold and variegated selections, and even reblooming cultivars. Some species and forms, like *W. subsessilis* 'Canary', have added to the color palette with yellow flowers. Weigelas are perhaps best when used in mixed shrub hedges or at the back of perennial beds in full sun, where other plants continue the display after the weigela flowers are finished.

Weigela florida 'Variegata' is a showstopper in spring.

Yucca

Yucca, Spanish bayonet

BLOOM PERIOD: April to June

SIZE: 3–15 ft. tall, 3–8 ft. wide

HARDINESS: Zones 7–10

Yuccas are a group of strappy-leaved plants native from the east coast through Mexico. Many prefer very well-drained, lean soils, but the native species—*Yucca filamentosa*, *Y. flaccida*, and *Y. gloriosa*—are quite tolerant of average garden soil. The first two make low mounded plants while the third grows with tall stems clothed in stiff foliage. Variegated forms of all three add extra color to the garden. The western tree-forming species, *Y. rostrata* and *Y. torreyi*, have silvery blue foliage adding a bit of cool color to the landscape. All species have tall spikes of creamy bell-shaped flowers in spring.

Yucca flaccida 'Garland Gold' is a showy variegated form of the native species.

Trees

Trees are the aristocrats of the garden, adding color with smaller flowering forms and a sense of permanence thanks to larger shade trees. Few plants help mark the changes of season like deciduous trees, whose flowering, fruiting, fall color, and winter forms are reliable year in and year out.

There is a saying that the best time to plant a tree was 20 years ago and the second best time is today. That old adage has a lot of truth to it. Trees provide some of the most important benefits in the garden. They offer habitat and food for wildlife, including birds and insects. They shade the garden and house from the harsh southern sun, helping to reduce energy costs. They protect coastal homes from the winds of hurricanes. Yes, they can occasionally fall on a house during a storm, but in the big picture, trees save many more roofs than they damage. Large trees spread and cross over property lines, turning individual lots into cohesive communities. Too many homeowners today don't plant trees destined to grow large, and housing developments without shade trees never feel like neighborhoods.

Proper siting of trees is important since they will be long-term residents in the garden. Gardens will evolve over time as the trees grow and change the sunlight and water available for other plants. Plan to relocate or remove plants that are getting shaded out by growing trees. Improperly placed trees can be expensive to remove or prune and cause headaches for years. Avoid future problems by considering the ultimate height of the mature tree when planting a young one.

Trees are vital for creating a backdrop and ceiling for the garden as well as providing color and texture.

Maple

BLOOM PERIOD: April to May

SIZE: 20–65 ft. tall, depending on species

HARDINESS: Zones 4–10

As a group, maples are well known by gardeners. The larger species of native maples for landscapes—the red *Acer rubrum* and the sugar *A. saccharum*—need no introduction except to note that southern gardeners should seek out forms selected for heat tolerance. *Acer leucoderme*, the chalkbark maple, is a better choice for Deep South gardens, growing to 35 ft. with great fall color. A similar-sized Asian maple deserving wider use is painted maple, *A. pictum*, with its smooth gray bark and dense rounded head of broad leaves that turn rich gold in autumn.

Smaller maples form an important part of the southern landscape, represented mainly by Japanese maple, *Acer palmatum*, certainly one of the finest specimen trees for any garden. Trident maple, *A. buergerianum*, a small Chinese species, is strangely undervalued despite its drought tolerance, beauty, and potential as an urban street tree. Less well known but becoming more popular are Asian evergreen maples. The hardiest evergreen, *A. fabri* or Faber's maple, has deep green un-maple-like leaves on a 20-ft. tree. Its bright red flowers are surprisingly showy, followed by red whirligig maple fruits. Plants in zone 7 gardens have grown well for close to two decades.

Japanese maples like *Acer palmatum* and this *A. japonicum* 'Filicifolium' make elegant landscape accents, often with variegated or colorful foliage, brilliant fall color, and great form. BOTTOM LEFT Warmer gardens should seek out southern selections of red maple such as *Acer rubrum* 'Fireburst' and 'HOSR' (or Summer Red as it is more commonly known). BOTTOM Trident maple is exceptionally urban tolerant and should be more widely utilized as a small to medium-sized street tree.

WHERE DO NEW PLANTS COME FROM?

Every time I show up at my local garden center, I seem to find a whole range of new and interesting plants. Most people don't give this influx of new plants a second thought, but where do these novel introductions come from?

There is no single pipeline for new plants to the industry. In some cases, plant species which have been grown for years in botanical gardens and collectors' gardens finally find their way to the general market. In other cases, plant collectors are actively searching the wild spaces throughout the United States and other countries for plants that have not been in cultivation before, or for new forms of already familiar plants. Many of these discoveries will not make it to market in the short term but might be used for breeding purposes, or after many years they might make it to the garden center.

Mutants and sports can also lead to new plants. As nurseries sow thousands of seeds for production plants, occasionally a seedling will pop up that looks different than all the rest. It might be extremely slow growing (giving rise to a dwarf form), or have foliage variegated with a different color, or possess some other unique characteristic. Often these seedlings are not recognized as anything special and are thrown out, but sometimes they are saved and may over time prove to be valuable plants. Established plants will also sometimes put out a sport or mutated growth. Perhaps a specimen with white flowers will have one branch with pink blossoms. This sport can be propagated vegetatively and grown on its own, giving rise to a new plant.

Plant breeders actively work to produce new plants with different characteristics by hybridizing. This process typically takes multiple generations to produce a worthy plant. In the case of trees, this may mean decades of growing and hybridizing before a specimen is ready for the market. Plant breeders are often looking not only for different ornamental characteristics but also for greater disease resistance, drought tolerance, or other improved landscape traits.

Growing plants from seed can sometimes give rise to novel forms.

Aesculus

Buckeye, horse chestnut

BLOOM PERIOD: **April to June**

SIZE: **12–80 ft. tall, depending on species**

HARDINESS: **Zones 5–9**

☀ ◑ 🐝 📍

Buckeyes or horse chestnuts are native to the United States, China, and southern Europe, where they become either large flowering trees reaching at least 40 ft. or small, multi-stemmed plants topping out at 25 ft. Many of the larger species can be devastated by fungal diseases in the Southeast, losing their foliage by midsummer. All buckeyes have palmately compound leaves with spires of white, pink, red, or yellow flowers. *Aesculus pavia* and *A. sylvatica*, red and painted buckeye respectively, make multi-stemmed small trees with open panicles of red to yellow flowers. Another southeastern native, *A. parviflora* or bottlebrush buckeye, makes a shrubby mound with spikes of white flowers. Most species are best in a moist, well-drained location.

Gold fall color on bottlebrush buckeye adds interest to the garden late in the season. RIGHT The red flowers and bold foliage of red buckeye make it one of the showiest native trees and a favorite for hummingbirds.

Butia

Pindo palm, jelly palm

BLOOM PERIOD: May

SIZE: 12–20 ft. tall

HARDINESS: Zones 8–10

☀ ◑ ♠

Butia capitata or pindo palm is among the hardiest of the feather palms with 6- to 10-ft.-long, arching, bluish fronds composed of about 100 leaflets. The trunk is typically stout and slow growing. Large heads of small yellow to pinkish flowers give rise to clusters of 1-in. orange fruits from September to November. The fruits have a jelly-like consistency and taste like pineapple mixed with citrus flavors. Pindo palm is suitable for coastal regions of the Southeast, where it makes a striking specimen. The much taller *B. yatay* is also occasionally grown in the Southeast.

Carpinus

Hornbeam, musclewood, ironwood

BLOOM PERIOD: March to April

SIZE: 25–50 ft. tall

HARDINESS: Zones 5–9

☀ ☼ ◑ ◉

The nearly 50 species of hornbeam form small to medium trees of tidy habit with saw-edged leaves, winged fruit clusters, and smooth, sinuous bark. The most widely grown is the relatively large European *Carpinus betulus*. Dwarf, weeping, and columnar selections have been made over the years, and the species performs well even in difficult urban spots such as tree pits and parking lots. The native *C. caroliniana* is a smaller tree suited for naturalistic settings. In recent years, the Asian species have been gaining interest, especially *C. fangiana*, with its extra long flower and fruit panicles.

The long blue fronds of pindo palm make a graceful statement in the garden. RIGHT The tight upright form of *Carpinus betulus* 'Nana Columnaris' makes it ideal as a focal point in the landscape. OPPOSITE The long fruit clusters of *Carpinus fangiana* make it a highly sought-after garden specimen.

Cedrus

Cedar

BLOOM PERIOD: **Non-flowering**
SIZE: **40–90 ft. tall**
HARDINESS: **Zones 7–8**

The true cedars make large specimens in the landscape, suitable only where plenty of space is available. The needles of cedar are usually 1–2 in. long, with color ranging from deep green to silvery blue. In the Southeast, *Cedrus deodara*, with drooping branch tips, is widely grown for its dense, quick growth, but *C. atlantica* is often a better performer with age. In smaller landscapes, the dwarf, spreading, and weeping forms may be more suitable. They are best in an open situation with very good drainage.

Spreading forms like *Cedrus deodara* 'Prostrate Beauty' fit into smaller landscapes much better than the typical species.
RIGHT The pendulous forms of katsura tree—like *Cercidiphyllum japonicum* 'Morioka Weeping', 'Tidal Wave', and 'Amazing Grace'—make beautiful specimens with age.

Cercidiphyllum

Katsura tree

BLOOM PERIOD: **Insignificant**
SIZE: **50–80 ft. tall**
HARDINESS: **Zones 4–9**

This genus is composed of two species of very similar appearance found in China and Japan. Both are large trees although the Chinese form, somewhat confusingly named *Cercidiphyllum japonicum*, will grow taller than the Japanese form, *C. magnificum*. Katsura trees bear heart-shaped foliage with a scalloped edge, emerging with a burgundy tinge and becoming blue-green, then turning yellow, peach, and orange in the fall. When the leaves change in autumn they give a distinctive fragrance of caramelized sugar or cotton candy, especially on a morning after frost. Several weeping and smaller forms have been selected.

Cercis

Redbud

BLOOM PERIOD: **March to April**

SIZE: **12–25 ft. tall**

HARDINESS: **Zones 4–9**

Our native *Cercis canadensis* is among the best spring-flowering trees found in the Southeast, where the lavender to pink flowers brighten the woodlands and the lovely heart-shaped leaves add interest through the season. In recent years, several weeping, variegated, and gold- and purple-leaved forms have been introduced, adding greatly to the variety available to gardeners. Some of the Asian species, like *C. chinensis*, make excellent garden specimens as well, especially the seedless 'Don Egolf' and extra floriferous 'Kay's Early Hope'.

Chinese redbuds tend to grow as multi-stemmed plants. This displays the heavy flowering nature of *Cercis chinensis* 'Kay's Early Hope' to good effect.

Falsecypress, Atlantic white cedar

BLOOM PERIOD: Non-flowering

SIZE: 2–60 ft. tall, depending on selection

HARDINESS: Zones 5–8

Falsecypress is a group of tall, pyramidal conifers generally represented in gardens by selections ranging from basketball-sized mounds to large trees colored gold, green, or blue. Most widely grown are the forms of Hinoki falsecypress, *Chamaecyparis obtusa*, and Sawara falsecypress, *C. pisifera*. Both are variable and have selections suitable for rock gardens, foundation plantings, hedges, or specimen use. Our own native Atlantic white cedar, *C. thyoides*, is not as widely used, but its best forms, such as 'Heatherbun' and 'Little Jamie', are outstanding. Unlike most conifers, white cedar will grow in damp soils and in part shade, making it a valuable garden addition.

The native Atlantic white cedar is typically a soft-textured plant, but the form *Chamaecyparis thyoides* 'Rubicon', also known erroneously as 'Red Star', is a columnar exclamation point. LEFT Dwarf forms of falsecypress like *Chamaecyparis obtusa* 'Juniperoides' make excellent container specimens and provide evergreen structure in smaller garden spaces. RIGHT Hinoki falsecypress is often clipped and shaped for Japanese-style gardens like this classic gold selection *Chamaecyparis obtusa* 'Crippsii'.

Desert willow

BLOOM PERIOD: **June to August**

SIZE: **18–30 ft. tall**

HARDINESS: **Zones 7–9**

☀ ☼ 🐝▸ ◉

Chilopsis linearis is a dryland species from the south-western United States and Mexico. It makes a small multi-stemmed tree or large shrub with twisted trunks and stringy, peeling bark. It typically forms a rather loose, open plant with long, narrow leaves. This species is notable for its exceptional drought tolerance and long bloom period through the heat of the summer. The large flowers are usually pale pink, but dark burgundy and white forms are also available. It is best grown in very well-drained soils in full sun. The stems can be brittle and shatter under ice or heavy wind, but established plants will resprout quickly.

Fringetree, old man's beard

BLOOM PERIOD: **May to June**

SIZE: **25–40 ft. tall**

HARDINESS: **Zones 5–9**

☀ ◖ ☼ ◉

Fringetrees are small to medium flowering trees with airy, lacy flower panicles in spring. Among the finest of all flowering trees is the Asian species, *Chionanthus retusus*. It bears deep green leaves and has attractive blocky bark. The white flowers are borne in dense masses and will give rise to bluish olive-like fruit on female plants. Chinese fringetree is exceptionally drought tolerant and tough in the landscape. Our native species, *C. virginicus*, grows along stream banks and is probably best suited to moist conditions. Fall color on both species can range from attractive gold to nonexistent.

Our native fringetree *Chionanthus virginicus* tends to make a smaller, more open specimen well suited for more naturalistic plantings. LEFT As its name suggests, desert willow is exceptionally drought tolerant and combines well with succulents and agaves in dry gardens.

Few plants can match a mature *Chionanthus retusus* in full flower.

Yellowwood

BLOOM PERIOD: **April to May**
SIZE: **35–50 ft. tall**
HARDINESS: **Zones 4–8**

  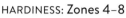

Our native yellowwood, *Cladrastis kentuckea*, is an underutilized, first-class flowering tree. Somewhat coarse, pinnately compound leaves provide a backdrop for the midspring show of white flower panicles that drip like icicles from the branches. It has relatively few pests or problems in the landscape and should be more widely used. Fall color is often a strikingly beautiful gold. A few selections with soft pink flowers are sporadically available to gardeners. While there are several Asian yellowwood species, none are readily available in the nursery trade.

A mature specimen of yellowwood in flower is striking.

Dogwood

BLOOM PERIOD: **March to June**
SIZE: **15–30 ft. tall**
HARDINESS: **Zones 5–9**

The Southeast's native flowering dogwood, *Cornus florida*, needs no introduction as it can be found growing in every neighborhood, virtually in every yard. Almost as well known is *C. kousa*, which flowers three weeks later than flowering dogwood, with white-bracted flowers glowing against the foliage. In recent years, evergreen relatives of kousa dogwood have found their way from Asia, including *C. hongkongensis* and *C. elliptica*. These are certainly more tender, but some forms have been hardy to at least zone 7, with kousa-like flowers and 1-in. red fruits highlighted by glossy foliage that takes on plum tones in winter.

While the large-bracted dogwoods are best known to gardeners, others have clusters of small white flowers. Among my favorites is the native pagoda dogwood, *Cornus alternifolia*, known principally by the white-margined 'Argentea'. Pagoda dogwood grows in a distinct tiered habit with blue-black fruit held on red stalks. It and the similar but larger-growing *C. controversa* are best grown in cooler regions of the Southeast or under high shade. Another small-flowered dogwood, *C. wilsoniana*, would perhaps escape notice were it not for its exceptional white bark. Along with the evergreen dogwoods, it is among the best plants for four-season landscapes.

The large red fruits of *Cornus kousa* are even showier than our native dogwood's. BOTTOM Evergreen dogwoods like *Cornus elliptica* are well suited to warm regions of the Southeast.

Cornus alternifolia 'Argentea' is sometimes known as the wedding cake tree for its tiered habit and striking white-variegated leaves.

Cryptomeria

Japanese cedar, cryptomeria

BLOOM PERIOD: Non-flowering

SIZE: 60 ft. tall

HARDINESS: Zones 6–9

 ☀ ☼ 🌲

Japanese cedar, *Cryptomeria japonica*, has become a conifer of choice in the Southeast, where the species and the more common large selections such as 'Yoshino' are grown as specimens or planted as screens. The tall, straight trunks and pyramidal form make elegant trees. The numerous selections—I have grown more than 70 myself—range from large trees to miniatures like 'Tenzan' which only grows to about 24 in. Cryptomerias perform exceptionally well in the Southeast, and there is a selection to fit almost every garden need. Some variegated forms will benefit from afternoon shade to prevent burning.

The pyramidal forms of mature Japanese cedars make outstanding specimen plants or tall screens to block nosy neighbors. RIGHT The Taiwanese *Cunninghamia lanceolata* var. *konishii* makes a shorter-needled, slightly more refined plant than the mainland China-fir.

Cunninghamia

China-fir

BLOOM PERIOD: Non-flowering

SIZE: 40–80 ft. tall

HARDINESS: Zones 7–9

 ☀ ☼ 🌲

Cunninghamia lanceolata, or China-fir, is a tall, coarse-textured conifer with flat, sharp needles spirally arranged around the branches. Old needles eventually turn orange-brown but do not drop for several years, giving plants a shaggy, unkempt appearance. The silvery blue form 'Glauca' is the most common selection, with dense foliage that shimmers in the summer sun. China-fir can be cut to the ground and will resprout with vigor. Plants are best in moist, rich soil with protection from drying winter winds. A Taiwanese variety, *C. lanceolata* var. *konishii* is similar to typical China-fir but has shorter needles and a somewhat finer texture.

239

Cypress

BLOOM PERIOD: **Non-flowering**

SIZE: **30–50 ft. tall**

HARDINESS: **Zones 7–9**

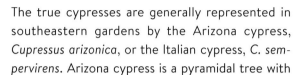

The true cypresses are generally represented in southeastern gardens by the Arizona cypress, *Cupressus arizonica*, or the Italian cypress, *C. sempervirens*. Arizona cypress is a pyramidal tree with fine texture and deep green to silvery blue, scaly needles, depending on selection. It is native to the Southwest but adapts well to the Southeast, where it makes an attractive, drought-tolerant screen. It takes shearing well and can be used to create clipped hedges or topiary. Italian cypress is generally represented in cultivation by one of its columnar forms. Grow cypress in full sun and very well-drained soil.

The blue needles of *Cupressus arizonica* 'Carolina Sapphire', like many Arizona cypress cultivars, sparkle in the southern sun.

Persimmon

BLOOM PERIOD: **April to May**
SIZE: **25–60 ft. tall, depending on species**
HARDINESS: **Zones 5–9**

Diospyros virginiana is well known in the South for its blocky bark and fall crop of yellow-orange fruit, which must be exposed to frost to be edible. It has separate male and female flowers, although both can sometimes be found on the same tree. It is often afflicted with leaf spot, although this doesn't affect the health of the tree. For the best fruit, choose a named selection like 'Early Golden'. Japanese persimmon, *D. kaki*, is becoming popular in the South where it makes a small tree, bearing bright orange fruit in fall. It is only hardy to about zone 7.

Bright fall color is only one of many reasons to grow Japanese persimmon. BOTTOM Japanese persimmon is an easy and trouble-free tree fruit for the Southeast.

Eriobotrya

Loquat

BLOOM PERIOD: November to January
SIZE: 15–25 ft. tall
HARDINESS: Zones 7–10

☀ ☀ ☀ ♠ ✿

Eriobotrya japonica is a large-leaved evergreen tree or shrub with stout branches. Flower buds form in late summer, covered with a thick layer of tan fuzz. The creamy flowers open between late fall and early winter, filling the garden with fragrance. Delicious yellow fruit ripens in spring in the Deep South, but fruits are rarely formed at the colder end of loquat's range. Best in a sunny spot, plants in colder areas may benefit from some high shade for winter protection. Another edible species is the more rare *E. deflexa* with bronze new growth.

Eriobotrya japonica is often grown as a large, multi-stemmed shrub. RIGHT The bronze new growth of *Eriobotrya deflexa* adds to the appeal of this rarely seen but garden-worthy plant which can also produce edible fruit.

Ginkgo, maidenhair tree

BLOOM PERIOD: Insignificant
SIZE: 50–80 ft. tall
HARDINESS: Zones 4–10

Ginkgo biloba is a striking shade tree from China. Its habit is quite variable when the tree is young but ultimately a rounded head is formed. The fan-shaped foliage is distinct and creates one of the finest displays of gold fall color of any southern tree. Male and female flowers are carried on separate plants; females will develop fruit with a foul fragrance, so planting named male clones is strongly advised. 'Jade Butterfly' is among the best of the several dwarf selections available. Established plants are exceptionally tough and make very effective street trees.

The unusual fan-like foliage of *Ginkgo biloba* turns brilliant gold in the fall, making it among the most reliable trees for autumn color in the South.

Halesia

Silverbell

BLOOM PERIOD: **April to May**

SIZE: **30–40 ft. tall**

HARDINESS: **Zones 5–9**

☀ ◑ ◉

Halesia tetraptera, Carolina silverbell, and the smaller *H. diptera*, two-winged silverbell, are multi-stemmed or low-branched native trees with pure white spring flowers. Carolina silverbell grows to 40 ft. in landscapes but can grow to double that height in the wild, while two-winged silverbell grows to only about 25 ft. Silverbells are exceptionally pest resistant and easy in the garden if given adequate moisture. Some pink-flowered forms are available in the trade but generally do not display good color in warmer climates. *Halesia diptera* var. *magniflora* has the largest flowers of any selection and is worth a choice spot in a woodland garden.

Few native trees are as showy as the large-flowered form of silverbell, *Halesia diptera* var. *magniflora*.

Lagerstroemia

Crepe myrtle

BLOOM PERIOD: June to September
SIZE: 15–25 ft. tall
HARDINESS: Zones 7–10

☀ ☼

Lagerstroemia indica, common crepe myrtle, is known for flowering up to 100 days in summer, especially if old flowers are removed. It makes a small tree with beautiful peeling bark and spectacular fall color. Breeders have introduced every size from 2-ft. groundcovers to 40-ft. trees and developed flowers ranging from white to lavender to red as well as foliage in deep purple hues. The Japanese crepe myrtle, *L. fauriei*, is a larger tree with cinnamon bark, white flowers, and good powdery mildew resistance. Hybridizing these two species has led to plants with exceptionally beautiful bark and disease resistance.

Breeding has created true dwarf forms of crepe myrtle such as *Lagerstroemia* 'Gamad1', or Cherry Dazzle as it is more commonly known, which can be grown like a summer-flowering azalea. BOTTOM The wide variety of flower color makes crepe myrtle invaluable for southern landscapes.

Magnolia

BLOOM PERIOD: **March to April**

SIZE: **25–50 ft. tall**

HARDINESS: **Zones 5–9**

☀ ◖ ⚙ ◉

Magnolias are familiar garden specimens throughout the Southeast; indeed, spring would be poorer without the large flowers adorning the bare branches of the deciduous types in March. Specialty nurseries offer hundreds of selections, in sizes ranging from large shrubs to sizable trees, and flowers in shades of white, purple-black, pink, and yellow. For small spaces, consider the star magnolia, *Magnolia stellata*, which often flowers late enough to avoid frost. The double pink form 'Chrysanthemumiflora' cannot be beat. The popular yellow magnolias, hybrids with the native *M. acuminata* in their parentage, are often large trees with good-sized flowers. Many become more cream than yellow under higher heat, but 'Yellow Lantern' is relatively late with good color. *Magnolia sieboldii* offers striking late-season flowers on a smaller-statured plant.

Evergreen magnolias supply multi-season interest instead of the single-season smack in the face of the deciduous species. One evergreen native is *Magnolia virginiana*, or sweetbay magnolia, but the southern magnolia, *M. grandiflora*, is synonymous with the South around the world. Many other species, however, are better suited to home landscapes. The purple-flowered banana shrub, *M. figo* var. *crassipes*, is a large shrub for warm (zones 7–10) gardens, with glossy foliage and fruit-scented, 1 ½-in. flowers. Another Asian evergreen is shrubby michelia, *M. laevifolia*, with leathery leaves and rusty, fuzz-covered flower buds that open to reveal 2- to 3-in. sweet-scented white flowers over a long period in midspring.

Magnolia sieboldii and its hybrids have relatively late porcelain-white flowers with red stamens. BOTTOM *Magnolia virginiana* 'Mattie Mae Smith' is brightly variegated. RIGHT *Magnolia grandiflora* 'Southern Charm', also known as Teddy Bear southern magnolia, has exceptional, uniform shape, dark green leaves with fuzzy tan backs, and restrained growth.

Dawn redwood

BLOOM PERIOD: **Non-flowering**
SIZE: **65–90 ft. tall**
HARDINESS: **Zones 5–9**

Often considered a living fossil, *Metasequoia glypto-stroboides* was only known from 100-million-year-old fossils until it was found growing in China in the 1950s. Plants have proved to be fast-growing, deciduous conifers with fluted, auburn bark. The form is pyramidal, becoming flat topped with age. The trunk can become wide with buttressed roots. Bright green, feathery branchlets turn russet in autumn and drop to reveal the striking winter silhouette. Several selections have been made, some with creamy variegation like 'Silhouette', gold needles such as 'Ogon', or dwarf habit as in 'Schirrmann's Nordlicht' and 'Matthaei Broom'.

Fast growth and a strong pyramidal form make *Metasequoia glyptostroboides* a popular conifer. LEFT Unlike most conifers, *Metasequoia glyptostroboides* has beautiful russet-orange fall color before dropping its needles in winter.

Nyssa

Tupelo, black gum

BLOOM PERIOD: **Insignificant**
SIZE: **30–50 ft. tall**
HARDINESS: **Zones 4–9**

Our native tupelo, *Nyssa sylvatica*, with its tough constitution, glossy leaves, and spectacular fall color adds to the landscape palette. It has a reputation of being difficult to transplant but container-grown plants establish readily. Gardeners should select a named variety like 'Wildfire' or 'Hayman Red', which is sold as Red Rage. The exceptionally uniform habit of 'NSUHH', sold as Green Gable, makes it a great choice for allées and formal landscapes. For those looking for a more distinct plant, the white-margined 'Sheri's Cloud' or contorted 'Zydeco Twist' make a statement. The Chinese *N. sinensis* has an upright habit and good fall color and deserves consideration for southern gardens.

Nyssa sylvatica is native to damp woodlands and river edges, but is tolerant of most garden sites.

Parrotia

Ironwood, parrotia

BLOOM PERIOD: February to March
SIZE: 25–40 ft. tall
HARDINESS: Zones 5–9

Persian ironwood, *Parrotia persica*, is a multi-stemmed tree with a broad, rounded habit and exceptional patchy, exfoliating bark. New leaves emerge with a burgundy cast before turning green, then orange to red in fall. Late winter flowers are not showy but the 1/2-in. masses of red stamens are pretty up close. Plants are quite tough once established. A species relatively recently discovered in China, *P. subaequalis*, is proving to be an outstanding multi-stemmed small tree. It grows quickly with a smaller leaf than its Persian sibling. Plants I have seen in cultivation have lovely dusky burgundy fall color.

Picea

Spruce

BLOOM PERIOD: Non-flowering
SIZE: 45–75 ft. tall
HARDINESS: Zones 4–7

Spruces are tall, pyramidal conifers much used in the upland and mountainous regions of the Southeast. The best spruce species for use in the Southeast are the Norway, *Picea abies*, the Colorado, *P. pungens*, and the Oriental, *P. orientalis*. The numerous forms of these species include dwarfs, weepers, creepers, and fastigiates as well as blue- and yellow-needled types. Dwarf forms seem to perform better in the Deep South, although mites can be a problem. Most resources underestimate the size of dwarf conifers in the South, so doubling the listed size is a good rule of thumb.

Norway spruce is typically a tall pyramidal conifer, but dwarf, weeping, and other growth forms are common, especially in the highlands. LEFT The rich plum to deep purple fall color of *Parrotia subaequalis* starts very early and lasts well into autumn, often for more than six weeks. RIGHT *Picea orientalis* 'Skylands' is a popular gold selection of Oriental spruce.

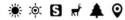

Pine

BLOOM PERIOD: **Non-flowering**

SIZE: **30–60 ft. tall**

HARDINESS: **Zones 4–9**

☀ ☼ Ⓢ ⚥ 🌲 📍

Pines are quite variable, often with a pyramidal habit in youth becoming flat topped with age. Needles in bundles of one to five can be 2–10 in. long. Generally, the fewer needles per bundle the more drought tolerant the plant. Long-needled natives like white pine, *Pinus strobus*, in cooler climes and loblolly, *P. taeda*, in the South make graceful landscape specimens. The Japanese pines, *P. densiflora*, *P. parviflora*, and *P. thunbergii* are often picturesque specimens, the last providing an excellent coastal windbreak where it tolerates sandy soils and salt spray. Selections of northern pines are available in every size and habit, but southern pines would benefit from more selections.

Podocarp

BLOOM PERIOD: **Non-flowering**

SIZE: **15–30 ft. tall**

HARDINESS: **Zones 7–10**

☀ ☁ ☼ Ⓢ ⚥ 🌲

The Chinese podocarp, *Podocarpus macrophyllus*, is a broad-needled conifer used in the Deep South for clipped hedges. Left unpruned it forms an upright oval. It is quite drought, salt, and heat tolerant. Variegated and dwarf selections as well as exciting colorful forms are available, like 'Akame' (sometimes seen as Royal Flush or Emerald Flame) with red new growth and 'Kinme', known as Golden Crown or Lemon Sparkler, with gold new growth. Several New Zealand species show promise in southern gardens, including *P. acutifolius*, *P. alpinus*, *P. nivalis*, and *P. totara*; the first three are low-growing shrubs. *Podocarpus totara* can be a shade tree but is typically a shrub in the Southeast.

The New Zealand *Podocarpus* 'County Park Fire' makes a small mound of brilliant foliage. LEFT The compact habit of *Pinus taeda* NCSU Dwarf Group is well suited to suburban landscapes.

Prunus

Flowering cherry

BLOOM PERIOD: **March to April**

SIZE: **20–40 ft. tall**

HARDINESS: **Zones 5–8**

The popular flowering cherries, including *Prunus serrulata*, *P. subhirtella*, and *P. ×yedoensis*, are represented in gardens by their various cultivars. 'Sekiyama' (usually listed as 'Kwanzan') with 3-in. double flowers is among the showiest and best known, but many others are widely available, including quite a few weepers. All these flowering cherries should be considered short-lived garden specimens as they are susceptible to various cankers, leaf spots, and other pests. Despite their problems, consider 15 to 25 years of incredible spring beauty to be time and money well spent, and replace as soon as a plant starts to go downhill.

Prunus is composed of a large group other than the flowering cherries, including evergreen trees and shrubs, fruit trees, and other flowering garden specimens. The winter blooming *P. mume*, Japanese apricot, has freeze-tolerant winter flowers from January to February in pastel colors with a spicy-sweet clove fragrance. Perhaps no other tree provides the level of winter interest of Japanese apricot, making it a valuable specimen despite a lack of charisma in other seasons. For smaller spots, the surprisingly problem-free Fuji cherry, *P. incisa*, is a multi-stemmed shrub or small tree with masses of pink or white flowers.

Spicy, clove-scented, frost-tolerant flowers in midwinter make Japanese apricot worth a spot in any garden. BOTTOM Fuji cherries like *Prunus incisa* 'Snowcloud' are delicate small trees or shrubs with very early spring flowers. NEXT PAGE *Prunus* 'Okame' is among the earliest flowering cherries available.

Golden larch

BLOOM PERIOD: **Non-flowering**

SIZE: **40–60 ft. tall**

HARDINESS: **Zones 5–8**

☀ ☀

Pseudolarix amabilis is a wide-spreading, pyramidal, deciduous conifer with a picturesque open crown at maturity. The lime-green spring needles are held in whorls on short spurs and turn bright orange-gold in fall, ending the season with style. The autumn color display does not last long but is spectacular and ranks high among my favorites for fall effect. Golden larch is easy but slow growing, making it suitable even for smaller landscapes. It is at its best in well-drained, organic soil in an open, sunny spot.

Although pyramidal when young, *Pseudolarix amabilis* can become a wide-spreading tree with age.

Oak

BLOOM PERIOD: **April to May**
SIZE: **25–80 ft. tall**
HARDINESS: **Zones 5–9**

☀ ◑ ♠ ⟁ ⚲

Many of our native oaks are too large to fit into typical landscapes or present difficulties in production. Of recent interest is the development of good heat-tolerant, fastigiate forms. The best of the half dozen I have grown is *Quercus* ×*warei* 'Long', sold as Regal Prince, which grows quickly in the landscape as a focal point or part of a screen. Southern landscapes are known for the massive, spreading form of live oak, *Q. virginiana*, which grows quickly in a favorable location with plenty of sun and well-drained soils. The form 'QVTIA', sold as Highrise, is an upright tree that fits in modern landscapes better than the species.

Asia and Mexico both have a high concentration of oaks, including evergreen species suitable for southeastern gardens. The hardiest of the Asian evergreen species is *Quercus myrsinifolia*, a medium-sized tree for gardens in zone 7 and warmer. Narrow, glossy leaves emerge burgundy, and specimens have been used as street trees in the South. Several Mexican evergreen oaks are proving to be excellent in the garden, including Mexican royal oak, *Q. germana*. It is a midsized, pyramidal tree with long, toothed leaves that emerge pinkish-red before turning deep green. It is hardy to zone 7, becoming semi-deciduous in cold winters.

A landmark live oak with Spanish moss. Located in City Park, New Orleans, this tree was one of my favorite play sites during childhood summers. RIGHT Many Asian evergreen oaks like *Quercus glauca* make elegant midsized trees which fit well in many landscape settings.

Sabal

Palmetto

BLOOM PERIOD: June to August
SIZE: 4–8 ft. tall or 20–40 ft. tall, depending on species
HARDINESS: Zones 8–11

Cabbage palmetto, *Sabal palmetto*, is among the hardiest of tree palms. The leaves are intermediate between fan-like and feathery. Old leaves are not dropped and will form a skirt of dead foliage persisting for several years, ultimately falling and leaving a basket-weave texture of leaf bases behind. Compulsive gardeners often remove this skirt, revealing the smooth, pale gray trunk. A dwarf palmetto species, *S. minor*, grows as an understory plant, often creating thickets in the wild. Palmettos are tolerant of salt spray and both sandy soils and wet clay. Bees love the flowers that are carried on long stalks in summer and give rise to blue-black fruits.

Cabbage palm, displaying its characteristic criss-crossed leaf bases up the stem, growing with the Asian windmill palm, *Trachycarpus fortunei*, and the shrubby dwarf palmetto.

Stewartia

Stewartia

BLOOM PERIOD: May to June
SIZE: 18–40 ft. tall
HARDINESS: Zones 5–8

Stewartias are among the most elegant of flowering trees. All the species bear white flowers with yellow, orange, or purple anthers, and have smooth gray or cinnamon bark. This bark often flakes to display a jigsaw of colors, offering brilliant fall hues. *Stewartia pseudocamellia* has large flowers, is the tallest in cultivation, and is best suited to the mountains of the Southeast. Better for warmer gardens are *S. monodelpha* and *S. rostrata*. Our native species—mountain and silky stewartia, *S. ovata* and *S. malacodendron*, respectively—can be difficult to grow in the garden, but are worth the effort. All species require moist, well-drained, organic soil.

Flowers of silky stewartia are among the most elegant of all southeastern natives.

Styrax

Snowbell

BLOOM PERIOD: May to June
SIZE: 25–45 ft. tall
HARDINESS: Zones 5–9

☀ ◑ ✿ ◉

Snowbells are elegant flowering trees with dangling white flowers. Our native *Styrax americanus* is a fine-textured shrub to 10 ft. that is lovely in a shady woodland. The most widely grown snowbell, *S. japonicus*, is a medium-sized tree with smooth gray bark, small leaves, and heavy flower set. The flowers give rise to attractive gray fruits. The selection 'Emerald Pagoda', made by J. C. Raulston, bears larger flowers and darker leaves. Pink-flowered forms and weepers have been selected, as have purple-leaved cultivars like 'Evening Light'. *Styrax obassia*, fragrant snowbell, is aptly named with racemes of intensely sweet-smelling flowers. Other Asian snowbells such as *S. wilsonii* often have a fine texture both in and out of flower.

The bark of *Stewartia pseudocamellia* can become quite spectacular with age. RIGHT Snowbells like *Styrax wilsonii* are exceptional flowering trees for any landscape, with white reflexed petals and gold stamens.

259

Taxodium

Bald cypress, pond cypress

BLOOM PERIOD: **Non-flowering**
SIZE: **60–90 ft. tall**
HARDINESS: **Zones 5–11**

Bald cypress, *Taxodium distichum*, is a native, deciduous conifer found in wet areas, where it forms a pyramidal tree. It can be grown in standing water but is also adaptable to drier sites. The feathery branchlets put on a russet display from October to November before dropping. Many selections are available, including the compact 'Peve Minaret', with congested branching, growing slowly to 25 ft. or more. Pond cypress, *T. distichum* var. *imbricatum*, is similar but with curious, strictly ascending branchlets. The narrow form, 'Prairie Sentinel', is among the best. Mexican Montezuma cypress, *T. mucronatum*, with a wide-spreading, semi-evergreen crown, is best suited for warm coastal gardens.

Taxodium distichum in full fall color. RIGHT Bald cypress is a quick-growing native tree tolerant of wet soils.

Tilia

Linden, basswood

BLOOM PERIOD: June to July

SIZE: 50–70 ft. tall

HARDINESS: Zones 4–8

☀ ☀ ✿ 🐝 📍

Lindens bear serrate, heart-shaped leaves and divinely fragrant, creamy yellow summer flowers. The littleleaf and silver lindens, *Tilia cordata* and *T. tomentosa*, respectively, make dense, round-headed shade trees. Silver linden is best in the cooler regions of the Southeast where the deep green leaves with silver backs always elicit comment. Many selections of littleleaf linden are available. The dwarf form *T. cordata* 'Halka', sold as Summer Sprite, only grows to about 15 ft. and is ideal for even the smallest landscapes. Our native basswood, *T. americana*, is striking, but its coarse texture, large leaves, and size make it suitable only for parks and open spaces.

Tilia cordata 'Greenspire' has an even crown making it useful as a street tree.

Trachycarpus

Windmill palm

BLOOM PERIOD: April to June

SIZE: 15–25 ft. tall

HARDINESS: Zones 7–10

☀ ☁ 🦌 🌲

Without doubt, the windmill palm, *Trachycarpus fortunei*, is the hardiest tree palm available. The slender stem is covered in a shaggy coat and topped with a head of fan-shaped fronds. The dense clusters of yellow male and female flowers are generally carried on separate plants, although occasionally both will be found on a single confused specimen. Blueberry-like fruits form on arching stalks. Windmill palms are easy to grow in anything from sandy to heavy clay soils, in full sun or shade.

Windmill palm gives a tropical feel to temperate landscapes.

Chaste tree

BLOOM PERIOD: July to August
SIZE: 10–20 ft. tall
HARDINESS: Zones 7–10

☀ ☼ 🦌 🐝▸

Vitex agnus-castus is a showy small tree for summer color, covering itself in spikes of lavender, white, pink, or blue flowers on a plant as wide as it is tall. In colder areas it will usually be killed to the ground in winter. Palmately compound leaves are dull gray-green on top and silvery gray beneath. The similar but hardier *V. negundo* is not as showy in flower, but cut-leaf selections like 'Heterophylla' add interest. Both species are very drought tolerant and a mature, well-maintained plant in flower is spectacular. Chaste trees need some regular pruning and thinning for optimal appearance.

When grown well, few summer-flowering trees can match *Vitex agnus-castus* in full flower.

Zelkova

BLOOM PERIOD: Insignificant
SIZE: 50–70 ft. tall
HARDINESS: Zones 5–9

☀ ☼ ☼

The Japanese *Zelkova serrata* is a uniform tree with numerous branches arching out in a vase shape. Small serrate foliage can be spectacular in fall some years but doesn't impress in others. The nice form, upward arching branches, and drought and urban tolerance make this a favorite for landscape designers. A gold-leaved form from Japan, 'Ogon' (often sold as Bright Park) adds a dash of color with its bright new growth in spring, and in winter the young orange stems glow. Several other species are available but don't add much that can't be found in Japanese zelkova.

Fall color can be striking on zelkova, but doesn't develop every year.

Vines

Vines are the final frontier in gardening. While adding immense interest to the landscape, they can be difficult for many gardeners to use effectively. Vines range from large, vigorous woody ramblers to herbaceous plants that die back to the ground each year. They can easily be grown on fences, arbors, and pergolas but can also be used as groundcovers, or allowed to grow up tall trees or through shrubs.

Quick-growing, large selections should be maintained regularly to keep them in bounds. With judicious trimming they require little other work.

Knowing how your vine grows makes maintenance much easier. Some vines need help to climb, others twine around supports or use tendrils or rootlets to climb on their own.

Smaller vines are ideal for growing into the lower limbs of trees or over shrubs, allowing for multiple plants in the same space. Different vines can also be planted together, which is especially effective for providing multiple seasons of flowering. Make sure paired vines have similar growth rates, though, or the more vigorous can choke out the slower vine.

Vines add texture and color to structures and extend the garden in another dimension.

Ampelaster

Climbing aster

BLOOM PERIOD: **September to November**

SIZE: **10 ft. tall with support**

HARDINESS: **Zones 7–10**

This native climbing aster makes a tangle of woody stems which can clamber to 10 ft. high if given support. The pale lavender flowers of *Ampelaster carolinianus* are borne in profusion from late summer into fall, putting an exclamation point on the growing season. If not given a support structure, climbing aster will make a 3-ft. mound which actually mingles well in a large perennial border. Plant in full sun in average garden soil for best growth.

Ampelaster carolinianus provides a burst of late season color.

Aristolochia

Dutchman's pipe, pipevine

BLOOM PERIOD: **May to August**

SIZE: **10–30 ft. tall with support**

HARDINESS: **Zones 7–10**

Aristolochia is a large genus with many tropical species of vines usually with more or less heart-shaped leaves. The native, hardier forms make excellent garden plants. *Aristolochia macrophylla* is the main food source for the larvae of the pipevine swallowtail butterfly, making this large vine useful in habitat gardens. Small 1-in. greenish-yellow flowers resembling pipes give the plant its common name. The smaller, fuzzy-leaved *A. mandshuriensis* has similar flowers that are bright yellow. A diminutive species, *A. fimbriata*, does not climb well but spreads along the ground providing an interesting feature with its silvery veins and fringed flowers.

Aristolochia fimbriata scrambles along the ground with attractive, white-veined leaves and small flowers.

Bignonia

Crossvine

BLOOM PERIOD: **April to May**

SIZE: **30 ft. tall with support**

HARDINESS: **Zones 5–10**

The native crossvine, *Bignonia capreolata*, is a vigorous evergreen to semi-evergreen vine with long tubular flowers borne in profusion in spring. The typical wild form has peachy orange flowers with yellow throats. Several selections for flower color have been made, such as the dark orange-red of 'Atrosanguinea' and the deep orange of 'Jekyll'. Crossvine will quickly cover a trellis, fence, or tree stump in sunny or relatively shady garden spots and is not particular about soils, making it a valuable addition to the landscape.

Crossvine is a vigorous grower, with flowers in shades of peach to red or bright orange, as in *Bignonia capreolata* 'Jekyll'.

Clematis

BLOOM PERIOD: **December to September,
depending on selection**
SIZE: **6–20 ft. tall with support**
HARDINESS: **Zones 5–10**

The genus *Clematis* includes a large group of plants ranging from vigorous, large-growing vines to small perennials. Considerable confusion has developed regarding care and maintenance of these plants. In general, they want full sun but a cool root zone in the South. Planting them where the base is well mulched or shaded by a shrub is often enough to satisfy this need. For clematis that flower on new wood in summer or fall, prune them almost to the ground in late winter. Spring-flowering clematis can be pruned immediately after flowering. Some forms bloom on old wood and then sporadically on new growth. I generally recommend pruning lightly after the first show in spring.

Most people picture the large-flowered clematis when they think of this group. Smaller flowered selections like the graceful blue *Clematis* 'Betty Corning' and the fall- and winter-flowering *C. cirrhosa* add elegance to the garden. For a shot of bright color, the gold *C. tangutica* is especially showy. Evergreen *C. armandii* with long glossy leaves and late winter flowers is too tender for colder gardens, making it best suited for zone 7 and warmer. The non-climbing *C. integrifolia* is ideal for weaving through other perennials in the border.

The large-flowered cultivars of *Clematis*, such as 'Roblom' (sold as Rüütel), prefer a sunny spot with cool, well-mulched roots.
RIGHT The non-climbing species is typically soft blue, but white- and rose-colored selections like *Clematis integrifolia* 'Rose Colored Glasses' are also available.

Gelsemium

Carolina jessamine, swamp jessamine

BLOOM PERIOD: March to May or
October to November

SIZE: 25 ft. tall with support

HARDINESS: Zones 7–10

The native Carolina jessamine, *Gelsemium sempervirens*, flowers in spring with sweetly fragrant gold flowers that shine against the glossy evergreen foliage. Sporadic reblooming occurs in the fall in many cases. 'Pride of Augusta' is a double-flowered form. Swamp jessamine, *G. rankinii*, is not quite as vigorous and is unfortunately not fragrant, but it flowers mainly in fall with sporadic spring flowering. Both species can be grown together to provide a bright show in spring and autumn. The former is drought tolerant while the latter will grow in boggy spots, but both are happiest in moist, well-drained soil.

Gelsemium sempervirens 'Woodlander's Pale Yellow' provides a softer color than the typical Carolina jessamine.

Redwing

BLOOM PERIOD: June to November

SIZE: 18 ft. tall with support

HARDINESS: Zones 7–11

☀ ☀ 🦌 ☀

Redwing, *Heteropterys glabra*, is a woody scrambling vine from Paraguay and Uruguay. It bears small, bright gold flowers all summer until frost. The blooms turn quickly to bright, rosy red, winged seeds resembling maple samaras. The combination of gold and red against the bluish-green foliage is attractive and unusual. Young plants often die back to the ground in zone 7 gardens but come back in late spring. Established plants are quite drought tolerant. The stiff, woody vines may need some tying to get them to climb where desired, or they can be allowed to grow as a sprawling shrub.

Redwing is surprisingly hardy for a South American vine.

Kadsura

BLOOM PERIOD: June to July

SIZE: 15 ft. tall with support

HARDINESS: Zones 7–11

☀ ● 🌲 ✿

The Japanese kadsura, *Kadsura japonica*, is the species most commonly encountered in gardens. Thick-textured evergreen foliage is carried on well-behaved woody stems with small, fragrant, creamy white flowers followed by brilliant red fruit in fall. Plants in gardens are often represented by the variegated forms 'Chirimen' with creamy marbling and 'Fukurin' with a white margin. Less common but worth seeking out is the Chinese *K. longipedunculata* with similar foliage but flowers carried on long, pendant stalks which are magical when grown overhead on a pergola or lattice.

The variegated *Kadsura japonica* 'Fukurin' brightens a shady landscape.

Honeysuckle

BLOOM PERIOD: March to May and sporadically through summer

SIZE: 20 ft. tall with support

HARDINESS: Zones 5–9

☀ ◑ ⛁ ✿ 🐝 ◉

Honeysuckles are among the best-known woody vines throughout the Southeast, recognized mainly from the invasive weed *Lonicera japonica*, with its white flowers that turn yellow. Instead of this weed, grow the the native semi-evergreen *L. sempervirens*, with long, tubular, reddish-orange flowers. Among the best forms are the dark-flowered 'Cedar Lane', which shows a tendency to rebloom strongly, and the long-blooming red 'Major Wheeler'. The hybrid *L. ×heckrottii* is perhaps the showiest hardy honeysuckle with deep red buds opening to show the creamy yellow flower interior with a pink exterior.

The eucalyptus-like leaves of *Lonicera reticulata* 'Kintzley's Ghost' provide long seasonal color even after the creamy yellow flowers fade. BOTTOM Both the typical form of *Lonicera sempervirens* and its yellow variant are attractive to hummingbirds.

Parthenocissus

Virginia creeper, silvervein creeper, Boston ivy

BLOOM PERIOD: Insignificant

SIZE: 40 ft. tall with support

HARDINESS: Zones 6–11

The native Virginia creeper, *Parthenocissus quinque-folia*, is a self-clinging vine with palmately compound, five-part leaves which turn brilliant scarlet in fall. Less well known is its Asian cousin, *P. henryana* or silvervein creeper, with similar-shaped foliage colored bluish to plummy purple with silvery white veins. It is much more restrained in growth and quite showy. Boston ivy, *P. tricuspidata*, an Asian species without a compound leaf, resembles a deciduous form of English ivy. The yellow-leaved form 'Fenway Park' is especially showy in spring and again in fall when the foliage turns vivid red.

Silvervein creeper's burgundy foliage with silver highlights provides easy color to cover a wall. RIGHT Typical for the genus, the gold *Parthenocissus tricuspidata* 'Fenway Park' is a self-clinging vine that will climb most surfaces.

Passiflora

Passion flower, maypops

BLOOM PERIOD: **June to October**

SIZE: **18 ft. tall with support**

HARDINESS: **Zones 7–11**

Passion flowers are native to much of the tropics with a couple of species growing as far north as Pennsylvania. The showy maypops, *Passiflora incarnata*, is a vigorous spreading vine with intricate blue flowers sporting a ring of thread-like filaments between the petals and the three-part stigma. The yellow fruit is sweet and can be eaten fresh or used for juice. The South American *P. caerulea* is similar in appearance. Several hybrids such as the blue *P.* 'Elizabeth' and the rosy violet 'Lady Margaret' are available for southeastern gardens. All serve as host plants for gulf fritillaries and other butterflies.

Few vines are as exotic looking as passion flowers like *Passiflora* 'Blue Eyed Susan'.

Schizophragma

False climbing hydrangea

BLOOM PERIOD: **June to July**

SIZE: **30 ft. tall with support**

HARDINESS: **Zones 5–10**

True climbing hydrangeas are slow to flower in the Southeast, but the vigorous *Schizophragma hydrangeoides* is a dead ringer with heart-shaped, serrate leaves and flowers at a young age. The blooms sport 10-in. lacy clusters of small flowers ringed with large white, paddle-shaped, sterile florets. The form 'Moonlight' has a silvery wash with darker veins over the leaves, which is arresting on a large healthy planting. A pinkish flowered form, 'Roseum', and a white leaf margined form, 'Ivory Majik', are also available. *Schizophragma integrifolium* is larger in all aspects—leaf, flower cluster, and sterile florets. Other species are coming into cultivation from Asia as well.

Schizophragma integrifolium is breathtaking when grown well.
LEFT *Schizophragma hydrangeoides* can have good fall color even in the shade.

Jackson vine, bamboo vine, greenbrier, catbrier

BLOOM PERIOD: Insignificant

SIZE: 30 ft. tall with support

HARDINESS: Zones 7–10

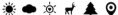

The vigorous, thorny stems of common greenbrier are the bane of hikers and many woodland gardeners, but the evergreen, largely thornless Jackson vine, *Smilax smallii*, is an elegant native for the South. Green stems clothed with narrow, glossy leaves can be trained along fences, over arbors, or against brick walls. Driving through old neighborhoods in Charleston, you will find it much in evidence. The several Asian species are not much in cultivation, but the dwarf, groundcovering *S. nana* makes a steel-wool-textured mat of zigzag stems with tiny green leaves.

Smilax nana is an underused plant with a distinctive texture in the garden.

Confederate jasmine, star jasmine

BLOOM PERIOD: April to June and sporadically until October

SIZE: 15 ft. tall with support

HARDINESS: Zones 7–11

Confederate jasmine, *Trachelospermum jasminoides*, is a tough evergreen vine or groundcover with creamy white flowers often with a yellow eye. The form 'Raulston Hardy' is reliable into zone 7 while the pink-flowered 'Pink Showers' adds color variation. Star jasmine, *T. asiaticum*, is typically smaller leaved and often grown as a groundcover. Several variegated forms are available, including 'Hatsuyuki' which emerges in spring with pink-and-white-speckled leaves before becoming mostly green and white. It has been sold as 'Tricolor' and 'Snow 'n' Summer' which are doubtfully different. The white-splashed 'Nagaba' is found as a groundcover through the South.

Confederate jasmine's fragrant flowers and evergreen foliage make it a popular vine for growing over fences and trellises throughout the South. BOTTOM *Trachelospermum asiaticum* 'Hatsuyuki' is among the best variegated forms of star jasmine.

Wisteria

BLOOM PERIOD: **April to May**

SIZE: **30 ft. tall with support**

HARDINESS: **Zones 5–11**

The Asian wisterias are among the showiest vines available and are simply spectacular in spring, but in the South they are so weedy that they should be avoided as landscape plants. Stick to the native species (*Wisteria frutescens* and *W. macrostachys*) with a good conscience. Both open later than the Asian species and have more rounded flower panicles. 'Amethyst Falls' and 'Longwood Purple' are two of the finest blues, while 'Nivea' and 'Clara Mack' are excellent white forms. *Wisteria macrostachys* tends to be somewhat more fragrant. It has longer flower racemes and it is a bit more tolerant of wet soils.

Wisteria macrostachys 'Aunt Dee' has long flower panicles like the aggressive Asian species. RIGHT *Wisteria frutescens* 'Longwood Purple' is among the deepest-colored native wisteria selections.

PLANTS FOR PROBLEM SPOTS

PLANTS FOR DRY SHADE

Acanthus mollis	bear's breeches	*Ilex crenata*	Japanese holly
Aesculus parviflora	bottlebrush buckeye	*Iris cristata*	crested iris
Amorphophallus spp.	voodoo lily	*Iris tectorum*	roof iris
Arisaema spp.	cobra lily	*Itea virginica*	sweetspire
Arum italicum	Italian arum	*Liriope* spp.	liriope
Aspidistra spp.	cast-iron plant	*Mahonia* spp.	mahonia
Athyrium filix-femina	lady fern	*Nandina domestica*	nandina
Aucuba japonica	Japanese aucuba	*Ophiopogon* spp.	mondo grass
Buxus spp.	boxwood	*Osmanthus* spp.	osmanthus
Cephalotaxus spp.	plum yew	*Pieris japonica*	Japanese pieris
Chamaecyparis obtusa	Hinoki falsecypress	*Pittosporum tobira*	pittosporum
Convallaria majalis	lily-of-the-valley	*Podocarpus macrophyllus*	podocarp
Cornus alba	redtwig dogwood	*Polygonatum odoratum*	Solomon's seal
Cryptomeria japonica	Japanese cedar	*Polystichum acrostichoides*	Christmas fern
Cyclamen spp.	cyclamen	*Pyrrosia* spp.	tongue fern
Cyrtomium spp.	holly fern	*Rohdea japonica*	sacred lily
Danae racemosa	poet's laurel	*Sabal minor*	dwarf palmetto
Disporopsis pernyi	evergreen Solomon's seal	*Sarcococca* spp.	sweetbox
Dryopteris erythrosora	autumn fern	*Serissa japonica*	Japanese snow rose
Epimedium spp.	fairy-wings	*Trachycarpus fortune*	windmill palm
Euphorbia amygdaloides subsp. *robbiae*	Mrs. Robb's bonnet	*Viburnum obovatum*	Walter's viburnum
Fatsia japonica	Japanese fatsia	*Waldsteinia* spp.	barren strawberry
Helleborus ×hybridus	hellebore	*Yucca filamentosa*	yucca

SALT-TOLERANT PLANTS FOR THE COAST

Aesculus pavia	red buckeye	*Hedychium* spp.	flowering ginger
Agapanthus spp.	agapanthus	*Helleborus* spp.	hellebore
Agave spp.	agave	*Hemerocallis* spp.	daylily
Amsonia spp.	bluestar	*Hibiscus* spp.	hibiscus
Aspidistra spp.	cast-iron plant	*Hydrangea macrophylla*	bigleaf hydrangea
Aucuba japonica	Japanese aucuba	*Ilex* spp.	holly
Baptisia spp.	baptisia	*Illicium floridanum*	Florida anise
Brugmansia suaveolens	angel's trumpet	*Juniperus conferta*	shore juniper
Buddleja spp.	butterfly bush	*Juniperus horizontalis*	creeping juniper
Callicarpa americana	American beautyberry	*Kniphofia* spp.	red-hot poker
Canna spp.	canna lily	*Liriope* spp.	liriope
Chamaecyparis pisifera	Sawara falsecypress	*Magnolia grandiflora*	southern magnolia
Chionanthus virginicus	fringetree	*Miscanthus sinensis*	maiden grass
Clethra alnifolia	summersweet	*Muhlenbergia* spp.	muhly grass
Crinum spp.	crinum lily	*Myrica cerifera*	southern waxmyrtle
Cryptomeria japonica	Japanese cedar	*Nerium oleander*	oleander
Cyrtomium fortunei	holly fern	*Nyssa sylvatica*	tupelo
Delosperma spp.	iceplant	*Ophiopogon* spp.	mondo grass
Echinacea purpurea	purple coneflower	*Panicum virgatum*	switchgrass
Euphorbia spp.	spurge	*Pennisetum* spp.	fountain grass
Fatsia japonica	Japanese fatsia	*Perovskia atriplicifolia*	Russian sage
Gaillardia spp.	blanket flower	*Phlox paniculata*	border phlox
Ginkgo biloba	ginkgo	*Phlox subulata*	moss phlox

Picea pungens	Colorado spruce
Pinus thunbergii	Japanese black pine
Quercus virginiana	live oak
Rhaphiolepis indica	Indian hawthorn
Rhapidophyllum hystrix	needle palm
Rudbeckia maxima	giant black-eyed Susan
Ruellia simplex	ruellia
Sabal spp.	palmetto
Salvia spp.	sage
Sedum spp.	stonecrop
Sempervivum spp.	hens and chicks
Spiraea japonica	Japanese spiraea
Taxodium distichum	bald cypress
Trachelospermum spp.	Confederate jasmine
Trachycarpus fortunei	windmill palm
Vitex spp.	chaste tree
Yucca spp.	yucca

PLANTS FOR RAIN GARDENS

Acer rubrum	red maple		*Ilex verticillata*	winterberry
Aesculus parviflora	bottlebrush buckeye		*Iris fulva*	copper iris
Alocasia spp.	upright elephant ear		*Iris virginica*	Virginia iris
Andropogon spp.	bluestem		*Itea virginica*	sweetspire
Arundo donax	giant reed grass		*Juncus* spp.	rush
Asclepias incarnata	milkweed		*Kniphofia* spp.	red-hot poker
Aster novae-angliae	New England aster		*Lindera benzoin*	spicebush
Callicarpa spp.	beautyberry		*Metasequoia glyptostroboides*	dawn redwood
Calycanthus floridus	sweetshrub		*Myrica cerifera*	southern waxmyrtle
Canna spp.	canna lily		*Nyssa sylvatica*	tupelo
Chamaecyparis thyoides	Atlantic white cedar		*Osmunda cinnamomea*	cinnamon fern
Chionanthus virginicus	fringetree		*Osmunda regalis*	royal fern
Clethra alnifolia	summersweet		*Panicum virgatum*	switchgrass
Colocasia spp.	elephant ear		*Sabal minor*	dwarf palmetto
Cornus (shrubby spp.)	redtwig dogwood		*Stokesia laevis*	Stokes' aster
Crinum spp.	crinum lily		*Taxodium distichum*	bald cypress
Cyperus papyrus	papyrus		*Viburnum nudum*	viburnum
Farfugium japonicum	leopard plant		*Zantedeschia* spp.	calla lily
Gelsemium rankinii	swamp jessamine			
Geranium maculatum	geranium			
Hibiscus coccineus	scarlet mallow			
Hibiscus mutabilis	Confederate rose			

SOUTHEAST GARDENING PRACTICES

THERE REALLY IS NO SUCH THING as a brown thumb, but selecting plants that will perform well in your area is just one step toward a thriving garden. The real key—whether you grow veggies, showy annual flowers, or trees and shrubs—is properly preparing your site and then taking care of the plants you've installed. If you take away only one thing from this book, it's this: proper soil preparation is the most important step you can take to ensure a successful garden.

Early in my career I was told that all I needed to know when planting was "green side up," but I've come to find that a bit more knowledge and understanding help get your plants off on the right foot. In this section we'll discuss how to develop great soils, whether you are starting from scratch or dealing with an established garden. The key is organic matter, and I'll explain my tried and true method for creating great compost. We'll take a look at garden pests—from deer and armadillos to the insects which can cause a gardener's breakdown—as well as review how to reduce disease in the garden. I've included a maintenance chart to provide month-by-month reminders for basic tasks, so you can spend less time working and more time enjoying the garden.

A well-prepared site will do more for the success of your garden than any other single factor.

GETTING DOWN AND DIRTY: BUILDING SOILS

Successful gardening is all about the soil and what is happening around the roots of your plants. Well-prepared planting beds will grow the healthiest plants and require less water, fertilizers, and pesticides. Soils throughout the Southeast range from areas of almost pure sand on the coast to deep, rich, organic silts along the Mississippi. The mountains and uplands often have thin, poorly developed soil over bedrock—usually precisely where you want to plant your prized specimen tree. By far the most common soil encountered across the region is the nearly ubiquitous red clay found from the inland regions of the coastal plain across most of the Piedmont and into the mountains. Red clay can be poorly drained and saturated during wet periods, then dry to the consistency of concrete during droughts. While it offers some challenges, the dirty secret of red clay is that it is exceptionally rich in nutrients, and if adequate drainage can be provided, few soils are better for growing a wide range of plants.

The first step is to understand what you have to work with in your garden. It's easy to skimp on the soil so you can start putting plants in the ground, but the secret to a green thumb is to properly prep before planting. A soil test from the local office of the Cooperative Extension Service is an easy way to get a baseline for your garden. If you breathed a sigh of relief after finishing with high school chemistry, this may give you cold sweats, but your extension agent will help interpret the results of your test if they are unclear and will also give you directions that are easy to follow. The main thing to look for on your soil test is the pH or acidity of your soil and the levels of phosphorous (P) and potassium (K). The nitrogen (N) is less important during the soil-building process.

Whether you have a sandy coastal soil or heavy red clay, adding organic matter in the form of compost is the single best way to build soil. Organic matter adds the capacity for holding water and nutrients in sandy soils. It also provides drainage and improved structure in clay soils. I have yet to come across a soil that wouldn't be improved by the addition of compost. Organic matter is typically somewhat acidic, and incorporating some lime may be necessary if the native soils and compost both have low pH.

When creating new beds, kill off any existing vegetation and till the soil as deeply as you can, at least 6–8 in. but preferably to 12 in. or more. Spread a 3- to 4-in. layer of your compost or mix of compost and topsoil over the tilled ground and turn that layer over by hand or with the tiller. If you want the bed to be bermed or raised, which can be beneficial for most plants, add a topsoil or compost mix to at least 6 in. above the final height. The tilled soil beneath the bed will allow water and roots to freely move through the ground. Expect your bed to settle over time as some of the airspaces compress. Adding an expanded slate product can be useful in extremely heavy soils.

Many people find themselves inheriting existing gardens and don't have the option of starting from scratch. Renovating existing beds can be as difficult or even more difficult than creating new beds. Small plants can be dug and potted to be replanted after renovation, but larger plants need to be worked around. Till the bed about 3 in. deep, steering clear of the root zones of existing trees. Alternatively, use a shovel or spading fork to loosen the soil by hand. Spread a 3-in. layer of compost over the entire area, including spaces where you could not till or loosen. Keep the compost about 24 in. away from tree trunks. Using the shovel or fork, turn the compost into the already loosened soil. Make sure to keep your existing trees watered over the next year, since many of the roots will have been damaged in this process.

Top-dress all beds with 1–2 in. of compost each year, to keep the organic matter replenished as it breaks down. Doing this will mimic the natural process that creates the topsoil lost during the construction of most houses. Over time, you will

Work organic matter into the soil to both improve drainage and hold water as well as to provide nutrients.

develop a new layer of beautiful, dark, loamy soil and a thriving community of beneficial insects and microorganisms that will help keep your garden healthy.

Creating compost

Making your own compost for the garden isn't rocket science, despite what some resources tell you. All that is needed is organic material, soil microbes, moisture, and air. Most recipes you'll find give various ratios or ordered layers of green material, sticks, and so on. Unfortunately, my garden doesn't produce waste in the layers these recipes give. Composting is really more like stir-fry than baking a cake—so while your results may vary depending on what you add, your compost should be fine.

Organic matter in the form of almost any garden waste is great for adding to the compost pile. Green material like trimmed-back perennials or end-of-season annuals are great. Raked up fall leaves, dead plants, and other brown material are also good. Small woody parts are excellent as well, including twigs, wood chips, and so on. Kitchen waste can be composted, but stay away from animal products like meat or dairy, as these can smell and attract rodents and other unwanted visitors. Some paper material (such as napkins and thin cardboard) can be composted, but a daily newspaper is probably more material than a compost pile can adequately break down. Horse manure is fine, but other manures or pet waste can be difficult to break down. Avoid weedy plants that have gone to seed and any diseased materials.

Soil microbes are essential for getting compost started. Often these microorganisms necessary for breaking down the organic matter are not present in large numbers. A few shovelfuls of good topsoil will get the process going, and if conditions are favorable, the microbes will get busy turning your waste

into black gold. Once you have a good compost pile going, the microbes will keep the ball rolling, and if you start a new pile, a bit of the older compost will supply everything needed. In fall, however, when the compost pile may consist largely of brown leaves and no green material, the microbes may need the help of some nitrogen fertilizer. A cup of 10-10-10 granular fertilizer per cubic yard is plenty.

Air and water are necessary ingredients to keep a compost pile working. If a compost pile is dry, all the breakdown processes will slow to a stop. Water the pile during dry periods to keep things moving along. Compost production also requires oxygen. A lack of oxygen will give rise to a strong ammonia smell. The composting barrel kits make sure plenty of oxygen is available, but they hold a fairly small amount of compostable material. For a larger compost pile, just turn it occasionally by hand with a garden fork or shovel to mix the matter and make sure the pile stays oxygenated. If you add a lot of green material which tends to mat or clump—grass clippings can be especially troublesome—you will have to turn the pile more often to keep air in the mix.

My preferred method of composting ultimately involves three piles. First, I begin a compost pile with organic garden material and a few scoops of native organic topsoil and leaf duff. I turn this pile occasionally. Once it gets to a good size and is breaking down, I start a second pile to begin the process with new material, adding some of the partially broken down compost from the first pile. When the first pile is ready to begin using in the garden, I start a third pile. This way I always have a bin of compost to use, a partially broken down pile, and a new pile for fresh material. During the summer's high heat, an active compost pile can break down in a matter of a couple months. When the weather is cold, the compost will take considerably longer.

GETTING STARTED ON THE RIGHT FOOT: PLANTING PERFECTION

Once your soil is ready for planting, it's time to site your plants. If you've prepped your beds well, planting is simple since the soil should be loose and friable. Perhaps no better time is spent in the garden than moving plants around before planting, to get a feel for how they will look. Keep in mind that the plants will grow, so try to picture them as mature specimens to see how they fit in your design.

Once you have rearranged your plants several times—like moving furniture around the living room—and decided on a layout, it's time to put them in the ground. Always make sure your new plants are well watered and hydrated before attempting to plant them. Remove a plant from its pot and check to make sure it has no circling roots. If it doesn't, simply rough up the sides of the root ball to encourage roots to grow out into the surrounding garden soil. If you do find circling roots, however, cut the roots apart with a shovel, saw, or serrated knife (one of the most underrated gardening tools around). Be ruthless now, though you will baby your new items once planted. Circling roots can lead to death several years down the road, and most plants can tolerate the tough love as long as you keep them watered while they're establishing.

Dig a hole as deep as the root ball and no deeper, but three times as wide with sloping sides. If the soil is well prepped this is less important, but if you are planting in areas that have not been tilled or turned over it becomes much more critical to help plants root out into the surrounding soil. Place the plant in the center of the hole and backfill with the soil you removed. Don't amend the planting hole with peat or other amendments. Always remember to add amendments to entire planting beds but not to individual holes. Water your plant in well and tamp the soil down around the root ball to eliminate any large air pockets. When watering your newly installed plants, water them in slowly and deeply with a hose, not a sprinkler.

New trees will sometimes need to be staked after planting to ensure they don't blow over. This is especially important in windy spots, high traffic areas, and where the head of the tree is large in comparison to the rootball. There are various products and systems to help stake your plant. Whatever method you use, make sure the tree can move some, as movement in a breeze is what helps the tree to develop reaction wood and ultimately form a sturdier, thicker trunk. Make sure to loosen the ties as your tree begins rooting into the surrounding soil, so the ropes or straps do not damage the trunk. Unless the site is especially windy, straps should rarely need to stay on your plant beyond a single full growing season.

In the Southeast, plants will benefit from a good layer of mulch, which helps keep moisture in the soil and suppresses weeds. Watering your new plantings is an important task, and there is no easy answer for what is the right amount. Watering will depend on weather, soils, and size of your plant. The key is to keep the rootball moist so the roots don't dry out, but not so wet that the roots rot. If planting in fall or early winter, which is by far the best time for planting in the South, your plants will be going dormant and won't require much water. Keep them hydrated with some water once or twice per week until the weather turns cold. Spring and summer plantings are a bit more difficult. These plants will need water at least twice a week in the absence of regular rainfall. Water long enough to make the soil thoroughly moist. If using sprinklers, run them for a long time and then dig a small hole to see if the water is soaking into the soil or just making the mulch damp.

When planting, make sure the new plant has no circling roots once it is removed from its pot.

MAINTAINING YOUR MASTERPIECE: GARDEN TASKS

With a well-prepared, well-thought-out garden, maintenance can be relatively minimal, but there will always be some activity in the garden. Weeding your beds is a must-do project on a regular basis. Don't let the weeds get out of hand or you'll find yourself too frustrated to go out at all. If you pull weeds regularly or spray them with an herbicide, it is a matter of a few minutes every week. By far the best methods for keeping weeds to a minimum are adding a good layer of mulch every year to reduce weed seeds from germinating, and planting your garden densely so the plants outcompete the weeds.

Herbaceous perennials will often live longer and stay more vigorous if dug and divided in fall every three to five years. Simply dig out your clumping perennial as it begins to go dormant, and using your spade or that serrated knife, split your plant into pieces. Compost the oldest parts and replant some of the younger pieces. Share the extras with your gardening friends and they're sure to share plants with you.

Flowering shrubs, perennials, and annuals will often continue flowering for much longer if they are deadheaded. Deadheading is the process of removing the old flowers before they begin forming seed. If you are growing plants for birds and other wildlife, leave some of the old flowers so they can produce seed and fruit for your winged visitors.

When it comes to pruning trees and shrubs, few garden tasks are met with such dread by some and enthusiasm by others. Prune young trees for shape to ensure a straight, single trunk with well-spaced branches. Older trees may be limbed up to allow more space under them. Also prune out dead, diseased, and crossing branches. Other than that, most trees need little in the way of pruning, other than a cut here or there to maintain shape. Remember that pruning will almost always stimulate more growth. Avoid cutting large limbs if possible, as these will not heal quickly and can be entryways for diseases and insects. Never top your trees by cutting the central leader and main branches back hard. The weak growth that follows topping is a much greater hazard than the original branches.

Most multi-stemmed flowering shrubs can be rejuvenated by cutting them back hard to 8- to 12-in. stalks, either in winter for summer-flowering plants or immediately after flowering for spring bloomers. Often removing the oldest quarter of stems near their base is better than cutting the whole plant to the ground. This serves to reduce the height, rejuvenate the plant, and allow some light into the interior of the shrub. Many shrubs can also be sheared or trimmed into hedges. Faster growing plants may need to be hedged two or three times per year, but one trim per year is enough for most.

An inevitable truth in gardening is that you will kill plants. Sometimes those deaths will be caused by neglect, sometimes by pests, sometimes through coddling, and occasionally for no apparent reason at all. Experienced gardeners know that this is simply part and parcel of the whole process. In fact, the more you garden, the more plants you will kill. Even when plants don't die but instead thrive a bit too well, you may need to get rid of them. They may have outgrown their space, they may be pest prone or require too much maintenance, or they may no longer provide the look you want. I've found that many gardeners will live with a plant they don't really love because they cannot stand the idea of killing off plants intentionally. There is no reason not to rid your garden of plants that don't provide what you want from them. Those plants have served their purpose, and much like getting a new couch or repainting the family room, a change will provide renewed interest and excitement in the garden.

QUICK-GLANCE MAINTENANCE CHART

GARDEN TASK	JAN	FEB	MAR	APR	MAY	JUNE	JULY	AUG	SEPT	OCT	NOV	DEC
Mulch beds	●	●	●							●	●	●
Add compost to garden beds	●	●	●								●	●
Plant trees and shrubs	●	●	●	●	●	●	●	●	●	●	●	●
Prune spring-flowering shrubs and trees						●	●	●				
Prune summer-flowering shrubs and trees	●	●	●							●	●	●
Prune roses			●									
Plant herbaceous perennials			●	●	●	●	●	●	●	●	●	
Divide perennials			●	●	●	●			●	●	●	
Plant spring bulbs	●								●	●	●	●
Plant summer bulbs			●	●	●	●						
Plant summer annuals and tropicals				●	●	●	●					
Plant fall mums									●	●		
Plant winter annuals									●	●	●	

QUICK-GLANCE MAINTENANCE CHART CONT'D

GARDEN TASK	JAN	FEB	MAR	APR	MAY	JUNE	JULY	AUG	SEPT	OCT	NOV	DEC
Start spring ornamental vegetable seeds indoors	●	●										
Plant spring ornamental vegetables		●	●				●	●				
Plant fall ornamental vegetables								●	●	●	●	●
Plant asparagus crowns		●	●									
Plant summer ornamental vegetables				●	●		●	●				
Use pre-emergent herbicides for lawn and garden		●	●							●		
Plant warm season grasses (bermuda, centipede)			●	●								
Plant cool season grasses (fescue)									●	●		

Coastal gardens may start 15 days earlier in spring and 15 days later in fall. Mountain gardens may start 15 days later in spring and 15 days earlier in fall.

UNWANTED GUESTS: PESTS AND INVADERS

A healthy garden is a thriving ecosystem of plants, worms, birds, frogs, lizards, and beneficial insects working together. Different gardeners appreciate some garden denizens more than others. For example, snakes are a sign of a healthy ecosystem and provide great rodent control, but many gardeners prefer that they dwell somewhere else. Squirrels can be a nuisance as they dig your flower bulbs and steal birdseed, but generally they are relatively harmless unless they steal all your ripening fruits. Some pests, however, are mostly reviled in the garden.

Wild and woolly

Deer have become one of the biggest garden pests, due to habitat loss and the elimination of natural predators. A hungry deer will eat nearly anything in the garden and is the reason a prudent nursery professional will label plants as deer resistant but never deer proof. In general, deer will hit tender and juicy plants before leathery-leaved or spiny-edged ones. Some more popular deer-resistant woodland plants include ferns and hellebores. Poisonous plants such as oleander and angel's trumpet are also usually safe. Plants with strongly fragrant foliage and a high concentration of aromatic oils often keep deer away. Especially effective are Mediterranean herbs like rosemary and thyme, which will only appeal to the hungriest of deer.

Trying to plant a garden composed entirely of deer-resistant plants would be difficult at best and certainly limit the palette. Keeping deer out of the garden is a much more effective method of control but often requires significant upfront costs. A deer fence is by far the best method of keeping your garden free of these four-legged foragers. A standard 4- to 6-ft. fence will simply not do the trick. At least 8 ft. of fence is the absolute minimum effective height. Luckily the fence can be effective even if it is constructed of a relatively lightweight material. There are some great black wire deer fences that disappear into the surrounding landscape. If fencing your entire property line is out of the question, putting a fence around some key areas like a vegetable garden or other special space can at least protect a portion of the garden.

A large dog can be effective at keeping deer at bay, especially in a yard with a low fence. Deer will quickly learn where dogs can't reach them, though, so they may feast in the front yard while your dogs are fenced in the back. Motion detectors which trigger sprinklers or noises can be relatively effective, especially if moved around the garden with some frequency. Other gimmicks are much less useful. Sprays made of wolf, bobcat, and even lion urine are available, but must be reapplied frequently. Some folks tie soap or bundles of human hair to tree branches, but these treatments simply do not keep deer away for long.

Rabbits are generally more annoying than damaging in ornamental gardens where they tend to nip off emerging stems and leave them lying around, but they can decimate a vegetable garden. An interesting fact about rabbits is that they will generally not try to go somewhere they can't see. A 12- to 16-in. board fence around your vegetable garden will provide effective relief from even large populations of rabbits. If they begin digging under your fence, install a 12-in.-wide chicken-wire band buried just under the soil parallel to the ground's surface outside your board fence.

Rabbits can be extremely detrimental to woody plants, sometimes gnawing the bark during winters. This tends to be a bigger problem in the highland areas, where food is less abundant than in the Piedmont and coastal plain, where herbaceous food is generally available year round. If it is a problem in your area, wrap tree trunks with hardware cloth.

Repellents are moderately effective with rabbits, especially since they do most of their damage when growth is very tender. Spraying early in the season with one of the many deterrents available can allow your plants to grow past the vulnerable stage and be fine the rest of the season. One popular deterrent is blood meal sprinkled around the property line or around vulnerable plants. If you own dogs, stay away from blood meal as dogs will dig like mad wherever they encounter it.

Cute as they are, rabbits have an annoying habit of nipping off new stems in ornamental gardens.

Perhaps the best method for controlling rabbits is to make your garden inhospitable to them. The rabbits found in our region do not dig their own burrows but instead rely on shelter in brush piles, tall grass, and cavities in rock piles. Removing cover will discourage rabbits from setting up shop, and dogs will worry them until they find a spot with fewer dangers.

Voles are small mouse-like rodents that burrow through the garden and create runways above ground connecting their burrows. Voles reproduce quickly and can cause considerable damage by eating bulbs, young shoots, roots, and bark around the base of trees. Often the first sign of voles is a rapidly wilting tree or shrub which when dug shows gnaw marks at its base or a severe lack of roots.

Since they are underground much of the time, voles can be difficult to control. Because they are active both day and night and all through the year, natural predators can help keep populations down. Leaving some tall trees around your property will encourage predatory birds like kestrels to hunt your garden. Snakes can keep your garden vole free, but unfortunately more gardeners rush for a shovel to kill the snake than encourage them to settle into the landscape. A good mouser is worth its weight in gold; however, mousing is mostly learned behavior in cats, and kittens are typically removed from their mothers before developing the skills.

Repellents can be used to protect some plants, but won't be effective in ridding your garden of an infestation. Mousetraps laid along the above-ground runways can work wonders but require a concerted effort. At least a dozen traps are needed; bait and check them frequently and keep them out and moved around in the garden until no voles are trapped for a week or two.

Voles will leave vulnerable plants alone if they must dig through rocky soil. A small amount of angular gravel or commercial expanded slate product can keep voles away from bulbs and tree roots if mixed into the soil around your plants. A large camellia garden I managed was devastated by voles, and after trying many labor-intensive and complicated measures, I found that a shovelful of sharp gravel mixed into the backfill soil was nearly 100 percent effective in protecting the camellias.

Armadillos have quickly become a serious garden pest. Before 1850, they weren't to be found in the United States at all. Today they cover a range from Texas to Florida and north to Missouri. They are making inroads into Tennessee and South Carolina, and we can expect them to spread through the entire Southeast in the future.

Armadillos will dig up your garden beds and seem oblivious to anything around them, as they tear up the landscape during the dark of night looking for grubs and worms. Their size and strength mean the damage they cause is significantly greater than most other mammals in as short a timeframe. Armadillos are not territorial and will wander all over, so even trapping one that is damaging your garden doesn't mean that another won't show up the next night.

Control of armadillos in the garden is not terribly easy. A very sturdy fence buried at least 12 in. deep is the best preventive measure. They are keen smellers, finding buried grubs by their nose alone, and some people report that spraying strongly scented products like vinegar or household cleaners around the property line will deter armadillos. Others claim they dislike the smell of pine, and mulching with pinestraw will keep them away. My first introduction to the species was in the pine woods of east Texas where the abundance of pine did not seem to bother them in the least.

Creepy crawlies

Insects are really a group of garden dwellers that need their own book, as the great variety of pests and beneficials in a garden can be so difficult to tell apart. A certain level of acceptance with insects is best—don't panic at the first sign of something munching on your plants. Often a healthy garden will keep pests in check before they become a real problem. Before treating any pest, make sure you know what is attacking your plant. Your local extension agent can have any insect identified and make recommendations on control if necessary.

I recommend trying to stay away from harsh chemicals as much as possible, because most insecticides won't distinguish between your pest and the community of beneficial insects in the garden. Indiscriminate sprays covering large parts of the garden should be avoided at all costs, and limit any necessary treatments only to the affected plants. Learning which insect invaders are regulars in your garden and how to nip an infestation in the bud is the best method for dealing with these regular pests.

Japanese beetles are among the most recognizable of southern garden pests, with their shiny iridescent carapace. While they don't attack every plant, the ones they do eat can be quickly skeletonized. Favorites include roses and rose family members such as cherries, as well as almost anything in the hibiscus family. Japanese beetles spend most of their lives as fat white grubs in the soil, where they munch on roots. Using the biological grub control called milky spore on your lawn can greatly reduce the population of adult beetles ravaging your roses. Another natural control method is to plant four o'clocks (*Mirabilis jalapa*) around susceptible plants. The foliage of four o'clocks is poisonous to Japanese beetles but won't harm the bees and butterflies attracted to the nectar.

NATIVES VS. EXOTICS

Some groups frequently cry that we should not plant anything that isn't native, and that all exotic plants are bad. The reasoning is often convoluted, with people saying in one breath that natives are better suited to the local conditions and in the next breath that exotics are all potential weeds which will outcompete our natives. There are certainly valid reasons for wanting to plant native plants and those who wish to should have ample opportunity to do so. Native plants do support native insects, birds, and other wildlife. They are also vital to giving an area a sense of place. The native plants of the Southeast certainly look out of place in southern California.

As far as natives being better suited for where they come from, that might be true in many cases in wild, undisturbed sites. But most suburban landscapes, roadsides, and businesses are nothing like the undisturbed native habitat. Planting our native species—which thrive in rich, organic, well-drained soil—on a compacted, red clay site where all the topsoil has been scraped away is often a futile exercise.

Exotics can certainly support a wide range of native insects (and non-native—honeybees are not native, after all), birds, mammals, and reptiles, and efforts to say otherwise are more than a little misleading. I for one certainly feel that our gardens would be much sorrier affairs without the diversity of plants we regularly use. Which isn't to say there isn't a place for natives. If they are good garden plants, they should always be part of our plant palette.

If you prefer native plants, that is of course your prerogative, and plantings around natural areas are likely best if local natives are used. Cityscapes with their unusual blend of constrained root space, pollution, high heat, and regular abuse are often better served by using a variety of plants that includes exotics.

While natives provide a sense of place, exotics help weave a richer tapestry in the garden.

Slugs can cause some of the ugliest damage to plants in short order. Tried and true natural controls include placing shallow dishes of beer around the garden. Apparently beer is irresistible to slugs, and they will congregate and drown in it. Plenty of wildlife like to eat slugs, and creating a bird-friendly garden can go a long way toward controlling these pests.

Mosquitoes are perhaps my least favorite garden pest. While they don't affect the plants, they will drive me from the garden when they are out in force. The number one control is to make sure there is no still water in the garden. Birdbaths should be refreshed every day or two to keep them from becoming havens for mosquito larvae. Empty pots and other potential water-holding containers should be kept water free. Rain barrels should always be covered or screened with fine mesh. Many products are available to treat ponds and should be used regularly. The numerous products for personal protection include botanical-based formulas that can be quite effective.

PLANT DISEASES

The number of diseases that can affect garden plants are too many and too varied to list separately. Much as with insects, your local extension agent can help you identify diseases and recommend treatments. When bringing a sample to your agent, follow these few simple guidelines:

- Take a sample that shows the transition between the healthy and diseased parts of the plant. A fully dead branch could have many secondary infections which are not affecting the healthy parts of the plant. The transition zone will allow the experts to isolate the true disease culprit.

- Bag your sample so you don't spread your plant's infections everywhere. No one wants to bring your fungal spores to their garden.

- Bring your sample as quickly as possible to the agent. If your sample bakes in a hot car all day while you're at work or running errands, don't expect miracles in identifying your problem.

The disease triangle

The general rules for helping prevent diseases in the garden start with understanding what it takes for a plant to contract a disease. A garden needs to have three components for disease to take hold of your plants. These three are known as the disease triangle. First, you must have a susceptible host plant. Some plants are extremely susceptible to certain diseases, but even those that would not generally be susceptible can become disease targets when stressed or wounded. Second, the garden must have the disease inoculant. If the disease isn't present, it doesn't matter how susceptible the plant might be. And third, the environment must be conducive to the disease for it to take hold in your plants.

The goal is always to reduce the lengths of the sides of the triangle. If you want to grow a plant that is prone to diseases in your area, try to make the environmental conditions as optimal for the plant and as detrimental to the disease as possible. Or if you have lost a plant to a disease, don't plant the same or a related plant back in the same spot, because the disease inoculant is likely present in high numbers there. Often one or two of the triangle's legs are somewhat out of our control, but we can control at least one of the legs to be as successful as possible.

Rhododendrons, for example, are typically susceptible to root rot in *Phytopthora* plants. This fungus is present in most soils, so two legs of the disease

Disease Triangle

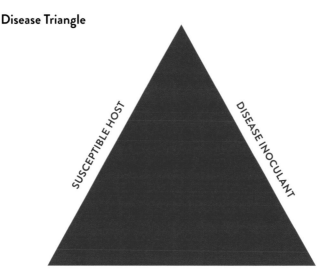

SUSCEPTIBLE HOST

DISEASE INOCULANT

FAVORABLE ENVIRONMENT

triangle are present. If the rhododendron is growing in poorly drained soil, the environmental conditions are ideal for the root rot to flourish and quickly kill your plant. If the soil is well-drained, the conditions are not ideal for the fungus and your rhododendron will have a much better chance of avoiding the disease. Also, some rhododendrons are much less susceptible to the disease, so they will tolerate less favorable growing conditions.

WEEDS

What is a weed? It is simply a plant where we don't want it. Often very desirable plants will set seed and grow in a spot that doesn't suit us. Consider a Japanese maple seedling. If you discover it growing in the corner of your yard where you had been thinking of planting a tree, you welcome it. But, if you discover it pushing up between the cracks in a pathway you use regularly, you consider it a weed that must be removed.

Weeds can be removed by hand and while this is a task most people dislike, I have learned more by getting up close and pulling the weeds around my garden plants than I have from any book I've read. If you weed your garden regularly, pulling weeds never becomes onerous, but if you take a month off, the weeds can quickly take over.

Plenty of chemical controls are available for ridding your garden of plants. Sprays that target broadleaf weeds are often used to kill lawn weeds but can also be used with care in a flower garden. Other sprays will kill only grasses, but these are less common. Most herbicides will be what are called broad spectrum, meaning they will kill all types of plants indiscriminately. Use care with all sprays and only after reading the label to check for safety precautions.

Staying ahead of pests and weeds in the garden will reap beautiful rewards.

Acknowledgments

SO MANY PEOPLE have helped me get to where I am today that it is difficult to know where to start. My professors at Virginia Tech, especially Alex Niemiera and Bob Lyons, were extremely influential in developing my love of plants. Mildred Pinnell-Foeckle at the Atlanta Botanical Garden exposed me to a world of plants I never knew existed, and encouraged me to continue my career in public gardening. My staff and colleagues at the Norfolk Botanical Garden helped turn me into a professional.

The plant exploration books of Roy Lancaster inspired me to get out and collect plants and their stories wherever I could. The time I spent with him at his home and garden, hearing those stories first-hand, continues to provide inspiration.

Tony Avent has been a continual source of information, encouragement, and opportunity, including my first plant-collecting trip to Taiwan and suggesting me to Timber Press for this book. Every time I visit his Juniper Level Botanic Garden, I leave both invigorated and knowing that I have a long way to go and many more plants to meet.

There is likely no place on earth quite like the JC Raulston Arboretum. The incredibly talented, knowledgeable, and enthusiastic staff constantly challenge and stimulate me, and the steady stream of new plants to geek out over is never ending. I'd especially like to thank Denny Werner for bringing me into such an incredible place and John Dole for supporting me as I transitioned into my dream job.

Most importantly, I'd like to thank my family for supporting me even when I work every spring weekend, for not forgetting who I am when I disappear on a three-week collecting trip to China, and for always bringing me more joy than any plant ever could. Both my children, Maggie and Jay, never cease to amaze me with their intelligence and humor. Last but certainly not least, my wife Mary can take the credit for anything I've managed to accomplish. She never stops believing in me, never stops pushing me, and never stops supporting me. Without her beside me, nothing else would matter.

Recommended Reading

Here is a sampling of books useful for new and intermediate gardeners. I have skipped the monographs, books about a single group of plants like magnolias or clematis, because there are just too many good ones to list. The Gardener's Guide and Plant Lover's Guide series from Timber Press both have numerous titles, and all are worth a place on a gardener's bookshelf.

DESIGN

Druse, Ken. 2015. *The New Shade Garden: Creating a Lush Oasis in the Age of Climate Change*. New York: Stewart, Tabori, and Chang.

Hartlage, Richard and Sandy Fischer. 2015. *The Authentic Garden, Naturalistic and Contemporary Landscape Design*. New York: The Monacelli Press.

Kingsbury, Noel and Piet Oudolf. 2013. *Planting: A New Perspective*. Portland, OR: Timber Press.

Rainer, Thomas and Claudia West. 2015. *Planting in a Post-Wild World: Designing Plant Communities for Resilient Landscapes*. Portland, OR: Timber Press.

Thomas, R. William. 2015. *The Art of Gardening: Design Inspiration and Innovative Planting Techniques from Chanticleer*. Portland, OR: Timber Press.

MAINTENANCE

Alexander, Rosemary. 2006. *The Essential Garden Maintenance Workbook*. Portland, OR: Timber Press.

Brown, George E. and Tony Kirkham. 2009. *The Pruning of Trees, Shrubs and Conifers*. 2nd ed. Portland, OR: Timber Press.

Cranshaw, Whitney. 2004. *Garden Insects of North America*. Princeton, NJ: Princeton University Press.

DiSabato-Aust, Tracy. 2017. *The Well-Tended Perennial Garden: The Essential Guide to Planting and Pruning Techniques*. 3rd ed. Portland, OR: Timber Press.

Hartman, John, Thomas Pirone, and Mary Ann Sall. 2000. *Pirone's Tree Maintenance*. 7th ed. New York: Oxford University Press.

TREES AND SHRUBS

Dirr, Michael. 2009. *Manual of Woody Plants: Their Identification, Ornamental Characteristics, Culture, Propagation and Uses*. 6th ed. Champaign, IL: Stipes Publishing.

Eckenwalder, John. 2009. *Conifers of the World: The Complete Reference*. Portland, OR: Timber Press.

Elias, Thomas. 2000. *The Complete Trees of North America: Field Guide and Natural History*. London: Chapman and Hall.

Hillier, John and Roy Lancaster, eds. 2014. *The Hillier Manual of Trees and Shrubs*. 8th ed. London: Royal Horticultural Society.

Hogan, Sean. 2008. *Trees for All Seasons: Broadleaved Evergreens for Temperate Climates*. Portland, OR: Timber Press.

Houtman, Ronald. 2004. *Variegated Trees and Shrubs: The Illustrated Encyclopedia*. Portland, OR: Timber Press.

Jacobson, Arthur. 1996. *North American Landscape Trees*. Berkeley, CA: Ten Speed Press.

More, David and John White. 2005. *The Illustrated Encyclopedia of Trees*. 2nd ed. Portland, OR: Timber Press.

NATIVES

Mellichamp, Larry. 2014. *Native Plants of the Southeast*. Portland, OR: Timber Press.

Sternberg, Guy and Jim Wilson. 2004. *Native Trees for North American Landscapes*. Portland, OR: Timber Press.

PERENNIALS AND BULBS

Hinkley, Daniel. 1999. *The Explorer's Garden: Rare and Unusual Perennials*. Portland, OR: Timber Press.

Mickel, John. 2003. *Ferns for American Gardens*. Portland, OR: Timber Press.

Rice, Graham. 2006. *American Horticultural Society Encyclopedia of Perennials*. New York: DK Publishing.

Ruksans, Janis. 2007. *Buried Treasures: Finding and Growing the World's Choicest Bulbs*. Portland, OR: Timber Press.

Schmid, W. George. 2002. *An Encyclopedia of Shade Perennials*. Portland, OR: Timber Press.

Resources

Southeastern region

Nearly Native Nursery
Fayetteville, GA
770-460-6284
nearlynativenursery.com

Almost Eden Plants
Merryville, LA
337-375-2114
almostedenplants.com

Brent and Becky's Bulbs
Gloucester, VA
877-661-2852
brentandbeckysbulbs.com

Brushwood Nursery
Athens, GA
706-548-1710
gardenvines.com

Camellia Forest Nursery
Chapel Hill, NC
919-968-0504
camforest.com

Edible Landscaping
Afton, VA
434-361-9134
ediblelandscaping.com

Lazy S'S Farm Nursery
Barboursville, VA
lazyssfarm.com

Mr. Maple
East Flat Rock, NC
828-551-6739
mrmaple.com

Niche Gardens
Chapel Hill, NC
919-967-0078
nichegardens.com

Nurseries Caroliniana
North Augusta, SC
803-278-2336
nurcar.com

Plant Delights Nursery
Raleigh, NC
919-772-4794
plantdelights.com

Woodlanders Nursery
Aiken, SC
803-648-7522
woodlanders.net

Elsewhere

Arrowhead Alpines
Fowlerville, MI
517-223-3581
arrowhead-alpines.com

Bluestone Perennials
Madison, OH
800-852-5243
bluestoneperennials.com

Cistus Nursery
Portland, OR
503-621-2233
cistus.com

Fairweather Gardens
Greenwich, NJ
854-451-6261
fairweathergardens.com

Far Reaches Farm
Port Townsend, WA
360-390-5114
farreachesfarm.com

Forestfarm
Williams, OR
541-846-7269
forestfarm.com

Klehm's Song Sparrow
Avalon, WI
800-553-3715
songsparrow.com

Old House Gardens
Ann Arbor, MI
734-995-1486
oldhousegardens.com

Rarefind Nursery
Jackson, NJ
732-833-0613
rarefindnursery.com

Yucca Do Nursery
Giddings, TX
979-542-8811
yuccado.com

WHERE TO SEE PLANTS IN THE SOUTHEAST

Alabama

Aldridge Botanical
Gardens, Hoover

Bellingrath Gardens
and Home, Theodore

Birmingham
Botanical Gardens

Donald E. Davis
Arboretum, Auburn

Huntsville Botanical
Garden

Mobile Botanical
Gardens

University of
Alabama Arboretum,
Tuscaloosa

Arkansas

Blue Spring Heritage
Center Gardens,
Eureka Springs

Botanical Garden
of the Ozarks,
Springdale

Garvan Woodland
Gardens,
Hot Springs

South Arkansas
Arboretum,
El Dorado

Georgia

Armstrong
Atlantic State Uni-
versity Arboretum,
Savannah

Atlanta Botanical
Garden

Atlanta Botanical
Garden, Gainesville

Atlanta History
Center

Callaway Gardens,
Pine Mountain

Coastal Georgia
Botanical
Gardens, Savannah

Gibbs Gardens,
Ball Ground

Meadowlark
Gardens, Griffin

Piccadilly Farm
Gardens, Bishop

State Botanical
Garden of Georgia,
Athens

Smith-Gilbert
Gardens, Kennesaw

Vines Botanical
Garden, Loganville

Zoo Atlanta

Louisiana

Audubon Park and
Zoological Garden,
New Orleans

Cohn Memorial
Arboretum,
Baton Rouge

Gardens of the
American Rose
Center, Shreveport

Hilltop Arboretum,
Baton Rouge

Hodges Gardens
State Park, Florien

Jungle Gardens,
Avery Island

Longue Vue House
and Gardens, New
Orleans

New Orleans
Botanical Garden

North Carolina

Airlie Gardens,
Wilmington

Biltmore Estate,
Asheville

Cape Fear Botanical
Garden, Fayetteville

Daniel Stowe Botanic
Garden, Belmont

Greensboro
Arboretum

JC Raulston
Arboretum,
Raleigh

Juniper Level Botanic
Garden, Raleigh

New Hanover
County Arboretum,
Wilmington

North Carolina Arbo-
retum, Asheville

North Carolina
Botanical Garden,
Chapel Hill

Paul J. Ciener
Botanical Garden,
Kernersville

Reynolda Gardens,
Winston-Salem

Sarah P. Duke
Gardens, Durham

South Carolina

Brookgreen Gardens,
Murrells Inlet

Kalmia Gardens,
Hartsville

Magnolia
Plantation and
Gardens, Charleston

Moore Farms
Botanical Garden,
Lake City

Riverbanks Zoo and
Garden, Columbia

South Carolina
Botanical Garden,
Clemson

Tennessee

Cheekwood
Botanical Garden
and Museum of Art,
Nashville

Dixon Gallery and
Gardens, Memphis

Knoxville
Botanical Garden
and Arboretum

Memphis Botanic
Garden

Reflection Riding
Arboretum and Nature
Center, Chattanooga

University of Tennessee
Arboretum,
Oak Ridge

University of Tennessee
Gardens, Knoxville

Metric Conversions

INCHES	CENTIMETERS
¼	0.6
½	1.3
¾	1.9
1	2.5
2	5.1
3	7.6
4	10
5	13
6	15
7	18
8	20
9	23
10	25
20	51
30	76
40	100
50	130
60	150
70	180
80	200
90	230
100	250

FEET	METERS
1	0.3
2	0.6
3	0.9
4	1.2
5	1.5
6	1.8
7	2.1
8	2.4
9	2.7
10	3
20	6
30	9
40	12
50	15
60	18
70	21
80	24
90	27
100	30

TEMPERATURES

$$°C = \tfrac{5}{9} \times (°F - 32)$$

$$°F = (\tfrac{9}{5} \times °C) + 32$$

TO CONVERT LENGTH:	MULTIPLY BY:
Yards to Meters	0.9
Inches to Centimeters	2.54
Inches to Millimeters	25.4
Feet to Centimeters	30.5

Photography Credits

All photos by the author or property of the JC Raulston Arboretum, except the following:

Marion Brenner, pages 42, 43

C. Colston Burrell, page 41 top and bottom

Ken Druse, pages 38–39, 40

Suzanne Edney, pages 6, 12

Pamela Harper, pages 44, 45

Plant Delights Nursery, Inc.; plantdelights.com, pages 61 left, 72 right, 73 right, 74 top

Wikimedia
Used under a GFDL and Creative Commons Attribution–Share Alike 3.0 Unported license:

Forest & Kim Starr, page 163 right

Infrogmation of New Orleans, page 256

M.L. Haen, www.mlhaen.com, page 294

Raffi Kojian, Gardenology.org, page 62 right

iStock
ratpatch, page 16

Index

Athyrium niponicum, 117
Atlantic white cedar, 232, 283
Aucuba, 177
Aucuba japonica, 177, 280, 281
    'Hosoba Hoshifu', 177
    'Natso-no-kumo', 177
autumn fern, 126, 280
azalea, 212
    Aromi hybrids, 212
    Asian satsuki, 212
    Exbury hybrids, 212
    southern indica, 212
Aztec lily, 90

bald cypress, 260, 282, 283
bamboo, clumping, 97, 102
bamboo vine, 276
Bambusa, 97
Bambusa multiplex, 97
    'Alphonse Karr', 97
    'Tiny Fern', 97
banana plant, 51, 60
banana shrub, 246
Baptisia alba, 118
Baptisia arachnifera, 118
Baptisia australis, 118
Baptisia / baptisia, 118, 281
Baptisia sphaerocarpa, 118
Baptisia spp., 281
barren strawberry, 171, 280
basswood, 262
bayberry, 205
bearded iris, 82
beardtongue, 139
beargrass, 207
bear's breeches, 112, 280
beautyberry, 179, 281, 283
bed of nails, 64
beds, creating or renovating, 286
bees, plants attractive to, 258, 295
beet, ornamental, 55
Begonia / begonia, 42
    'Passing Storm', 54
    rex-type, 42
Begonia grandis, 54
bellflower, 120
benches, 31, 35
bermuda grass, 292
Beschorneria, 118
Beschorneria septentrionalis, 118
Beschorneria yuccoides, 118
    'Flamingo Glow', 118
Beta / beta, 55
Beta vulgaris, 55
    'Bright Lights', 55
    'Bull's Blood', 55
big bluestem, 96

bigleaf hydrangea, 198, 199, 281
Bignonia, 267
Bignonia capreolata, 267
    'Atrosanguinea', 267
    'Jekyll', 267
bioswales, 37, 95
birdbaths, 297
Bird Hill, 40–41
birds in pest control, 294
bishop's cap, 128
black-eyed Susan, 109, 146
black gum, 249
blanket flower, 129, 281
bleeding heart, 40, 117, 125
Bletilla, 119
Bletilla ochracea, 119
Bletilla striata, 119
    'Ogon', 119
bloom period
    extending with tender
        perennials and annuals, 38
    winter-flowering plants, 21
    See also plant palette
bluebeard, 182
blueberry, 175, 217
    rabbit-eye, 217
    southern highbush, 217
bluestar, 114, 281
bluestem, 96, 283
Bodnant Castle (Wales), 31
border phlox, 140, 281
borders, 45
Boston ivy, 273
bottlebrush, 179
bottlebrush buckeye, 226, 280, 283
boxwood, 42, 178, 280
boxwood hedges, 38
brassica / Brassica, 55
Brassica oleracea, 55
    'Nagoya Red', 55
breeding of plants, 225
Briggs, Loutrel, 42
brown coneflower, 146
Brugmansia, 56
    'Jamaican Yellow', 56
Brugmansia suaveolens, 56, 281
buckeye, 226
Buddleja, 178
Buddleja davidii, 178
    'Black Knight', 178
Buddleja fallowiana, 178
Buddleja spp., 281
bugleweed, 156
bulbs
    defined, 48
    with evergreen foliage, 64, 82, 88, 100
    growing and maintaining, 69

planting times, 291
    See also plant palette, 69–93
Burrell, C. Colston, garden of, 40–41
bush-clover, 203
bushy bluestem, 96
Butia, 228
Butia capitata, 228
Butia yatay, 228
butterflies, plants attractive to
    annuals, 58
    bulbs, 78
    groundcovers, 156, 169, 170
    perennials, 117, 122, 127, 130, 139, 146, 152
    shrubs, 178
    vines, 274
butterfly bush, 178, 281
butterfly weed, 115
Buxus, 178
Buxus harlandii, 178
Buxus sempervirens, 178
    'Graham Blandy', 178
    'Suffruticosa', 178
Buxus sinica var. insularis, 178
Buxus spp., 280

cabbage palmetto, 258
Caladium bicolor, 56
Caladium / caladium, 56
    'Yellow Blossom', 56
Calamagrostis, 98
Calamagrostis ×acutiflora, 98
    Avalanche', 98
    'El Dorado', 98
    'Karl Foerster', 98
Calamagrostis brachytricha, 98
calamint, 122
Calanthe, 119
    'Kozu Spice', 119
Calanthe discolor, 119
Calanthe sieboldii, 119
Calibrachoa / calibrachoa, 57
calla lily, 93, 283
Callicarpa, 179
Callicarpa acuminata, 179
Callicarpa americana, 179, 281
Callicarpa dichotoma, 179
    'Duet', 179
Callicarpa spp., 283
calliopsis, 122
Callirhoe, 120
Callirhoe bushii, 120
Callirhoe involucrata, 120
    'Logan Calhoun', 120
Callirhoe involucrata var. tenuissima, 120
Callistemon, 179
    'Woodlander's Red', 179

Callistemon brachyandrus, 179
Calycanthus, 180
    'Aphrodite', 180
    'Venus', 180
Calycanthus chinensis, 180
Calycanthus floridus, 180, 283
Calycanthus ×raulstonii 'Hartlage Wine', 47, 180
Camellia / camellia, 14, 21, 180
camellia family, 216
Camellia handellii, 180
Camellia japonica, 180
    'Pink Icicle', 180
Camellia lutchuensis, 180
Camellia oleifera, 180
Camellia sasanqua, 180
Campanula, 120
Campanula poscharskyana, 120
Campanula punctata, 120
    'Cherry Bells', 120
    'Sarastro', 120
candela, 140
candy corn vine, 51, 60
Canna / canna, 39, 121
    'Australia', 121
    'Bengal Tiger', 121
    'Phaison', 121
canna lily, 121, 281, 283
Canna spp., 281, 283
cape jasmine, 194
Capsicum, 57
Capsicum annuum, 57
    'Chilly Chili', 57
    'Explosive Ignite', 57
cardiocrinums, 38
cardoon, 123
Carex buchananii, 99
Carex / carex, 95, 99, 145
Carex ciliatomarginata, 99
Carex eburnea, 99
Carex elata 'Bowles Golden', 99
Carex muskingumensis, 99
    'Oehme', 99
Carex oshimensis, 99
    'Everest', 99
    'Everillo', 99
Carex pennsylvanica, 99
Carex phyllocephala 'Sparkler', 99
Carex siderosticha, 99
Carex testacea, 99
Carolina allspice, 180
Carolina jessamine, 270
Carolina silverbell, 244
Carpinus, 228
Carpinus betulus, 228
    'Nana Columnaris', 228
Carpinus caroliniana, 228
Carpinus fangiana, 228

About the Author

Suzanne Edney

A self-professed plant geek, Mark Weathington is director of the JC Raulston Arboretum at North Carolina State University. He was previously horticulturist for the Atlanta Botanical Garden and director of horticulture for the Norfolk Botanical Garden. Undergraduate and graduate degrees in horticulture plus a degree in sociology have helped Mark understand the very real impact that plants and gardening have on people's lives. He serves on the leadership team for the Plant Collections Network of the American Public Gardens Association, the board of the Magnolia Society International, and committees of the Southern Region International Plant Propagators' Society. Mark lives with his wife and two children in central North Carolina, and tries to garden there, despite the interference of two plant-eating boxers.